I0810167

IMAGES
of America

WABAUNSEE COUNTY

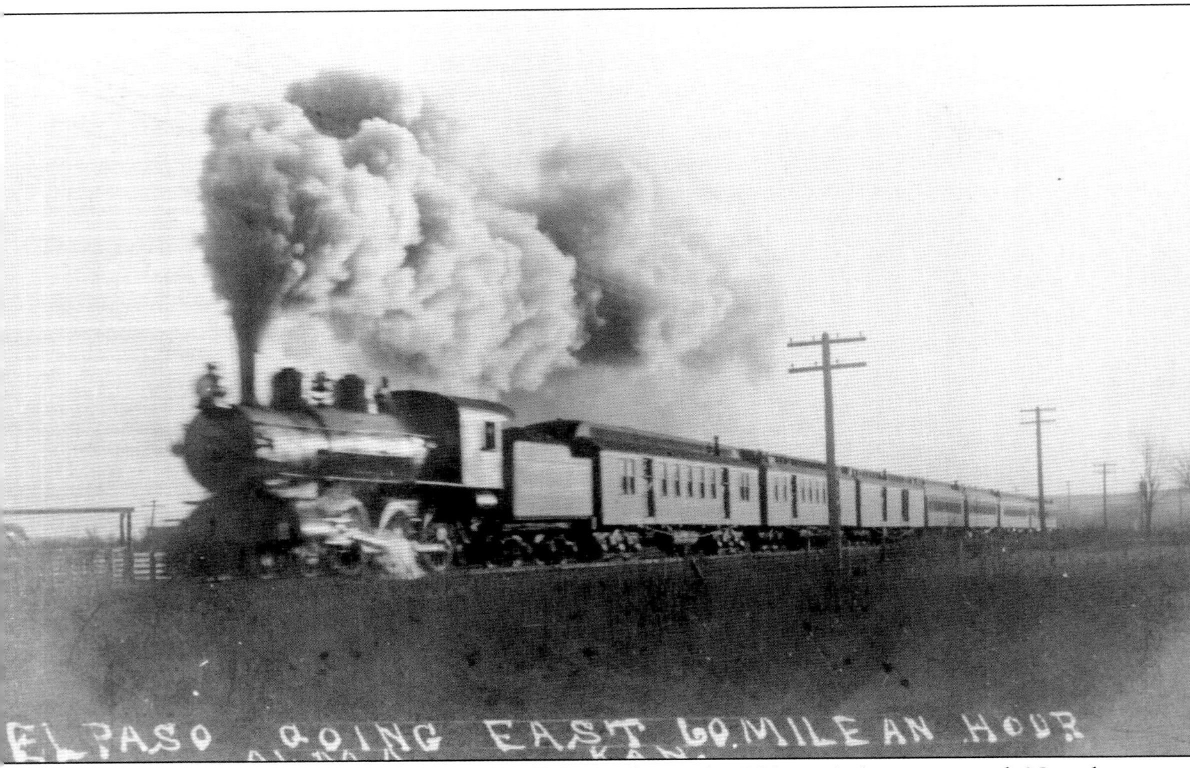

The El Paso Limited steams through Alma in this early-1900s real-photo postcard. No other single factor was so important to the growth and development of Wabaunsee County than the coming of the railroad in 1880 and the second rail line in 1887. The *El Paso*, above, was an extra-fare passenger train on the Chicago, Rock Island and Pacific Railroad line, which traveled from El Paso to Topeka in 31.5 hours. (Courtesy Paul Gronquist.)

On the cover: See page 15. (Courtesy Wabaunsee County Historical Society.)

IMAGES
of America

WABAUNSEE COUNTY

Greg A. Hoots

ARCADIA
PUBLISHING

Copyright © 2009 by Greg A. Hoots
ISBN 978-0-7385-6077-9

Published by Arcadia Publishing
Charleston, South Carolina

Printed in the United States of America

Library of Congress Catalog Card Number: 2008939974

For all general information contact Arcadia Publishing at:
Telephone 843-853-2070
Fax 843-853-0044
E-mail sales@arcadiapublishing.com
For customer service and orders:
Toll-Free 1-888-313-2665

Visit us on the Internet at www.arcadiapublishing.com

Contents

Acknowledgments		6
Introduction		7
1.	Early History of Wabaunsee County	9
2.	The Towns of Wabaunsee County	19
3.	Wabaunsee County at Work	67
4.	Community Affairs	83
5.	Ghost Towns of Wabaunsee County	103
6.	Disaster Strikes Wabaunsee County	111
7.	Wabaunsee County Farm and Ranch Tour	119
Bibliography		127

ACKNOWLEDGMENTS

The Wabaunsee County Historical Society asked me to prepare this book of over 200 photographs marking the 150th anniversary of the county's founding, celebrated in 2009. I wish to thank the many organizations and individuals who have contributed photographs, written material, and shared recollections with me.

First, I wish to express my appreciation to the Wabaunsee County Historical Society Board of Directors for trusting me with this project. The photographs displayed at the Wabaunsee County Museum have been the backbone of this collection. Also, the board has allowed me to enter into an agreement with the Kansas State Archives to exchange digital images of Wabaunsee County. I wish to recognize Nancy Sherbert, curator of the Kansas State Archives photograph collection, for making this agreement possible. Additionally, I want to thank her for all the effort that she has made in making historic Kansas photographs available to the public through the Web site kansasmemory.org.

I would also like to thank Michael Stubbs, who has been extremely helpful in the creation of this book. He is the leading authority on Wabaunsee County history. He serves on the board of directors of both the Wabaunsee County Historical Society and the Kansas State Historical Society. He has been a leading organizer of the Kansas City Symphony in the Flint Hills concerts. Michael has graciously agreed to write the introduction to this book, and he has provided a number of photographs to the project.

I would like to thank the other photographic contributors who have shared their family and community photographs with me. Each contributor is noted in the caption, and every contribution is important.

Finally, I would like to thank my wife, Cheryl, who has allowed me to spend so much of my time in preparing this book. I am sure I have not been much help around the house for the last few months.

Thank you all.

INTRODUCTION

The Wabaunsee County story is a tale of America and the West. It is a story of pioneer homesteaders and former slaves, farmers and ranchers, and entrepreneurs. It is a story of the tallgrass prairie and the Kansas Flint Hills.

Wabaunsee County is named for a venerated chief of the Potawatomi Nation. Called Nal-k-ses in his youth, he earned a reputation as a fearless warrior. It was said that he caused his enemies' faces to turn pale with fear. After these exploits, he was given the name Wa-bon-seh—"causer of paleness like the early light of dawn." Wabaunsee never came to Kansas; he died in Iowa in 1845 from injuries sustained in a stagecoach accident.

In May 1854, shortly after Kansas Territory was created, Peter Sharia, a French-Canadian from Michigan, recorded a town near Antelope Creek on the south side of the Kaw, 64 miles west of Lawrence. It was the fourth new town to be recorded after Lawrence, Topeka, and Manhattan. It remained nameless until the name Wabaunsee was suggested by a former Indian agent, who described it as meaning "dawn of day."

With the arrival of the free-state Connecticut Kansas Colony in 1856, Wabaunsee became the most populated settlement in the county. This colony received national attention due to the notoriety of its being armed with Sharps rifles and Bibles, provided in part by the famous abolitionist minister Henry Ward Beecher. It became popularly known as the Beecher Bible and Rifle Colony.

Several farms in the Wabaunsee community became stations on the Underground Railroad. Over 20 individuals assisted fugitive slaves escaping to freedom in Canada. Other stations in the county were located at Mission Creek and the Harvey settlement.

Wabaunsee County was originally named Richardson County, when the 1855 proslavery "bogus" legislature named counties after its own members. William P. Richardson had been one of its most influential members. In 1859, when free-state forces controlled the legislature, they voted to change those names. Since by that time everyone in the territory was familiar with the Wabaunsee settlement, and it was the only town in the county, its name was chosen to replace Richardson. As the leader of the colony said, "Had the name [Wabaunsee] been applied to the whole country [that is, state] it would have been beautifully significant of that new era of freedom for our land, the 'dawn' of which was coincident with the settlement of Kansas."

When Congress created the territories of Kansas and Nebraska in 1854, Kansas was still officially Indian Territory. In the 1830s and 1840s, over 30 eastern tribes had been forced to move to Kansas and settle on land once belonging to the Kansa Tribe. Portions of the Shawnee, Kansa, and Potawatomi reservations covered about a third of Wabaunsee County.

Nine thousand years earlier, Paleo-Indians had shared this landscape with woolly mammoths and long-horned bison. Evidence of these inhabitants has been found under 30 feet of sediment along lower Mill Creek. Archaeologists say some 480 generations of people have occupied this landscape since the first humans arrived here.

Around 1700, the Osage and the Kansa used this area as a vast hunting preserve. In 1717, the French explorer Etienne de Bourgmont traveled extensively in the area. He described the region as "the finest country and the most beautiful land in the world; the prairies are like the seas, and filled with wild animals . . . in such quantities as to surpass the imagination."

In the 1870s, when the Potawatomi reservation was diminished and the tribe no longer owned land in the county, some of the best farmland was opened to settlement. Wabaunsee County's population increased as immigrants from other states and foreign countries took advantage of the Homestead Act and available railroad land. This began the era of small family farms. Social organization centered around district schools, neighborhood churches, and star route post offices. The latter were usually operated out of postmasters' homes.

The construction of the Manhattan, Alma and Burlingame Railroad (eventually included in the Atchison, Topeka and Santa Fe Railway) in 1881 brought life to the towns along its route. In 1887, a railroad that later became the Rock Island System also crossed the county, adding to the area's prosperity. In 1900, the county's population peaked at 12,000. It fell steadily for the next century until the year 2000 when the trend was finally reversed and new growth occurred. In 2008, the population was nearing 7,000.

Social and political forces also brought changes. When rural free delivery was instituted in 1902, the social centers and community life that the star route post offices provided to neighborhoods was lost. By the 1920s, when the automobile became affordable for most rural families, neighborhood services like general stores, blacksmith shops, and churches began to disappear. As the decades passed, this trend then grew to include the decline of services in the county's towns. During the Great Depression in the 1930s, Lake Wabaunsee was built under the auspices of the federal government's Works Progress Administration. It put to work hundreds of laborers constructing the lake. In 1956, the first section of the nation's interstate highway system crossed part of Wabaunsee County when construction was completed between Topeka and Maple Hill. This new road and other highway improvements made it possible for residents to commute to employment outside the county.

The cold war came to Wabaunsee County in the form of an Atlas E missile launcher built at Keene in 1961. It was one of nine missile installations located in a ring around Topeka's Forbes Air Force Base. Each site contained an intercontinental ballistic missile armed with a thermonuclear warhead. By 1965, the Atlas E missiles were considered obsolete, and the base at Keene was decommissioned. Today the former missile defense complex is a private residence.

In the 1970s, the appearance of big-box stores and discount businesses in Manhattan, Topeka, and Emporia made it very difficult for local retailers to survive.

At the same time, middle- and upper-middle-class urban residents, usually with farming or ranching backgrounds, began to buy acreage in the county for hunting and recreation purposes. This trend continues today, with retirees and second-home owners retreating from crowded cities to the pastoral serenity of the Flint Hills.

Despite the ups and downs of the last century, Wabaunsee County residents retain a strong sense of family, community, and pride in the land. The slogan "small towns, big opportunities" has been adopted by the county's economic development council and reflects the positive view residents have for the future. In 2007, the state-sponsored Native Stone Scenic Byway was created, running through the county from Dover to Eskridge to Lake Wabaunsee and Alma.

Wabaunsee County residents have always been proud of their history and have maintained a strong and active historical society and museum. When it became necessary in the 1990s for the county to officially adopt road names for GPS and 911 purposes, county leaders wisely agreed to honor local history and cultural identity by approving names associated with that history and tradition. The list of road names reads as a history of Wabaunsee County, helping to keep the stories reflected in those names alive. It is hoped this book of historic photographs will serve the same purpose.

—Michael Stubbs

One

Early History of Wabaunsee County

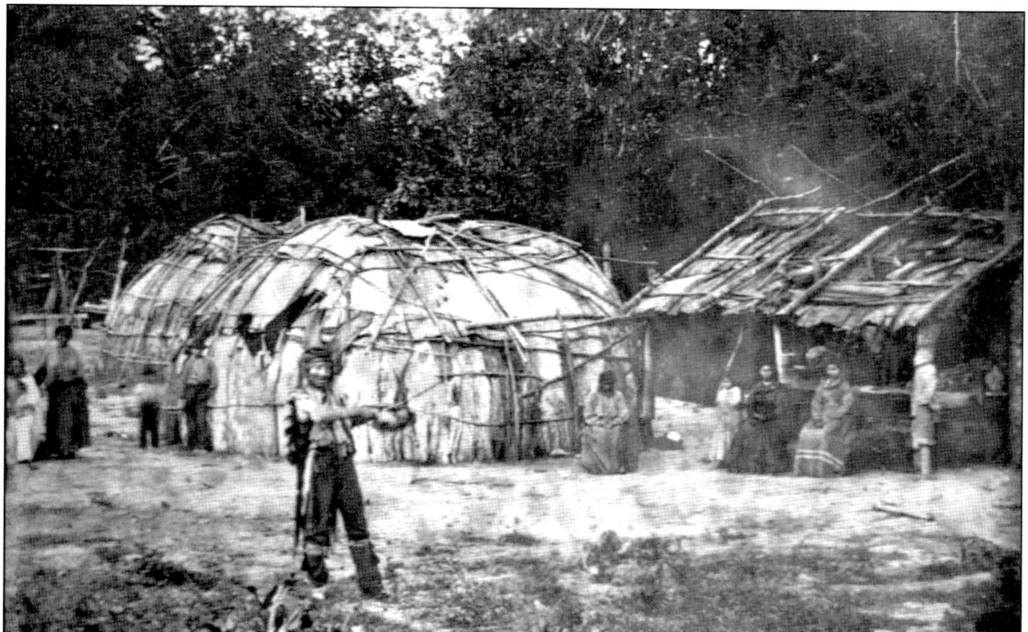

Seen above, "The Last of the Pottawatomie, Newbury, Kansas," this stereo card photograph by L. A. Ramsour from the 1870s, depicts the bark wickiup of a Potawatomi family in Newbury township. The location is believed to be about five miles southeast of Alma. In the 1830s, the area now known as eastern Kansas was designated Indian Territory and divided up into reservations for over 30 tribes. Much of what would become Wabaunsee County fell within the Kansa and Shawnee Reserves. (Courtesy of Michael Stubbs.)

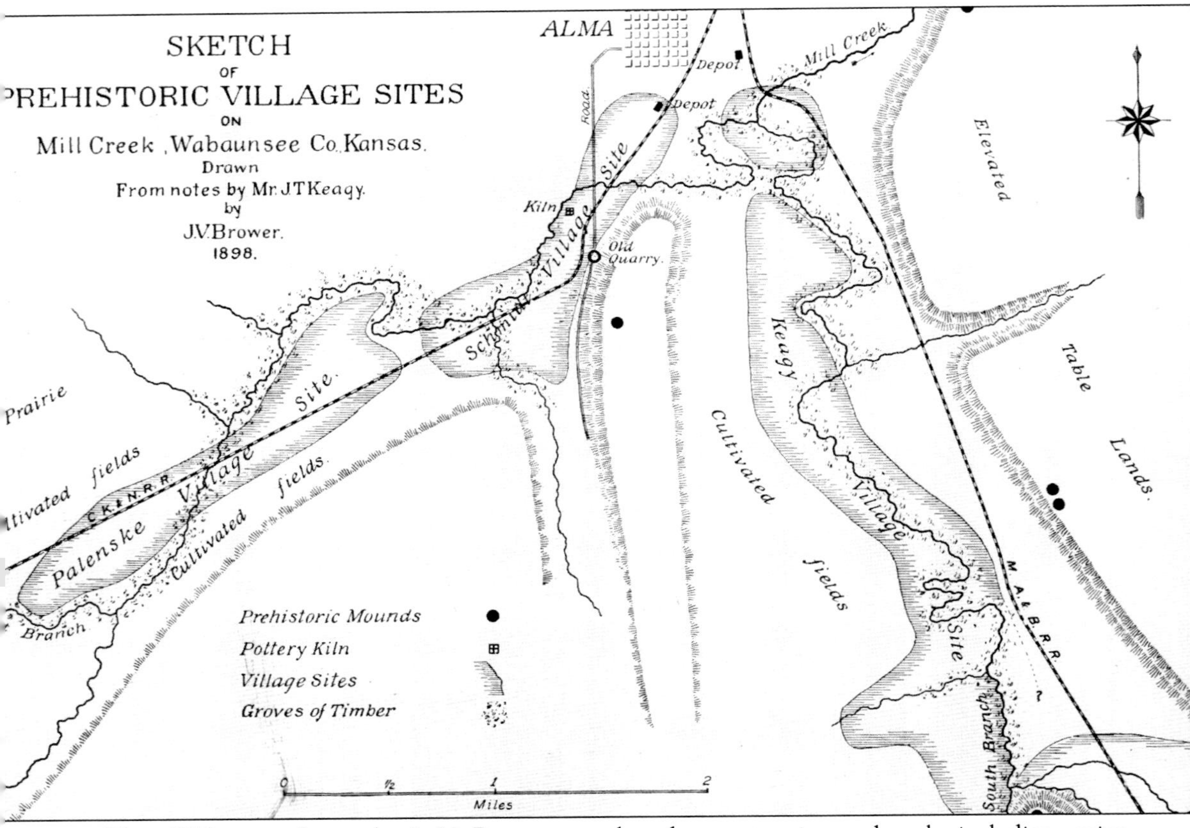

This 1898 map, drawn by J. V. Brower, was based on extensive archaeological discoveries made by J. T. Keagy, Wabaunsee County pioneer and county attorney. Brower, a writer and amateur archaeologist, met Keagy while the former was staying at the Alma Hotel. Keagy, an avid arrowhead hunter, commenced intensive searches for artifacts south and west of Alma. Matt Thomson wrote of Keagy in 1901, "No man in Wabaunsee County takes a greater interest in archeological research than does Mr. Keagy, his collection of prehistoric curios furnishing ample proof of the statement." On the basis of Keagy's finds, Brower created this map. Fifty years later, Alma resident Bob Grunewald began hunting artifacts in the same area, building the most extensive collection ever amassed in the county. An archaeological dig, sponsored by the University of Kansas and conducted on Mill Creek near Kuenzli Creek Road in 2003, revealed artifacts dating from 8,800 years ago. This confirmed what many amateur collectors in the area have long proven with their personal finds, that ancient cultures existed in the area for the last 10,000 years. (Courtesy of Wabaunsee County Historical Society.)

This 1855 map of Richardson County, Kansas Territory, shows the original county boundaries that existed prior to a realignment of the borders with Morris County in 1870 and Riley County in 1871. Approximately 72 square miles were removed in the first action and 54 square miles in the latter. Notice the Potawatomi Reservation in the upper right section of the county and the Kaw Reserve in the lower left portion. (Courtesy of Michael Stubbs.)

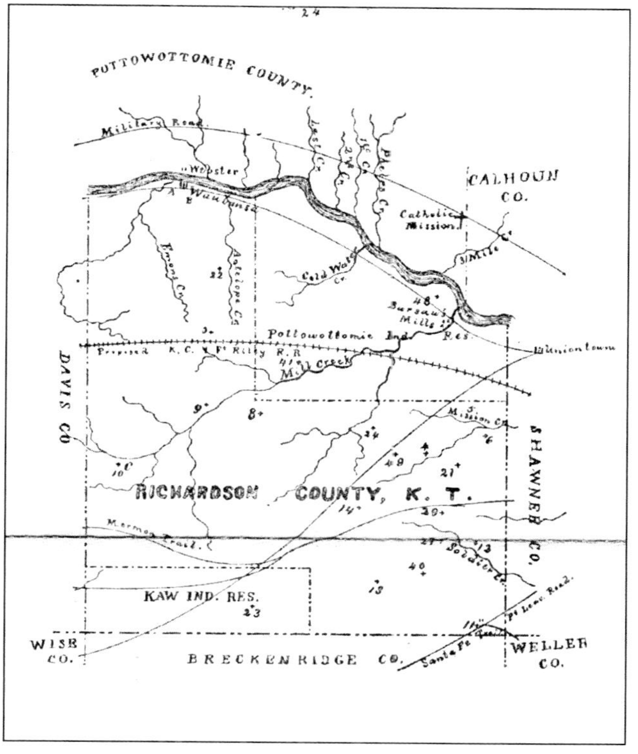

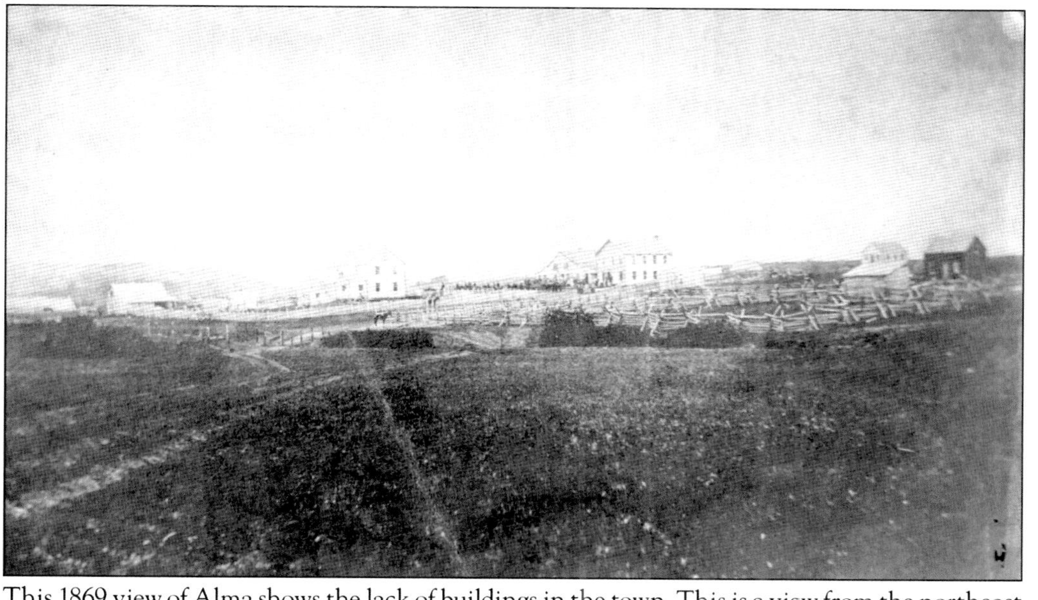

This 1869 view of Alma shows the lack of buildings in the town. This is a view from the northeast part of town, looking to the southwest. The large white building left of center is the Winkler Hotel, which was located at 224 Missouri Street. Across the street one can see the Schmitz and Meyer Store and the Kaufman building, which was the first courthouse in Alma. (Courtesy of Wabaunsee County Historical Society.)

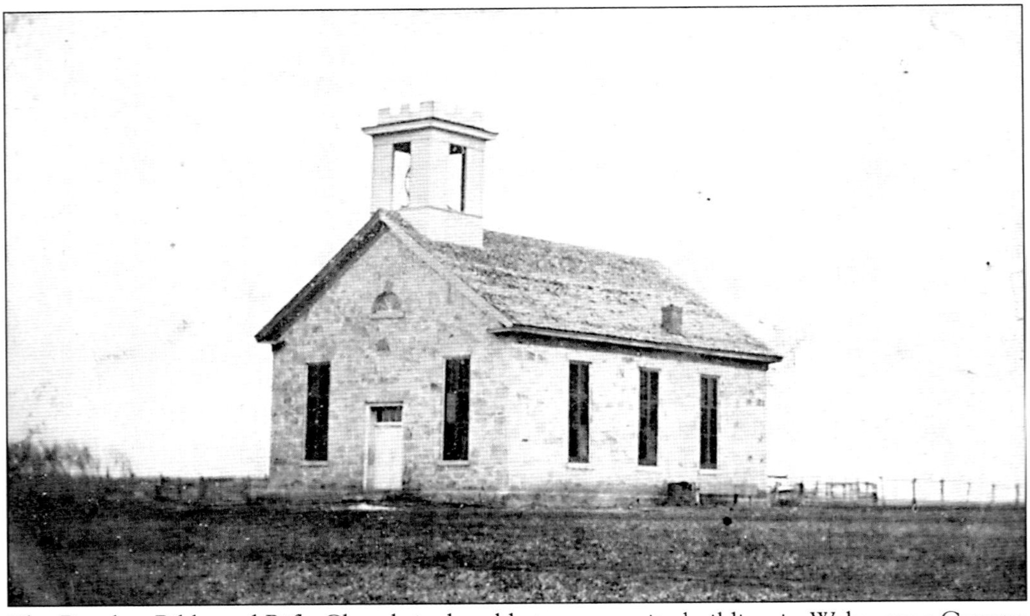

The Beecher Bible and Rifle Church is the oldest community building in Wabaunsee County. After two years of fund-raising, construction began on a stone church that still stands today in Wabaunsee. The stone was hauled from nearby hilltop quarries. Women helped mix the mortar by hand, and the long shingles, called shakes, were made with crude hand tools. The church was dedicated in May 1862. (Courtesy of Wabaunsee County Historical Society.)

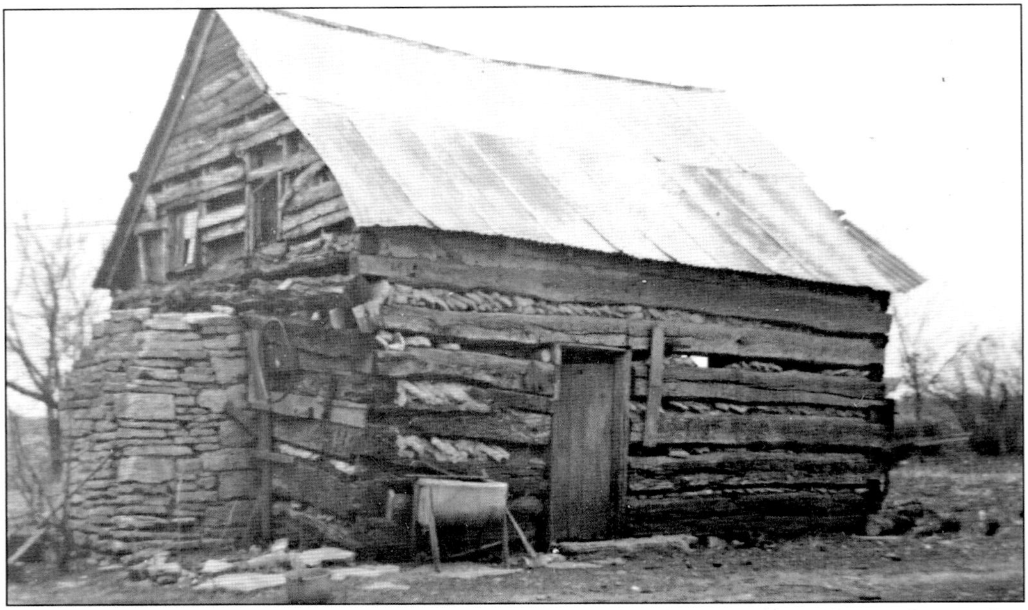

This log cabin, built in 1865, was the home of Caleb and Rebecca Zefferis Harvey. Located at 11792 Old Log House Road, it served as the Harveyville Post Office from 1870 to 1880. When the mail arrived by horseback from Burlingame, it was dumped in the middle of the floor where neighbors made a mad scramble for it. The salary for the postmaster was $12 a year. (Courtesy of Wabaunsee County Historical Society.)

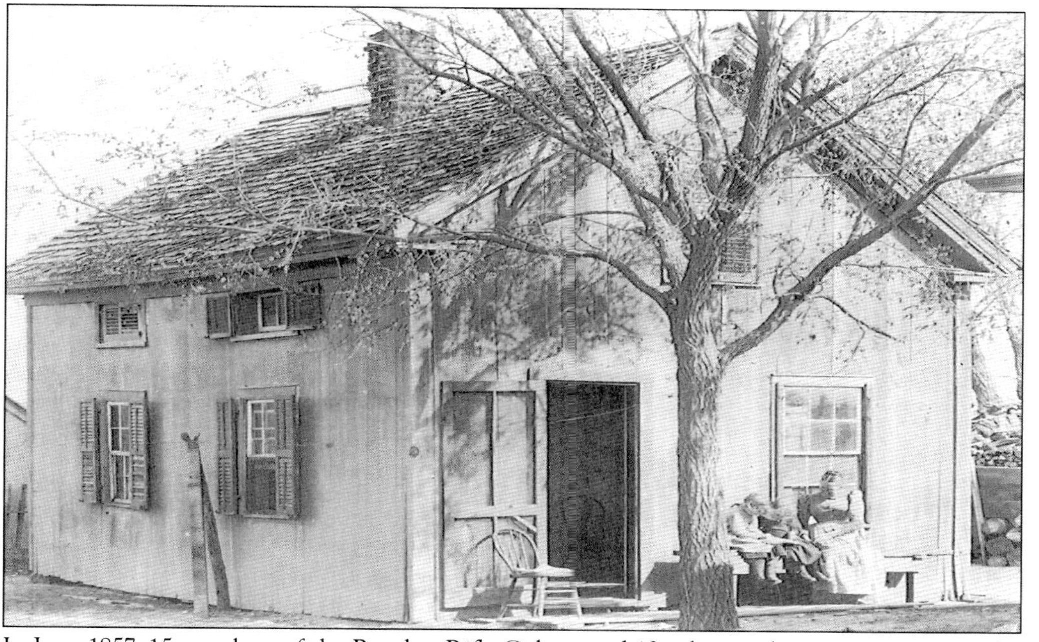

In June 1857, 15 members of the Beecher Rifle Colony and 13 other settlers met to organize the First Church of Christ in Wabaunsee. The Reverend Harvey Jones was pastor. This temporary church building was one of the first structures in the county to be built with milled lumber. It was used for religious services and community events until the present stone church was completed in 1862. It later became the home of the A. J. Bowman family (pictured). (Courtesy of Wabaunsee County Historical Society.)

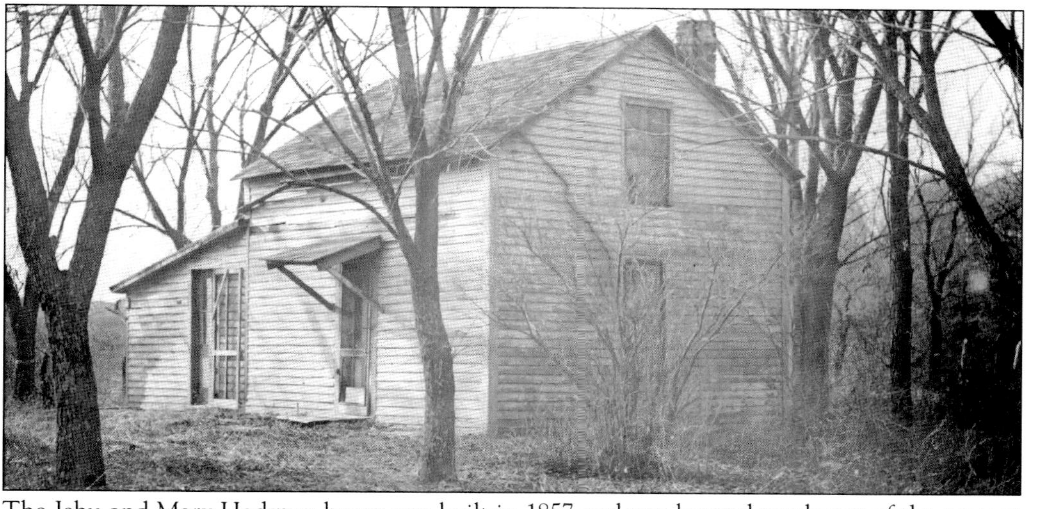

The Jehu and Mary Hodgson house was built in 1857 and was located southwest of the present Harveyville cemetery. Hodgson's son Frank recalled when his parents were assisting "Charley the slave" on his journey to freedom on the Underground Railroad. When a neighbor came to visit, Charley hid under the bed on which the neighbor chose to sit during her visit. The Harvey family, Morris Walton, and the Hudsons appear to have been the principal Underground Railroad participants in the community. (Courtesy of Michael Stubbs.)

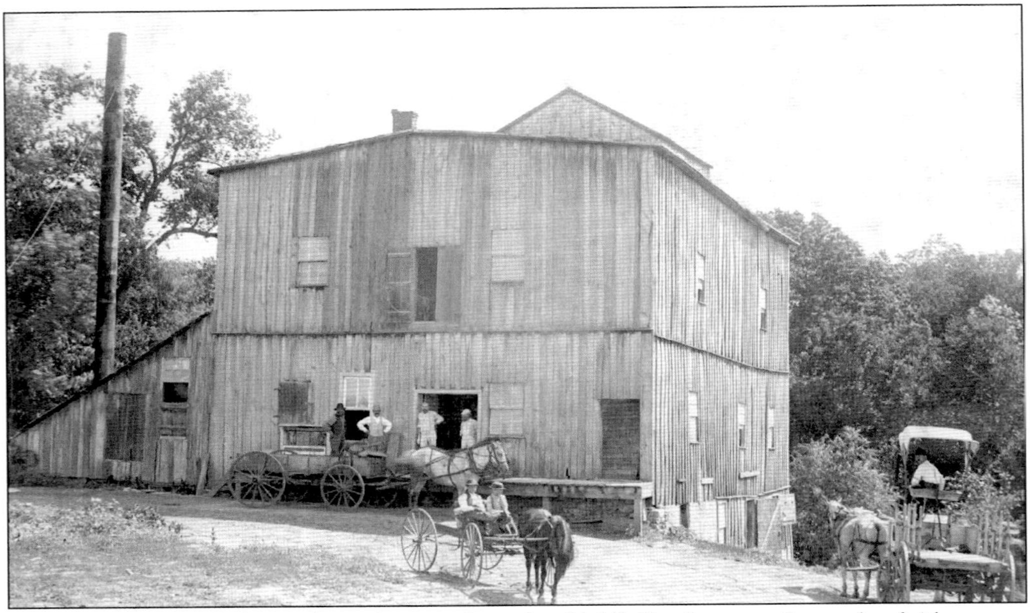

Lorenzo Pauly's mill, located on the west branch of Mill Creek one mile south of Alma, was constructed in 1858 by Alma founder Gottlieb Zwanziger, who sold the mill to Pauly in 1875. Pauly, a successful bread maker in Topeka for several years, made Pauly Brothers Mill a success by expanding its size and production capabilities. Pauly later sold the mill to H. J. Palenske, who operated it for many years. (Courtesy of Wabaunsee County Historical Society.)

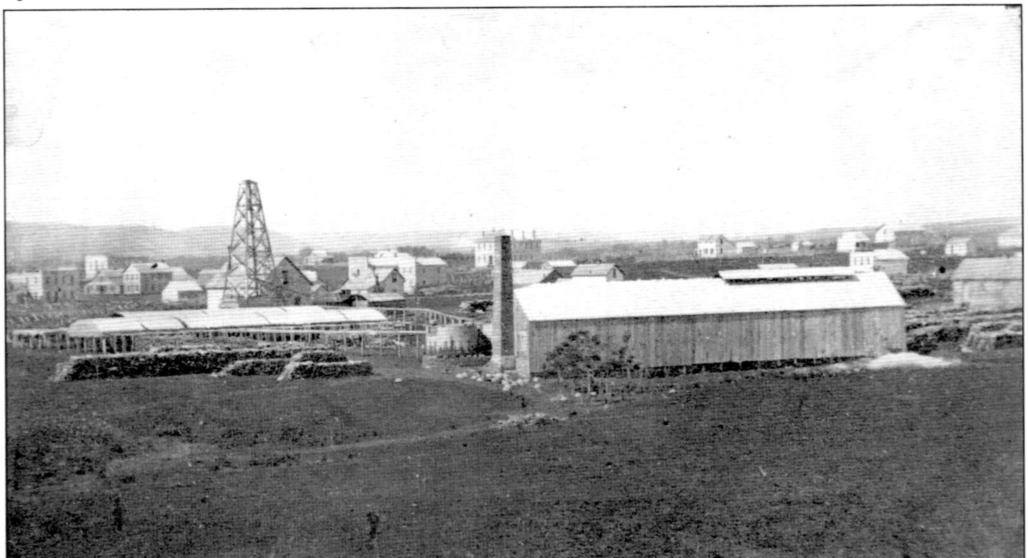

Alma Salt Works, seen here in 1874, was located at Seventh and Grand Streets. The factory evaporated water from a brine well, capturing the remaining salt. Notice the large stacks of wood used for boiling the water out of the brine. Notice the Palenske Hall building, the Schmitz and Meyer store, and the Kaufman building at the left edge of the photograph. The saltworks closed in 1876, and the Salt Works Addition became a residential section of Alma. (Courtesy of Wabaunsee County Historical Society.)

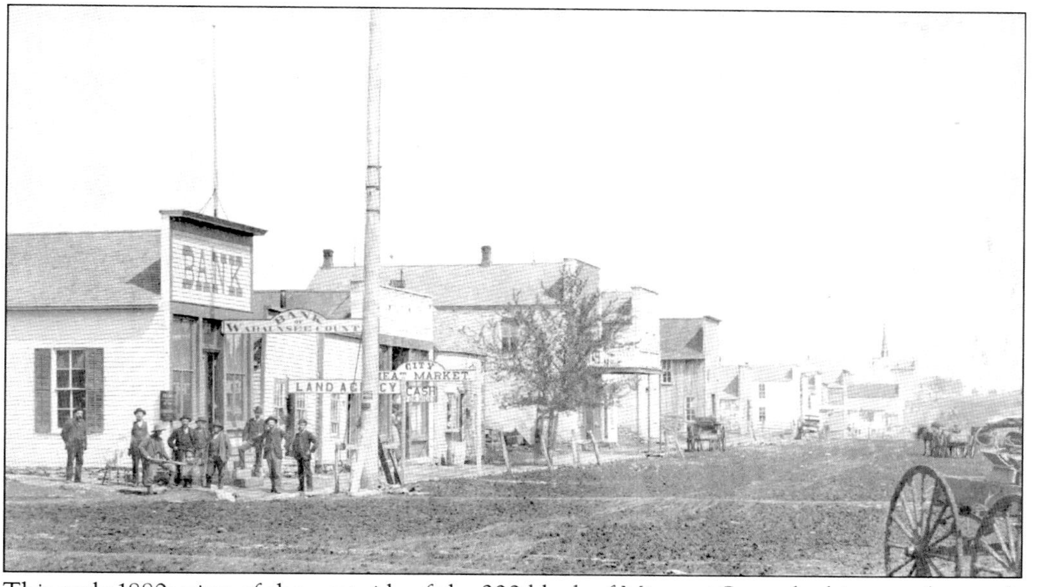

This early-1880s view of the west side of the 300 block of Missouri Street looking north reveals that many of the early business buildings were constructed of wood. Many of these structures were built during the boom years following Alma being declared the county seat in 1871 and the arrival of the railroad in 1880. This is the earliest-known view of the business district in Alma. A portion of this photograph appears on the front cover. (Courtesy of Wabaunsee County Historical Society.)

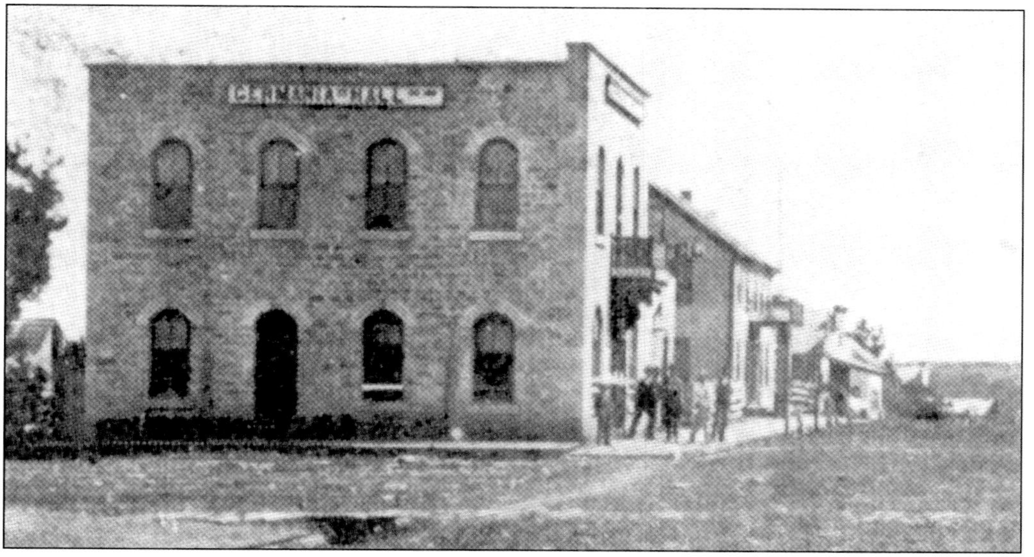

From Matt Thomson's book *Early History of Wabaunsee County, Kansas, with Stories of Pioneer Days and Glimpses of Our Western Border*, this photograph shows Germania Hall, a hotel built in 1873 by Peter Dagan. The building was rebuilt after a fire in 1890, extending it double in length. In 1908, Louis Palenske purchased the building to house the new Commercial National Bank, and the Feiden Brothers constructed a new front for the building and rebuilt the interior. Just beyond Germania Hall, one can see the first Winkler Hotel, the third building constructed in Alma. (Courtesy of Michael Stubbs.)

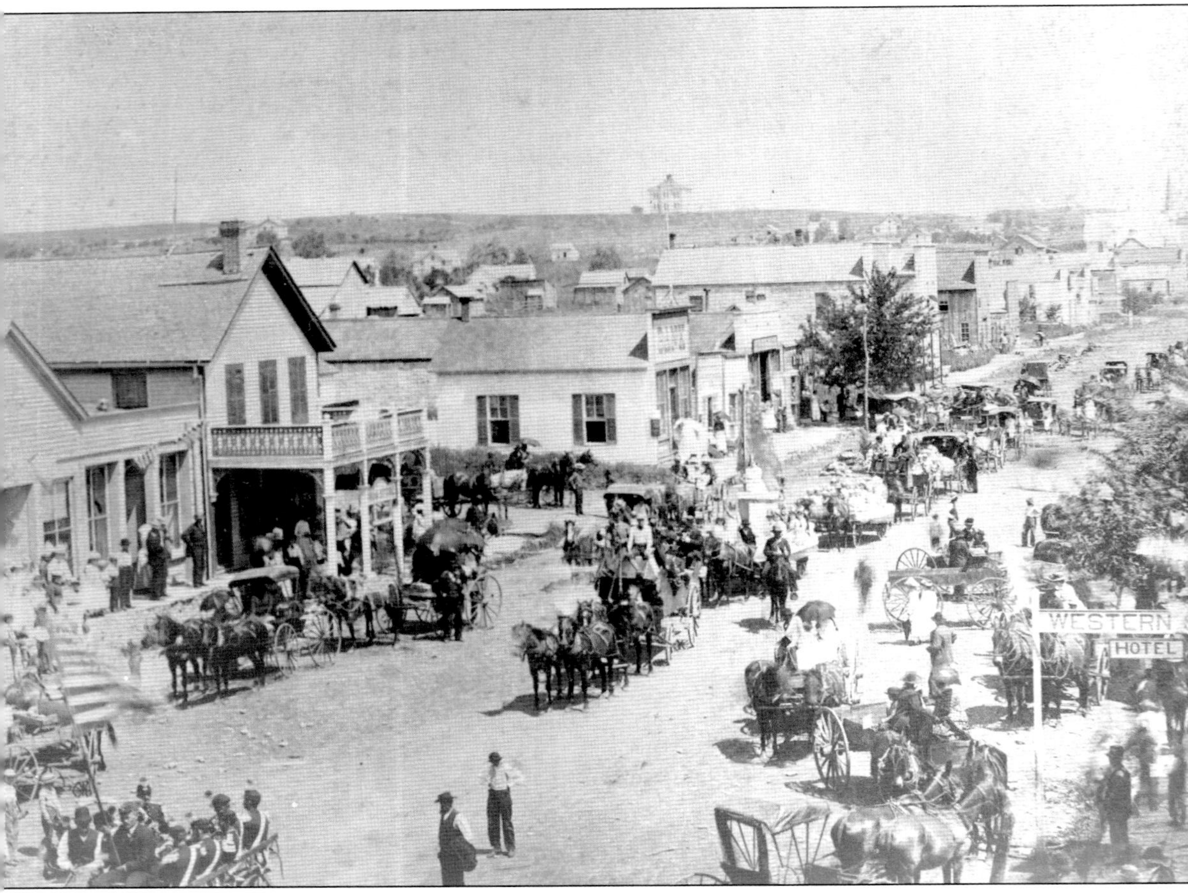

This parade scene looking at the west side of Missouri Street was taken about two years after the view on the previous page. One sees E. Meyer's store at the far left, with the Kaufman building to its right, sporting a second-story balcony. The third building from the left is the Bank of Wabaunsee County; however, notice that the ship's mast, seen in front of the bank in the photograph on page 15, had disappeared. Alma's first stone schoolhouse can be seen on the horizon on the hill near where the water tower is located today. As quickly as the wooden buildings began to spring up on Missouri Street, they began to burn, one by one, and soon, building codes required masonry structures with fire walls in the business district. By 1890, limestone had become the material of choice for building construction in Alma. (Courtesy of Wabaunsee County Historical Society.)

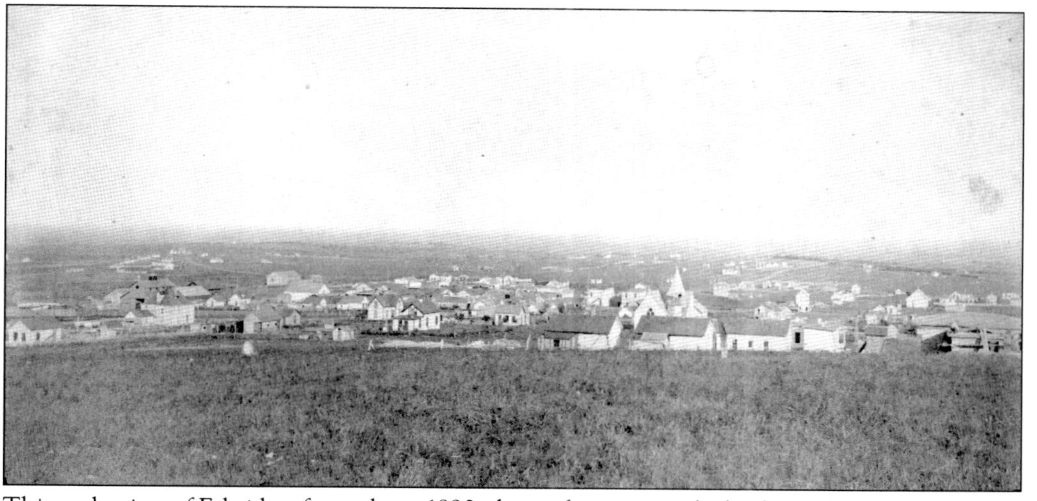

This early view of Eskridge, from about 1890, shows the amazing lack of trees in the town at the time. The town was platted by the Atchison, Topeka and Santa Fe Railway in 1880 and moved from its previous location about one mile east to a location more proximate to the depot. Dr. M. F. Trivett moved the first house into the new town in 1880 and located it at the southwest corner of Second Avenue and Cedar Street. (Courtesy of Wabaunsee County Historical Society.)

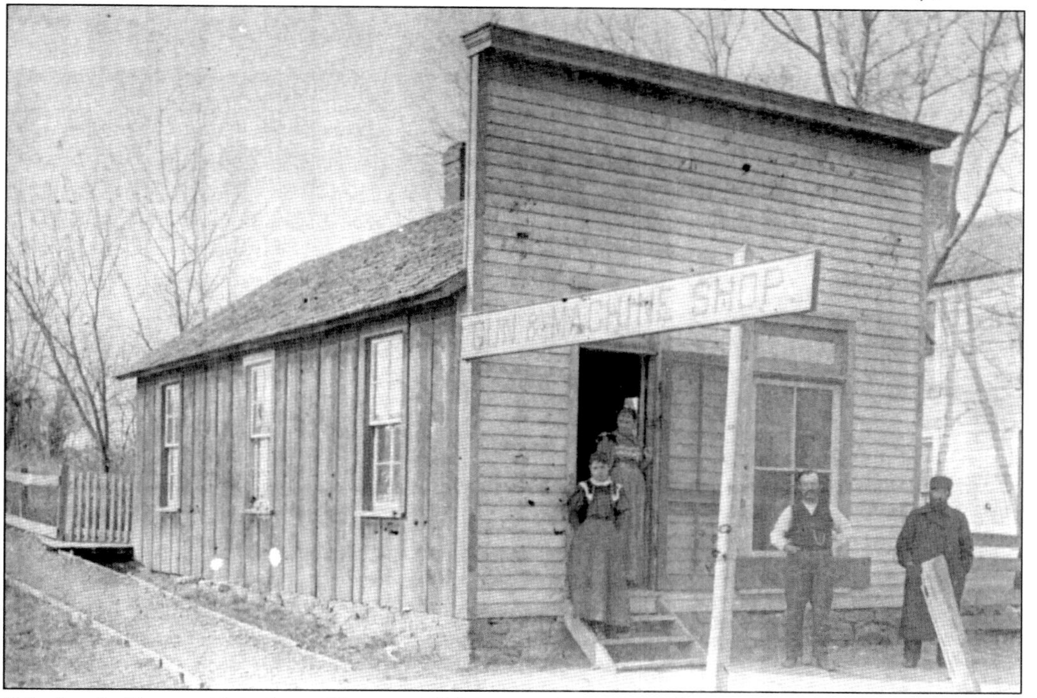

Schubert's Gun and Machine Shop at 401 Missouri Street in Alma, constructed in the 1870s, is the last remaining frame building in the business district today. Carl Schubert, his wife, Barbara, and their daughter Mary lived in the back of this building while operating the machine shop in the front. They are pictured above with an unidentified man at the far right. Today the building is owned by Keen Umbehr and serves as a law office. (Courtesy of Wabaunsee County Historical Society.)

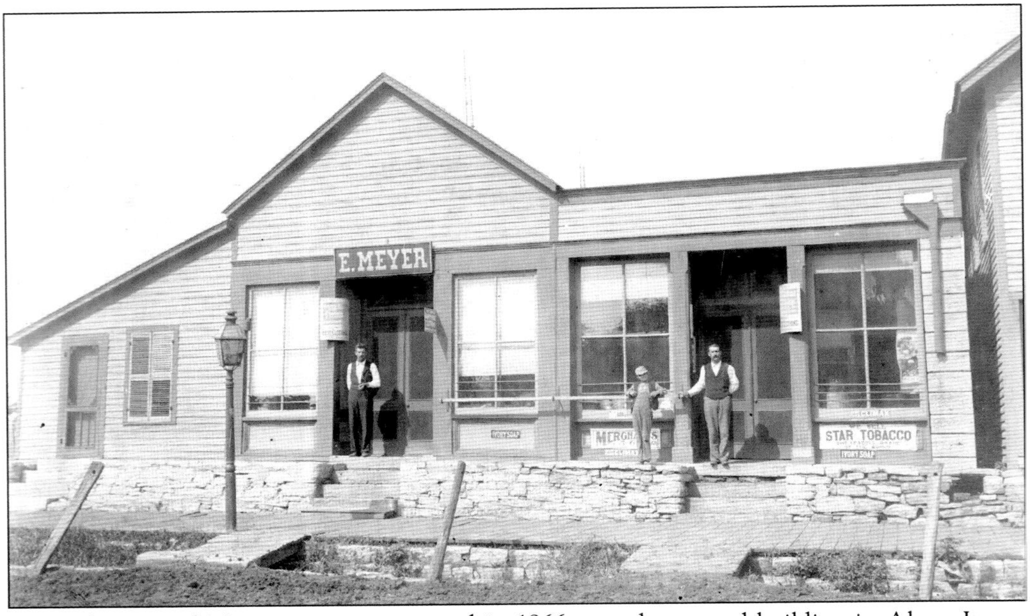

The Schmitz and Meyer store, constructed in 1866, was the second building in Alma. It was constructed after the erection of the Kaufman building next door that housed the first courthouse in Alma. Henry Schmitz sold his interest in the store in 1875 to Emillie Meyer, who operated it for many years. The building was demolished in October 1908 to make way for a new store constructed of limestone (see page 33). (Courtesy of Wabaunsee County Historical Society.)

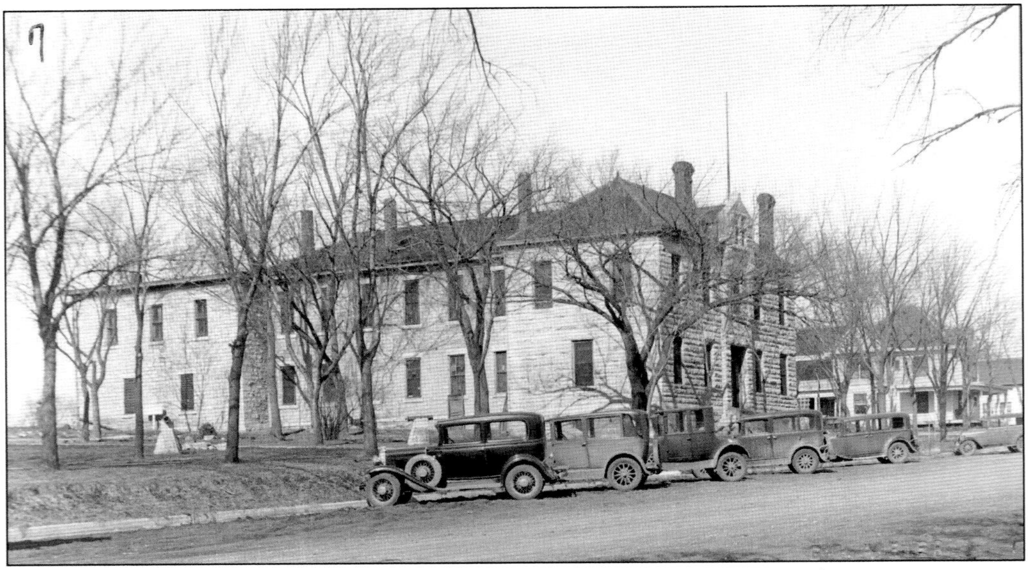

Alma's second courthouse was constructed in 1872 after a February 21, 1871, election, once again, challenging the location of the county seat. During the election, Alma promised to build a stone courthouse if it was affirmed as the county seat. Alma won the election and built the courthouse at a cost of $8,000, with half the money coming from private donations. The addition to the rear was added in 1893. The building was demolished in 1932, and much of the stone was crushed and spread on the streets of Alma. (Courtesy of Wabaunsee County Historical Society.)

Two

The Towns of Wabaunsee County

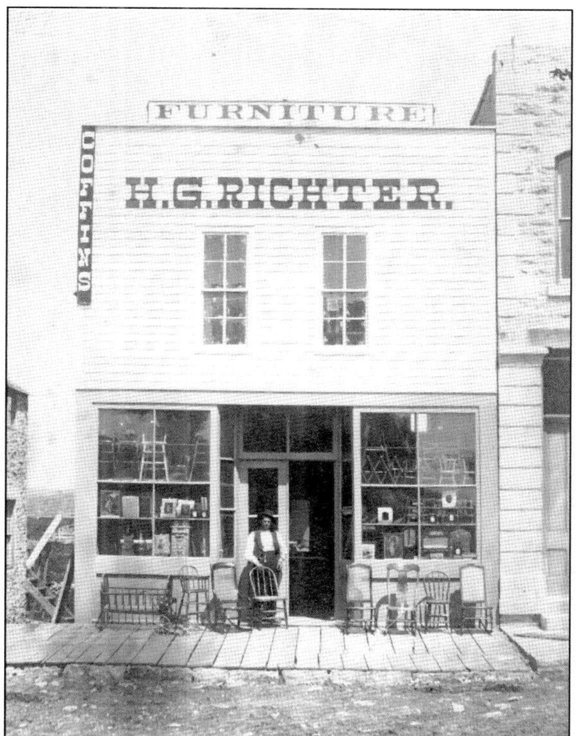

Chapter 2 looks at the development of Wabaunsee County's towns in photographs. Herman Richter is seen in front of his furniture store and undertaking business at 312 Missouri Street in this photograph from the 1880s. Richter lived in the stone house in what is today's Alma City Park, and he was a prominent early businessman in Alma. This building burned on February 4, 1896. (Courtesy of Wabaunsee County Historical Society.)

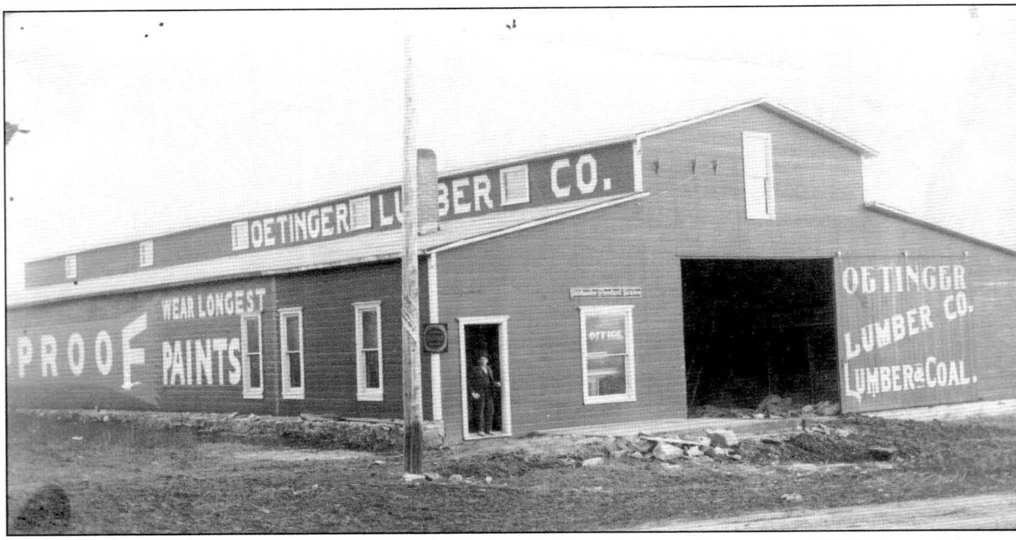

Oetinger Lumber, seen here as it opened on April 15, 1906, was located at 102 Missouri Street. Later the business was sold to Wolgast Lumber and then was operated by John Haefke as Alma Lumber Company. Today this is a parking lot for Hormel Foods factory. (Courtesy of Wabaunsee County Historical Society.)

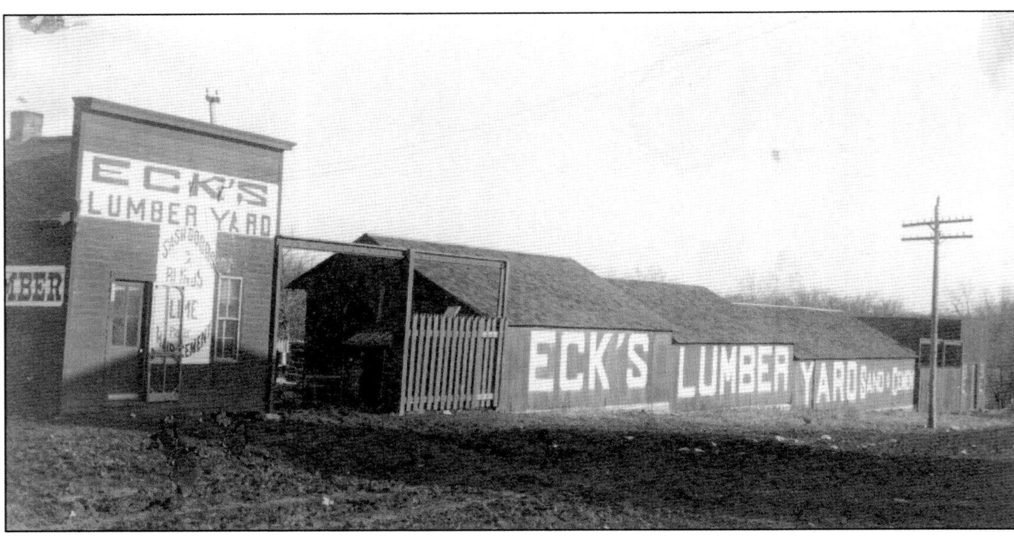

Eck Lumber Company was located in the old south town on the south end of Ohio Street in Alma. A number of business buildings and residences existed in this south section of town at the end of the 19th century. None remain today. Today the Hormel Foods plant is located here. (Courtesy of Wabaunsee County Historical Society.)

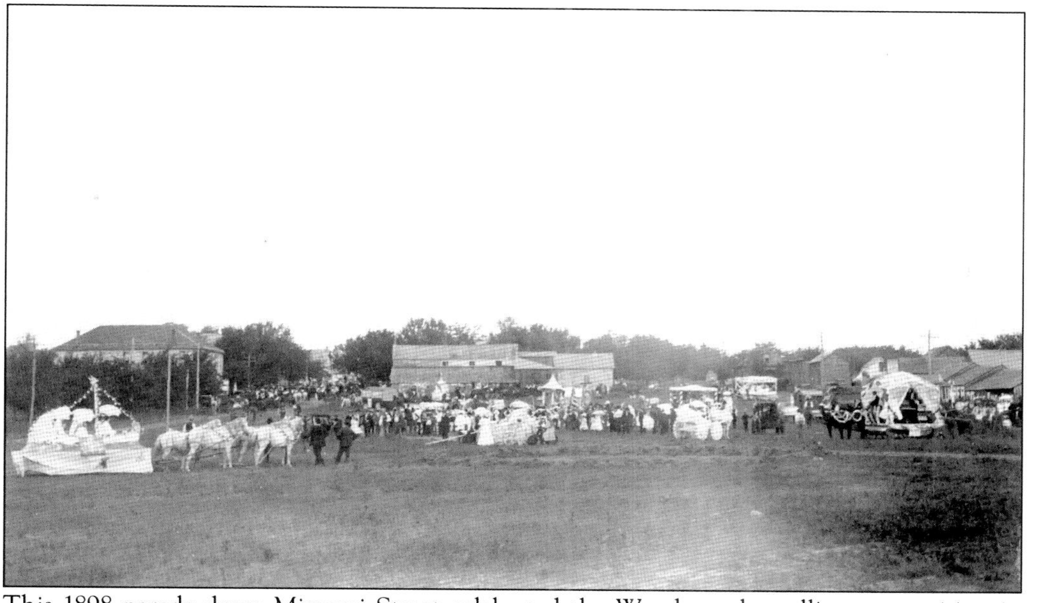

This 1898 parade down Missouri Street celebrated the Woodman log-rolling competition in Alma. Often these competitions brought as many as 10,000 people to the event. One can see the old south town, including Eck Lumber Company, to the far right. A. J. Schepp, donor of the photograph, wrote on the back, "Herman and I attended this event and saw the first automobile in Wabaunsee County." (Courtesy of Wabaunsee County Historical Society.)

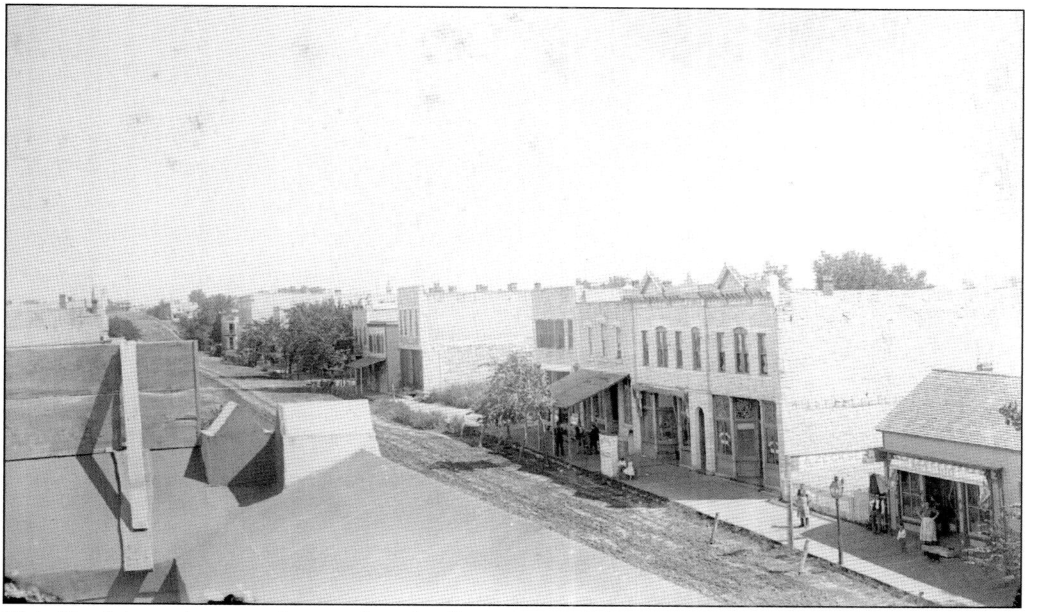

This Gus Meier photograph provides a bird's-eye view of the east side of the 200 block of Missouri Street taken around 1893. From right to left, the buildings include Zeckser's Shoe Shop, Alma State Bank, L. Palenske's Bookstore, Gus Meier Photo Studio, a drugstore, Allen Brothers Store, one frame building, and the Horne building (now Palenske Hall). (Courtesy of Wabaunsee County Historical Society.)

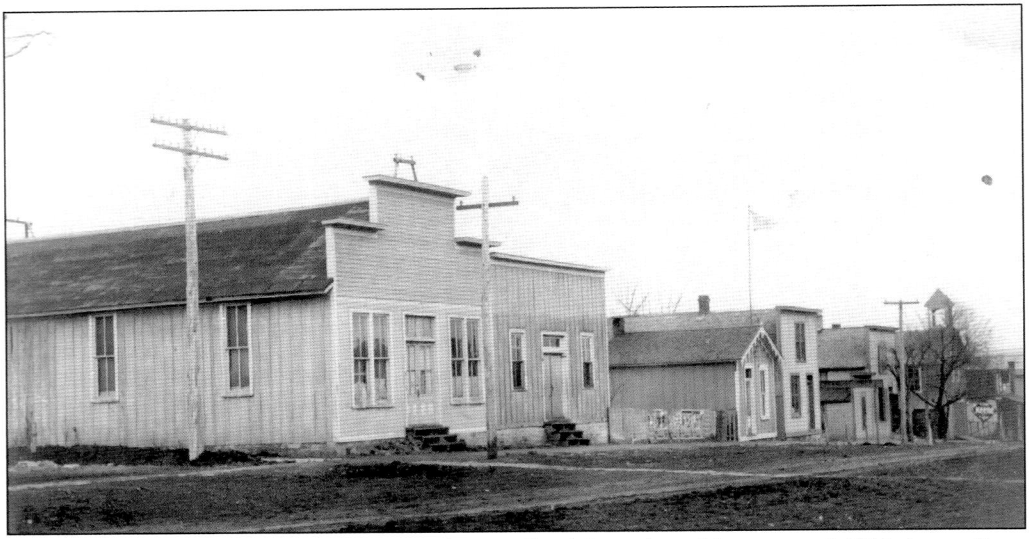

A view of the north side of Main Street (West Third Street) in Alma around 1910 shows, from left to right, Falk Opera House, Alma Marble Works, A. C. Campbell's the Alma Tailor, Ferd Herrmann's Shoe and Harness Shop, the Free Methodist Church, and Freeman Mercantile. (Courtesy of Wabaunsee County Historical Society.)

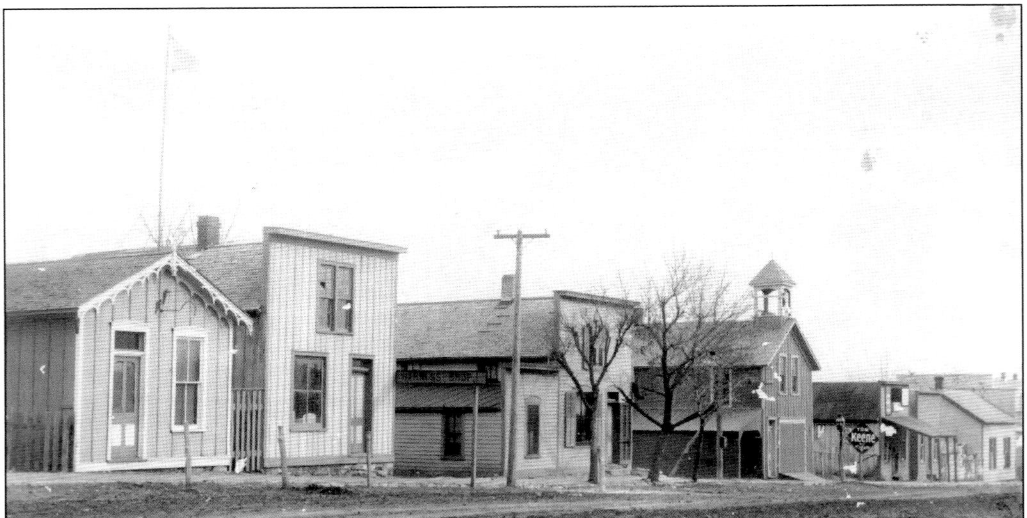

After the arrival of the railroad, Alma became a boomtown. In 1884, 52 buildings were erected. Many of these structures, including these on Main Street, as West Third Street was known until around 1920, were constructed of wood. (Courtesy of Wabaunsee County Historical Society.)

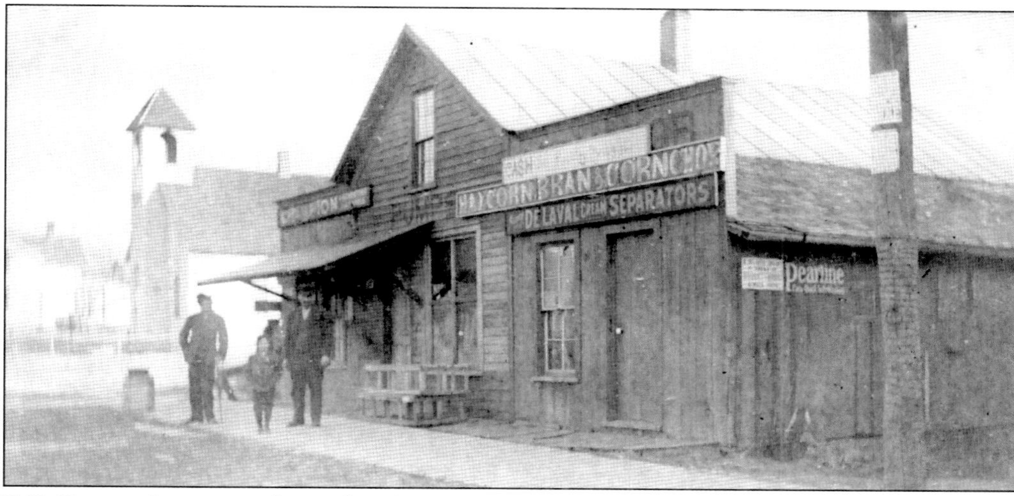

F. D. Freeman's store was located at the corner of Main Street (West Third Street) and Missouri Street in Alma, facing south, prior to the dawn of the 20th century. Seen here from left to right are Raymond Johnson, Charles Freeman, and F. D. Freeman around 1906. Freeman Produce began as a broom and produce business and then expanded, becoming a buyer of poultry and eggs. (Courtesy of Wabaunsee County Historical Society.)

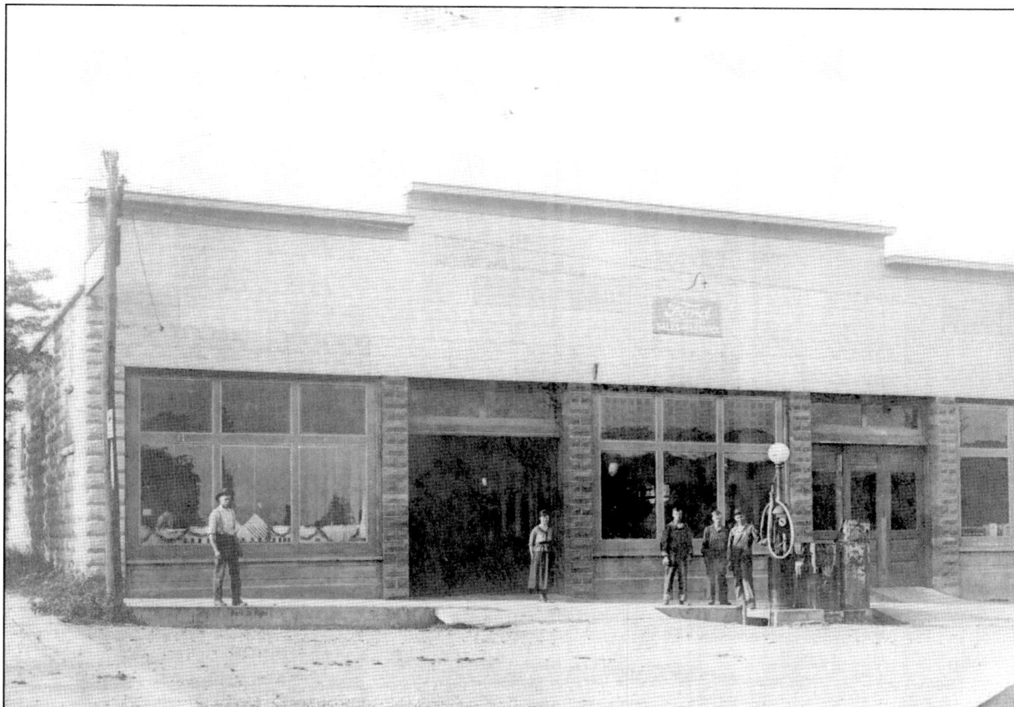

The opera house building was rebuilt and refaced, the stage was removed, and then it became Haller Motor Company. In this unusual view, Haller's was a Ford dealership. It was only that year that Haller's sold anything except Chevrolets. Maxine Haller remembers the cars were delivered to them off the rail by mistake, and rather than return them, they chose to sell Fords that year. (Courtesy of Wabaunsee County Historical Society.)

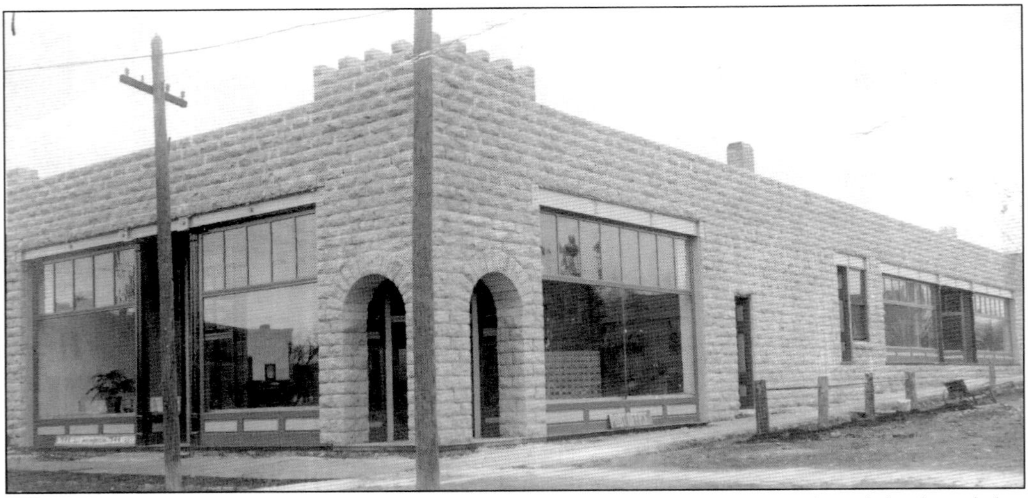

In 1906, the first courthouse building in Alma, the Kaufman building, was demolished, and this stone building was constructed by John Feiden. It housed a bank, the post office, and a drugstore over the years. This building was donated to the Wabaunsee County Historical Society in 1968 by Fred C. Palenske. (Courtesy of Wabaunsee County Historical Society.)

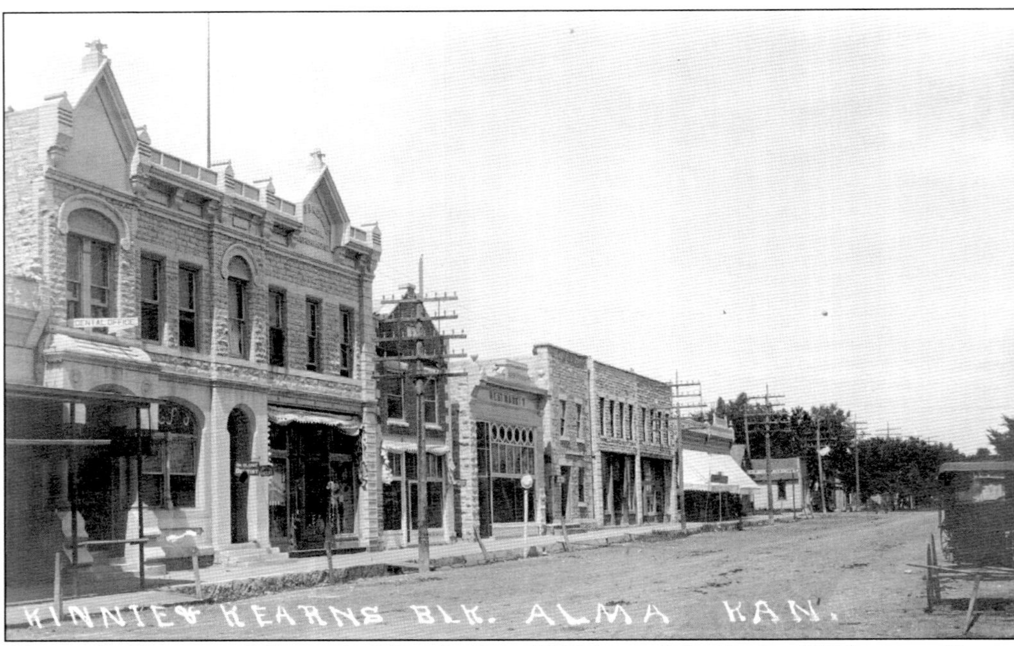

Above, the Kinnie and Kearns building, built in 1897, housed the Bank of Wabaunsee County before its failure on January 23, 1889. Kinnie and Kearns operated a mercantile and grocery store in the north half of the building at 311 Missouri Street, while the bank was located at 309 Missouri Street. (Courtesy of Wabaunsee County Historical Society.)

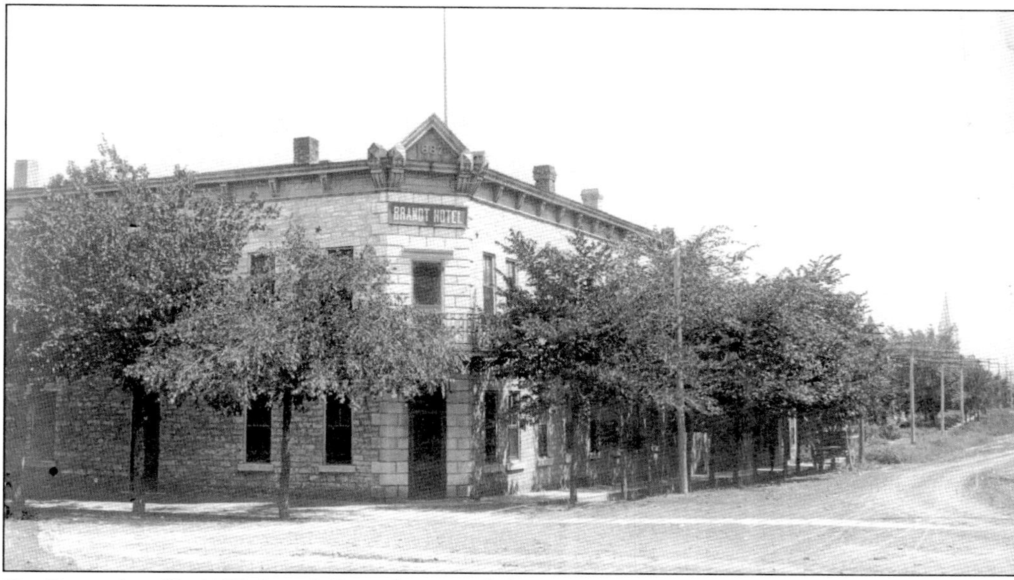

On December 12, 1887, Joseph Brandt opened the Brandt Hotel at 402 Missouri Street in Alma. He had previously operated the Western Star Hotel, a block to the south. By 1890, Brandt had turned the hotel over to M. G Whellan, and by 1901, it sold to Theresa Horne, who had previously operated a hotel in the old Palenske Hall building. After Brandt's departure, it was known as the Alma Hotel. This view is from about 1910. (Courtesy of Wabaunsee County Historical Society.)

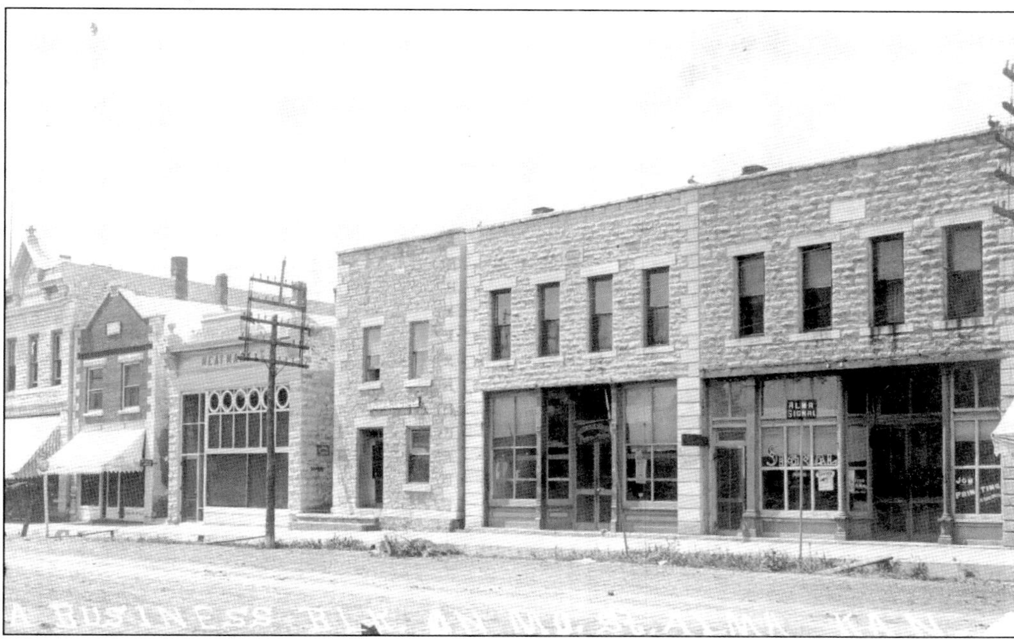

This view of the west side of the 300 block of Missouri Street in Alma shows the complete transformation of the business district to masonry buildings by 1910. Notice two newspapers, the *Alma Enterprise* at 319 Missouri Street and the *Alma Signal* at 323 Missouri Street, were separated by Dr. G. W. B. Beverley's office. (Courtesy of Wabaunsee County Historical Society.)

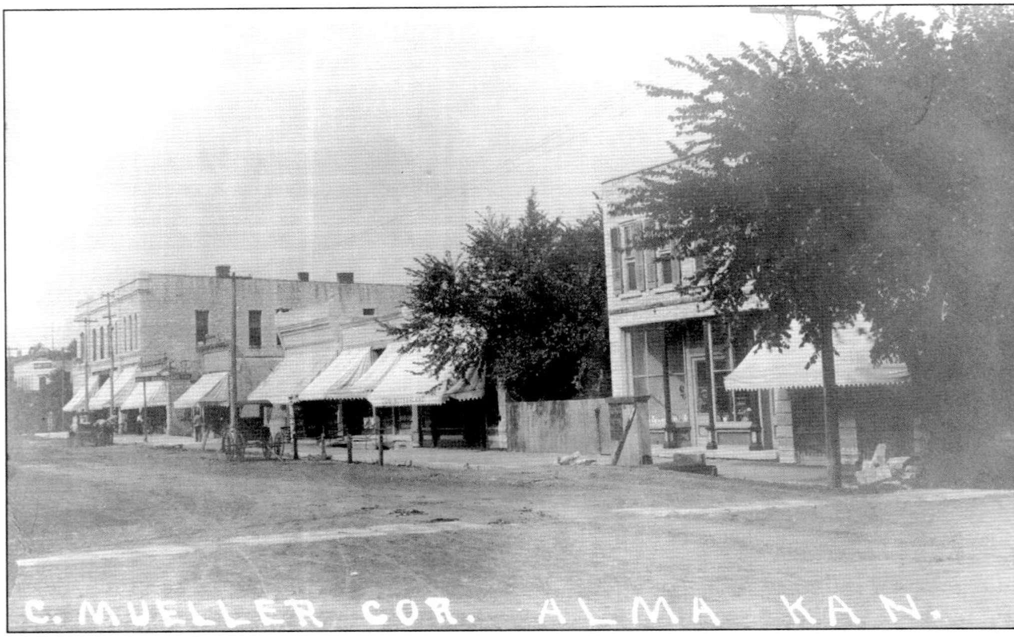

Conrad Mueller was an early Alma businessman, owning Mueller Hardware at 304 Missouri Street as well as the building next door in which he operated a saloon and pool hall in the late 1800s. In this real-photo postcard from about 1910, the east side of the 300 block of Missouri Street was at a peak for the number of structures. (Courtesy of Paul Gronquist.)

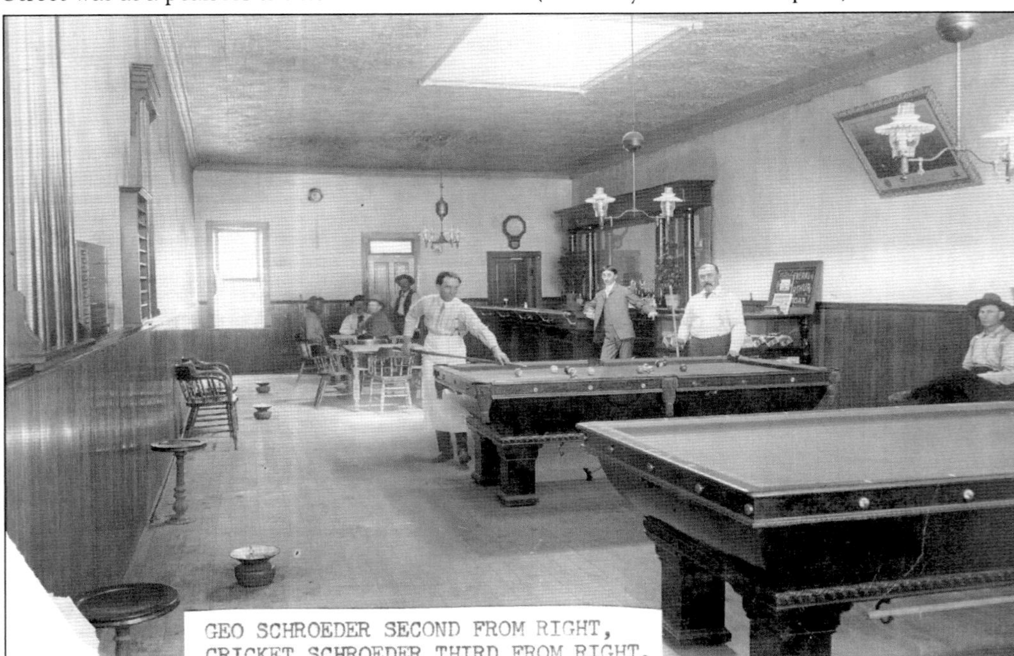

Palace billiard hall, located at 300 Missouri Street in this photograph, offered pool, billiards, cards, and drinks for Alma men. Conrad Mueller owned this building as well as his hardware store next door at 304 Missouri Street. (Courtesy of Wabaunsee County Historical Society.)

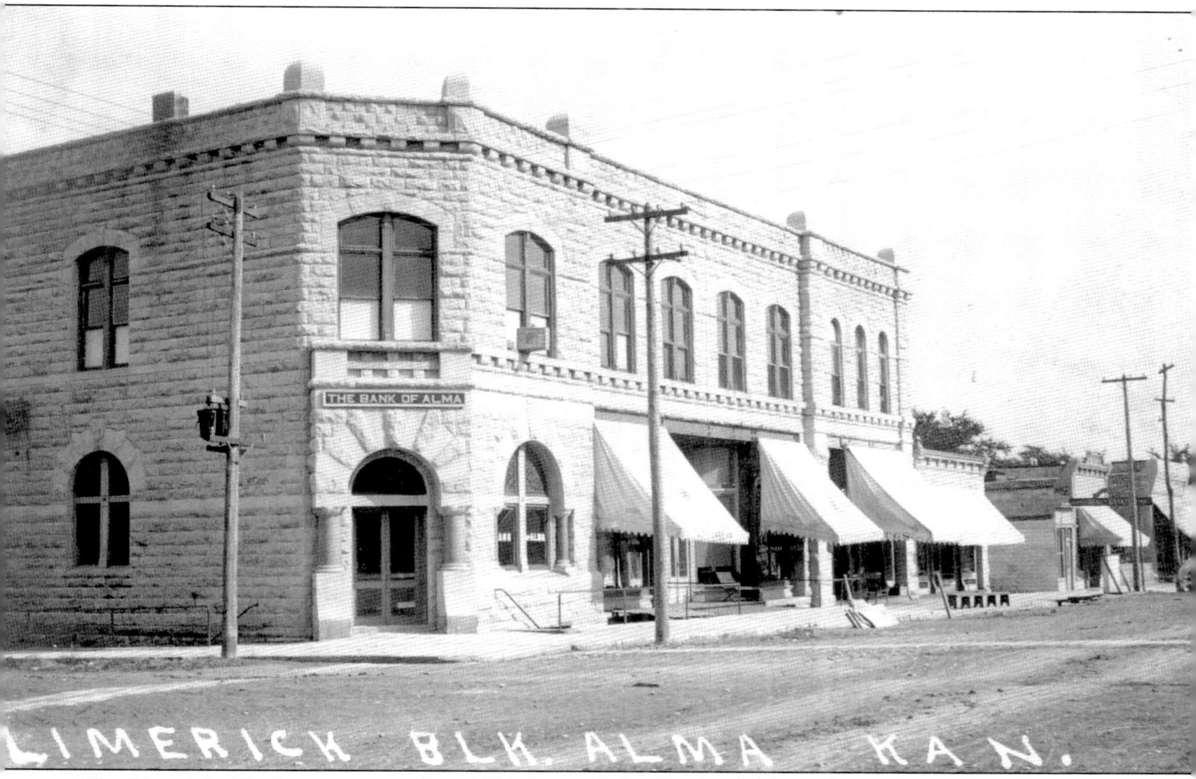

The Limerick block, constructed in 1890, housed the Bank of Alma that J. F. Limerick owned with his brother G. W. Limerick of Wamego. The building was also known as the Limerick and Crafts block, as druggist Fred Crafts joined the building venture and operated his drugstore in the south building in the structure (see page 29). The Limerick brothers also owned a land office, an insurance business, a brokerage business, and a coal-mining enterprise (see page 68). The bank failed and closed on November 9, 1890. Although Limerick left town with his business empire in shambles, his monument to greatness, the Limerick block, stands today as one of Alma's prominent stone landmarks. Today the building houses Alma's city hall, the Alma Antique Mall, and the Alma Post Office. (Courtesy of Wabaunsee County Historical Society.)

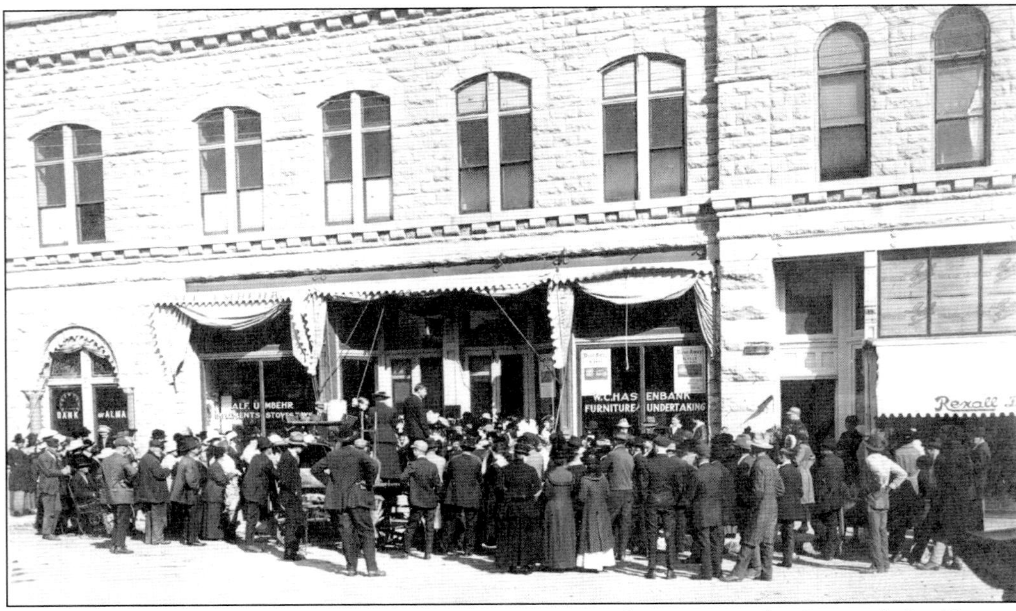

When Hasenbank Furniture Store moved into its new location in the Limerick building at 322 Missouri Street in this 1915 photograph, Stuewe Brothers Bank, Alf Umber's racquet store, and Fred Crafts's drugstore shared the building. This view was at the grand opening of the new store that had previously been located at 204 Missouri Street (see page 30). (Courtesy of Wabaunsee County Historical Society.)

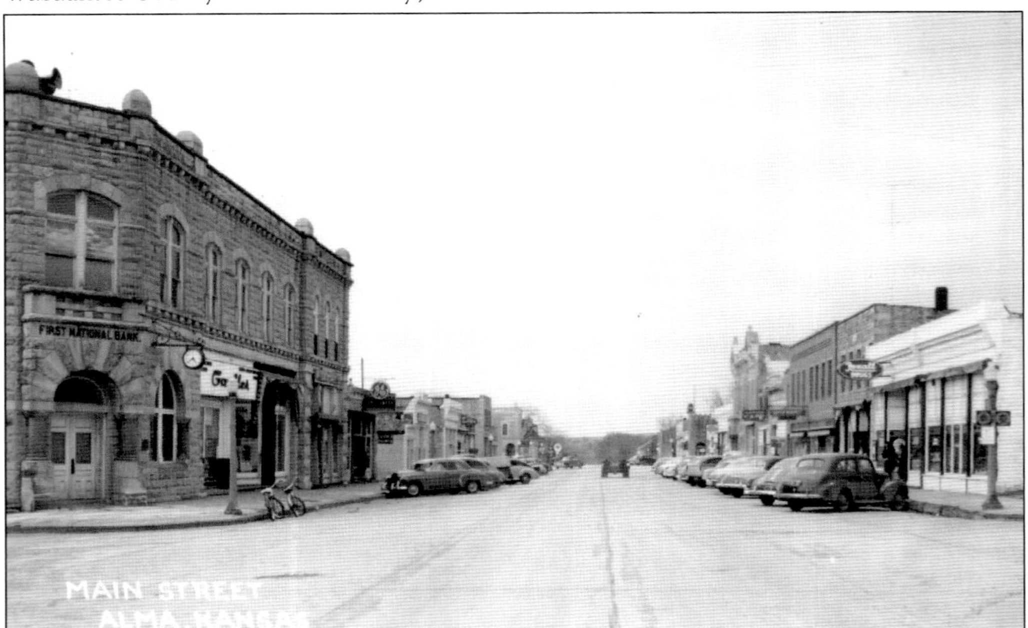

This early-1950s view of the 300 block of Missouri Street in Alma looks south. Notice that few of the storefronts were modernized at this time. Notably, the new brick front had been placed on the buildings at 319 and 321 Missouri Street on the right. This is the first view where that change had occurred. (Courtesy of Paul Gronquist.)

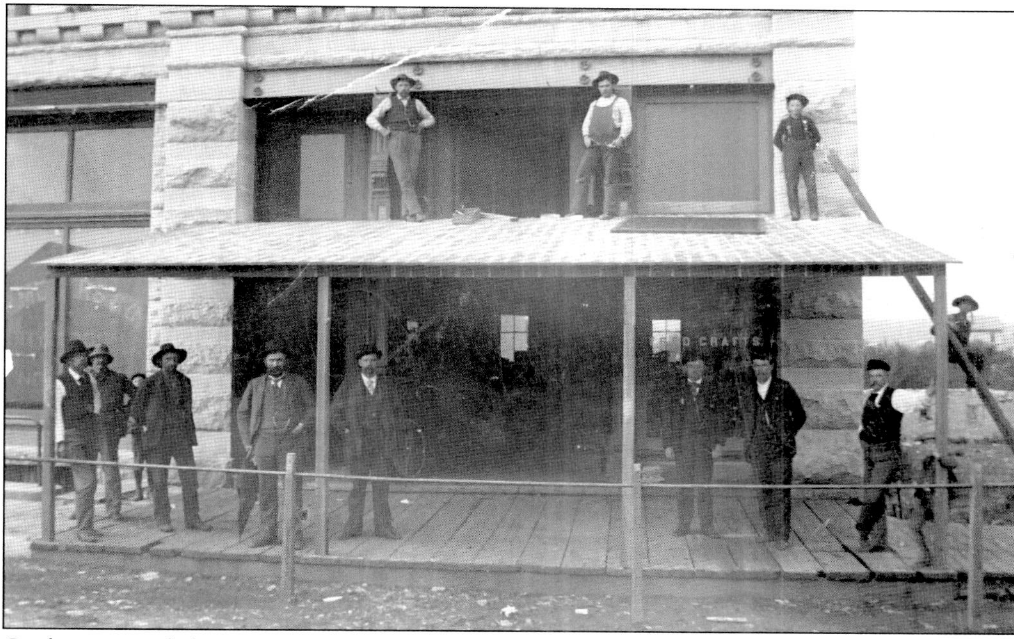

Crafts operated drugstores in Alma after moving there in 1875. In 1879, he was appointed postmaster. He partnered with J. F. Limerick to construct the limestone building in 1890. His drugstore is seen here, located at 320 Missouri Street, where the Alma Post Office is today. (Courtesy of Paul Gronquist.)

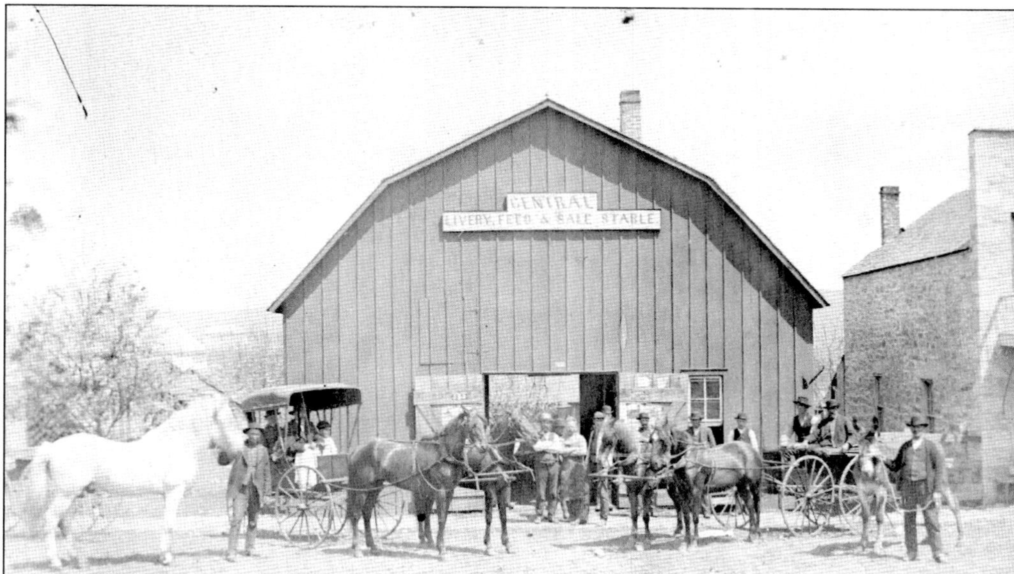

August Utermann's Central Livery Stable was among the earliest of buildings in Alma's business district, located at 316 Missouri Street, where a vacant lot exists today. It was built in 1884, and this view is from 1890. Around 1900, Utermann built a new livery stable a block north at 504 Missouri Street, where the American Legion building was constructed in 1936. (Courtesy of Wabaunsee County Historical Society.)

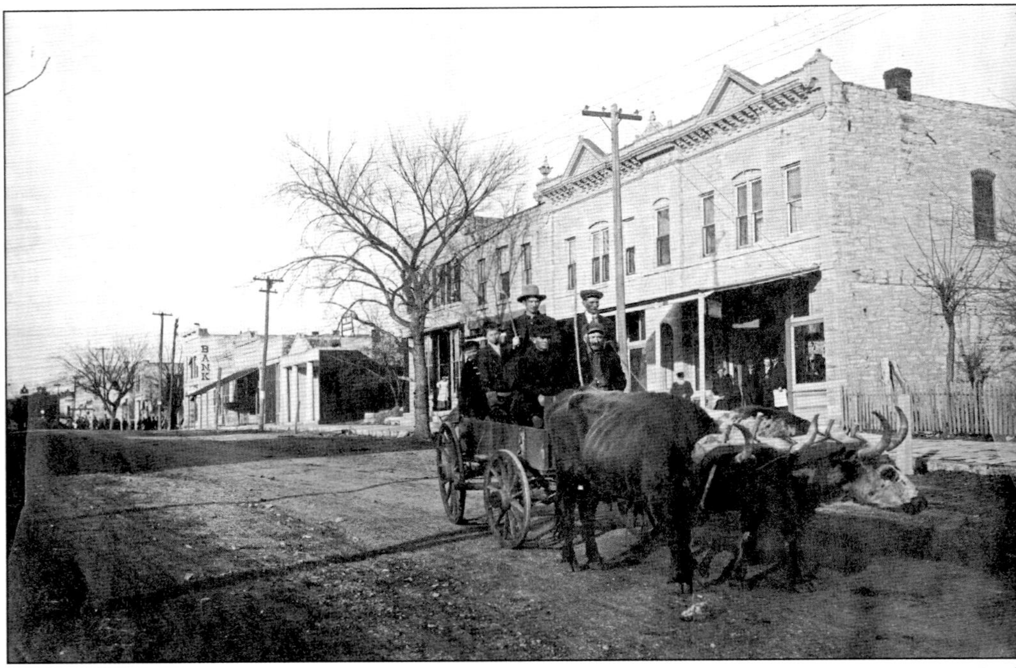

John Hasenbank drives a team of oxen down Missouri Street in Alma in this 1910 view. Dick Thoes (far right, holding newspaper) and W. C. Hasenbank (to his right) stand in the doorway of Hasenbank's furniture and undertaking business at 204 Missouri Street. (Courtesy of Wabaunsee County Historical Society.)

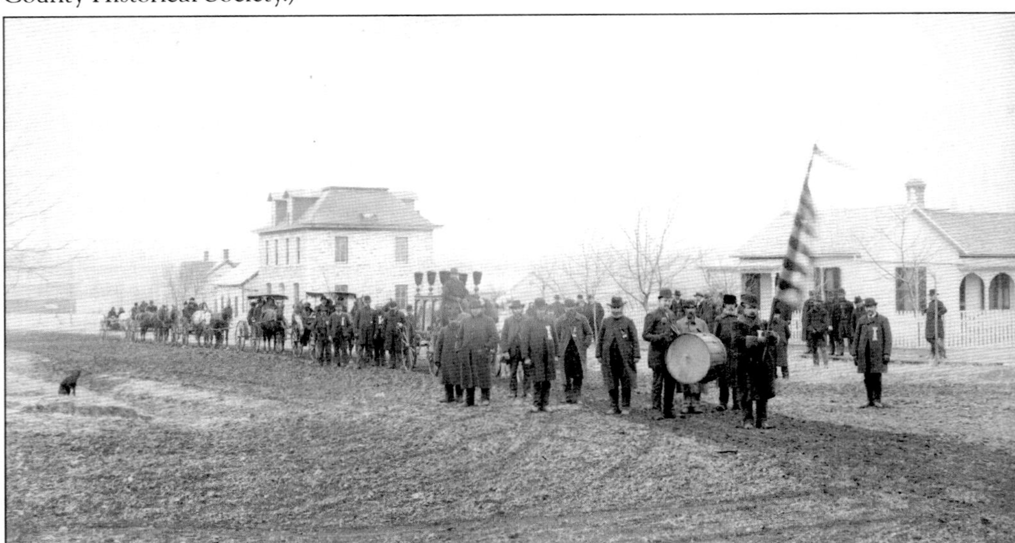

The funeral procession of William Schroeder is seen leaving his home on East Fourth Street in Alma. Herman Richter was the funeral director in this photograph from February 19, 1892. It was common in the 19th century for wakes and funerals to be held at the homes of the departed. In small towns, undertakers were usually the furniture makers who also manufactured coffins. In Alma, both Richter and Hasenbank undertakers operated furniture stores. (Courtesy of Wabaunsee County Historical Society.)

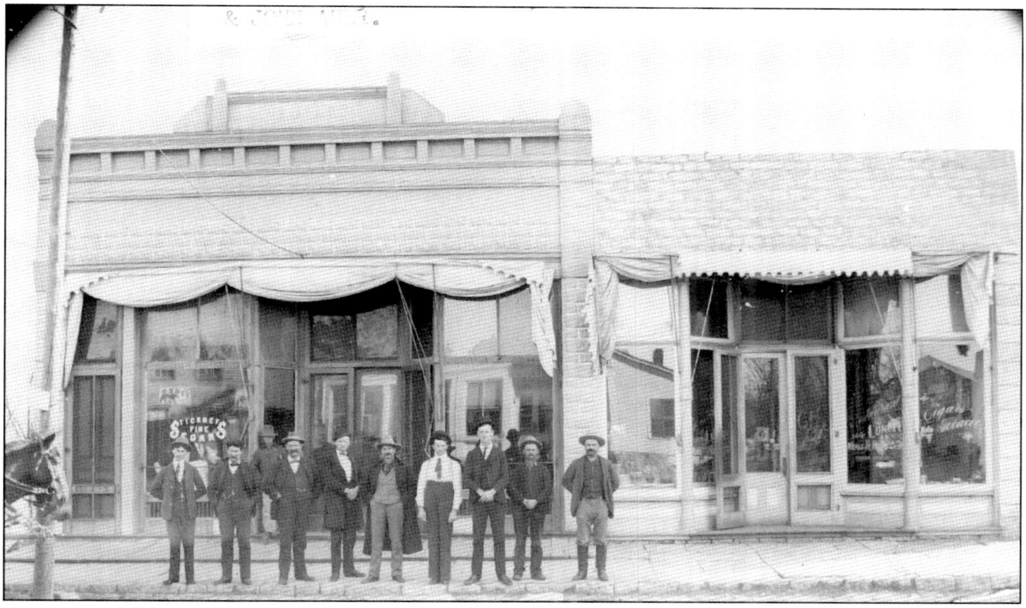

A group of Alma men pose in front of Hickory Jones's tobacco shop at 224 Missouri Street in Alma around 1900. This building was constructed in 1897. The telephone company was located in this building at the dawn of the 20th century. This building burned by 1920, and the lot remained vacant for a number of years. Today the building on this site is the Campanella-Gentry Funeral Home. (Courtesy of Wabaunsee County Historical Society.)

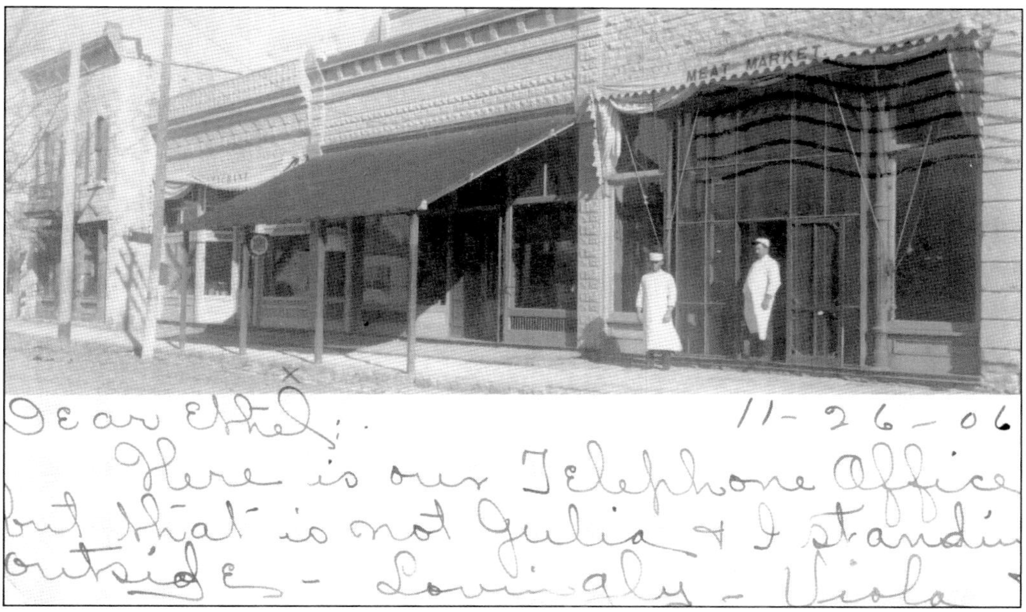

This postcard view, dated November 26, 1906, shows the evolution of the 200 block of Missouri Street. At the far left is the Horne building, now Palenske Hall, shortly before it was gutted and a new front placed on the structure. To the right of that building is a restaurant, then the telephone office, and finally, Eugene Schmitz's meat market. (Courtesy of Wabaunsee County Historical Society.)

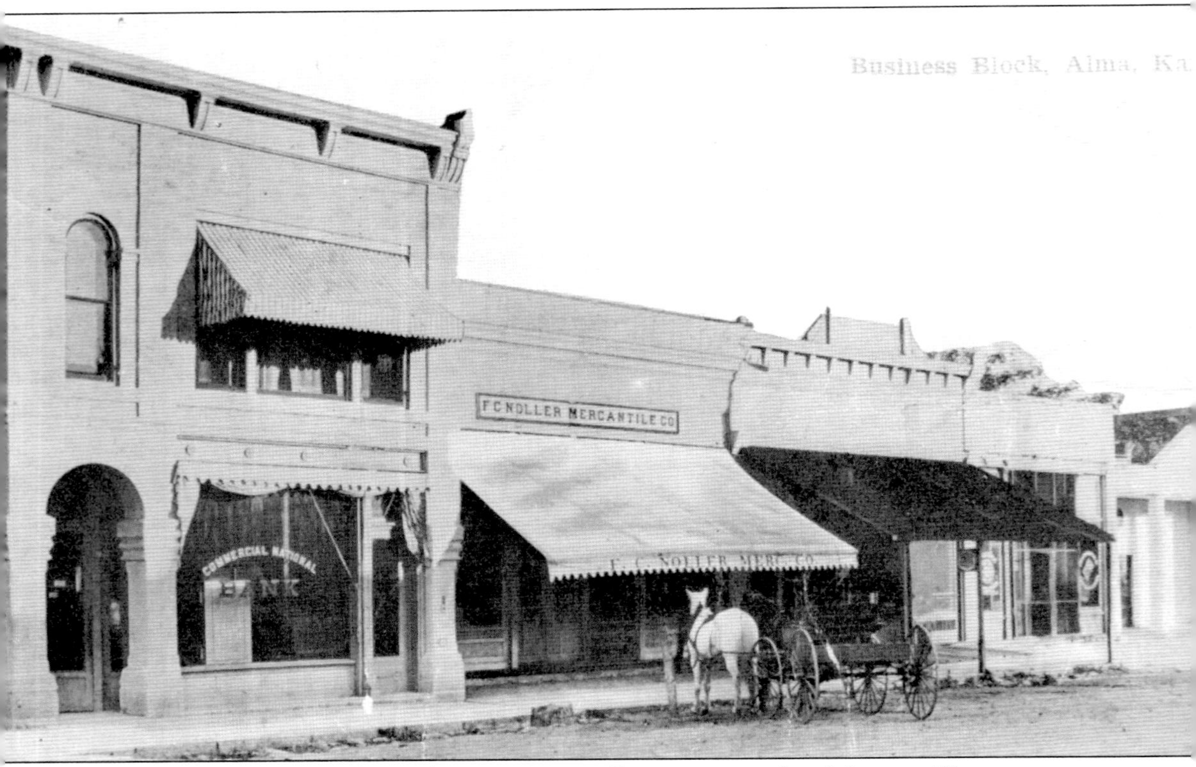

Palenske Hall (far left), located at 226 Missouri Street, is steeped with history. The structure was built in 1873 as a hotel and a meeting building called Germania Hall (see page 15). It was later known as the Horne building when Theresa Horne operated her hotel there. W. W. Thompson purchased it in 1908 and then sold it a few days later to Louis Palenske, who remodeled the building before opening the Commercial National Bank there in 1909. Over the years, the building housed a hotel, a bank, a saloon, and a produce business. Fred C. Palenske donated this building and the museum building across the street to the Wabaunsee County Historical Society in 1968. Born and raised in Alma, he founded Industrial Rubber Goods Company in St. Joseph, Michigan. He held three U.S. patents for rubber insulating material. After his wife's death in 1959, he sold his business, and in 1961, he sent anonymous donations of $5,000 to every private college in Michigan. Albion College was the only college that sent a thank-you letter. He then made substantial donations to that institution to complete a science complex, which bears his name, Fred C. Palenske Hall. (Courtesy of Wabaunsee County Historical Society.)

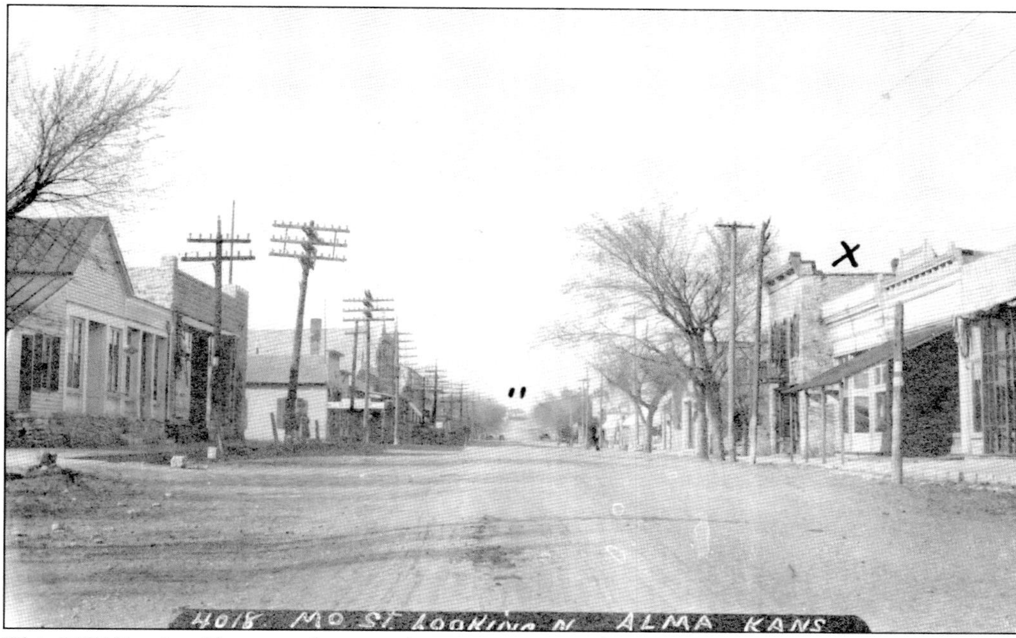

This 1907 Zercher Photography view shows a transitional Missouri Street, looking north. Notice that the museum building was constructed on the left; however, the old Meyer store was still standing. It was replaced in 1908; notice the view below. The Palenske Hall building on the east side of the street still bore its original front. (Courtesy of Paul Gronquist.)

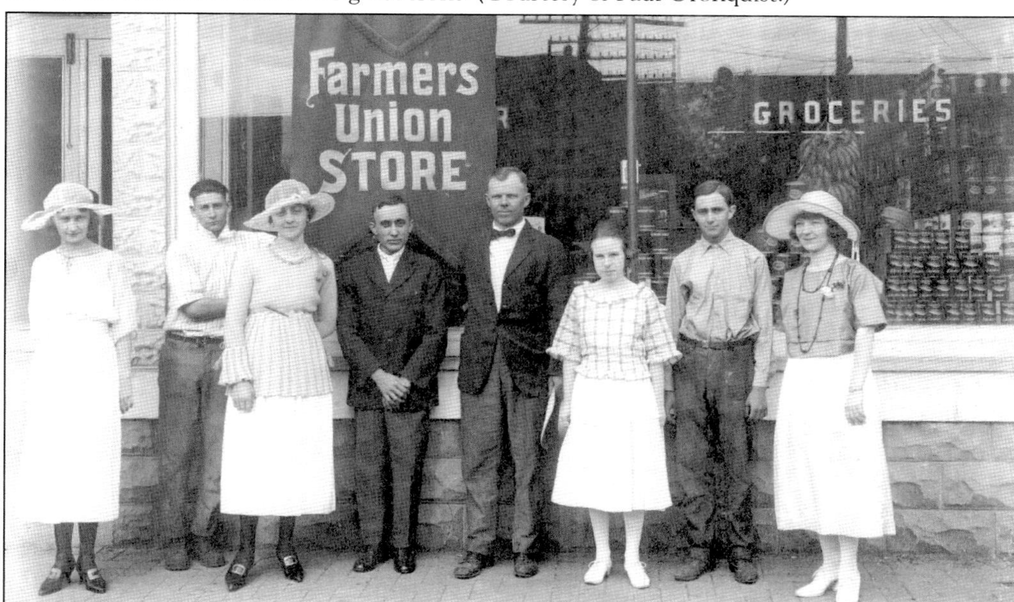

Construction began on the Farmers Union Store in October 1908 by the Feiden Brothers, replacing the old Meyer store at 225 Missouri Street. The new store opened early in 1909. From left to right are Marguerite McCrumb, Raymond Baker, Sophia Laging, August Guth, C. B. Thowe, Esther Fisher, W. E. Thowe, and Goldie Hess. (Courtesy of Wabaunsee County Historical Society.)

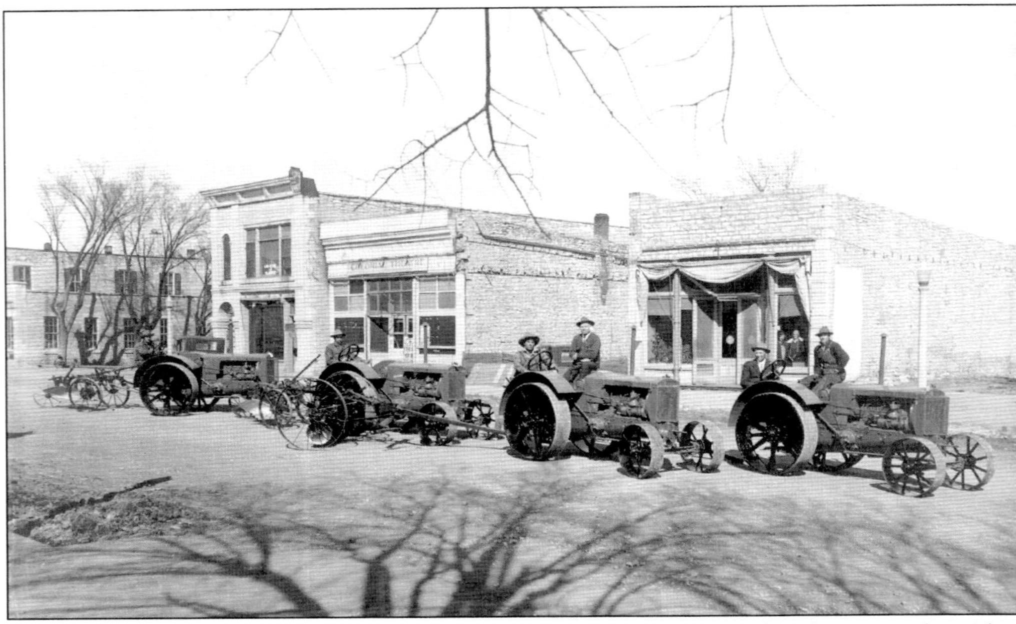

Area farmers proudly display four new Wallis tractors and equipment after their arrival in Alma via rail. Notice that Hickory Jones's tobacco store, seen on page 31, has disappeared by the time of this mid-1920s photograph, and a new building, the Colonial Theater, has been constructed next to the bank building. One of these very tractors is a pasture art display at the ghost town of Volland today. William Bowes's law office was upstairs in the Palenske Hall building in this view. (Courtesy of Wabaunsee County Historical Society.)

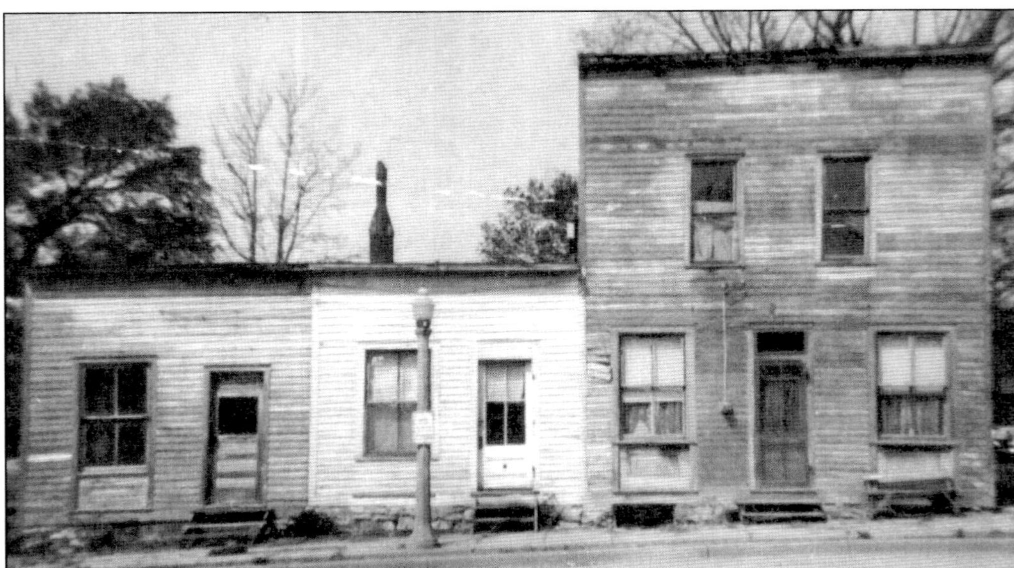

The Blossom House Café, the two-story building to the right, was located on the west side of Missouri Street in the 200 block and owned by William Dieball. These three frame buildings were constructed in the late 1800s and were demolished and replaced by Alma Co-op's grain elevators in the 1990s. (Courtesy of Wabaunsee County Historical Society.)

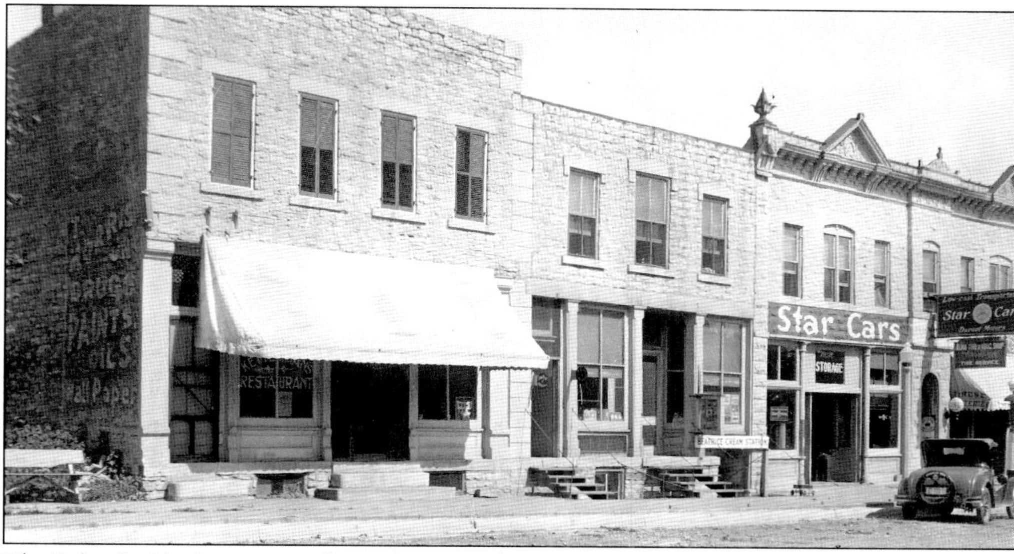

The Palenske block is seen in this early-1920s photograph by Gus Meier. This is among the Meier photographs that have been in the state archives since Mary Meier's death in 1966. The Kansas State Historical Society has graciously made these images available for this publication. From left to right are Ketterman's Restaurant, an army-navy surplus store in the old Palenske bookstore building, the Star car dealership, and Alma Tire and Battery Company. The last two businesses were operated by the Steinmeyer Brothers. (Courtesy of Kansas State Historical Society.)

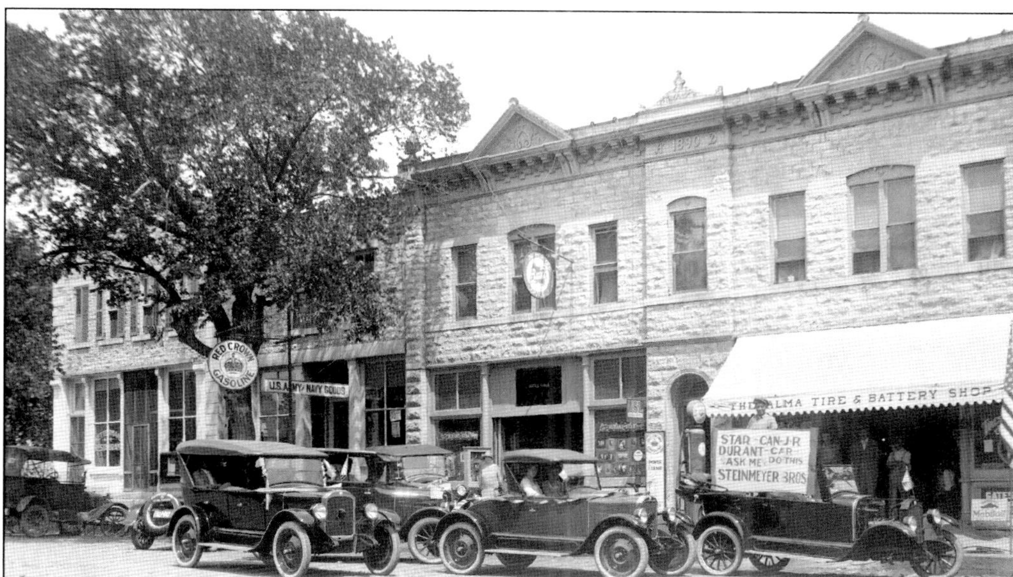

This Gus Meier view of the Palenske block looking to the north shows the Steinmeyer Brothers announcing the new Star car. Star, manufactured by the Durant Motor Company, produced cars from 1922 to 1928. In 1923, Star was the first car company to produce a factory-manufactured station wagon. Notice the Red Crown gas pump almost directly in front of the center door of the new Palenske building. (Courtesy of Kansas State Historical Society.)

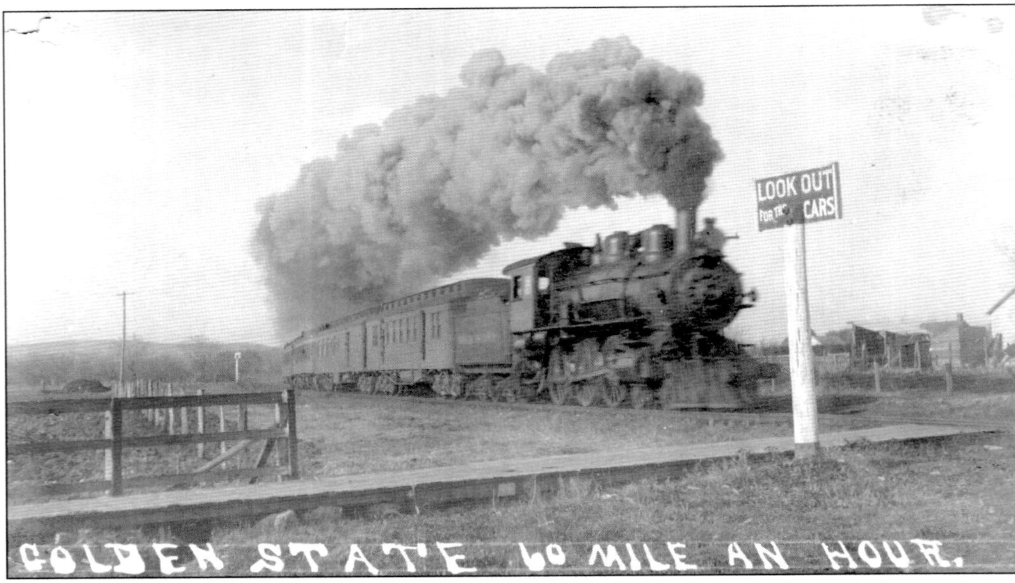

The Golden State Limited steams through Alma at 60 miles per hour in this real-photo postcard from about 1908. The Golden State, the first extra-fare train, was a partnership venture between the Chicago, Rock Island and Pacific Railroad and the Southern Pacific Railroad and provided express passenger service from Los Angeles to Chicago. The Golden State made its first run on October 2, 1902. The westbound Golden State was known as No. 3 while the eastbound was No. 4. (Courtesy of Wabaunsee County Historical Society.)

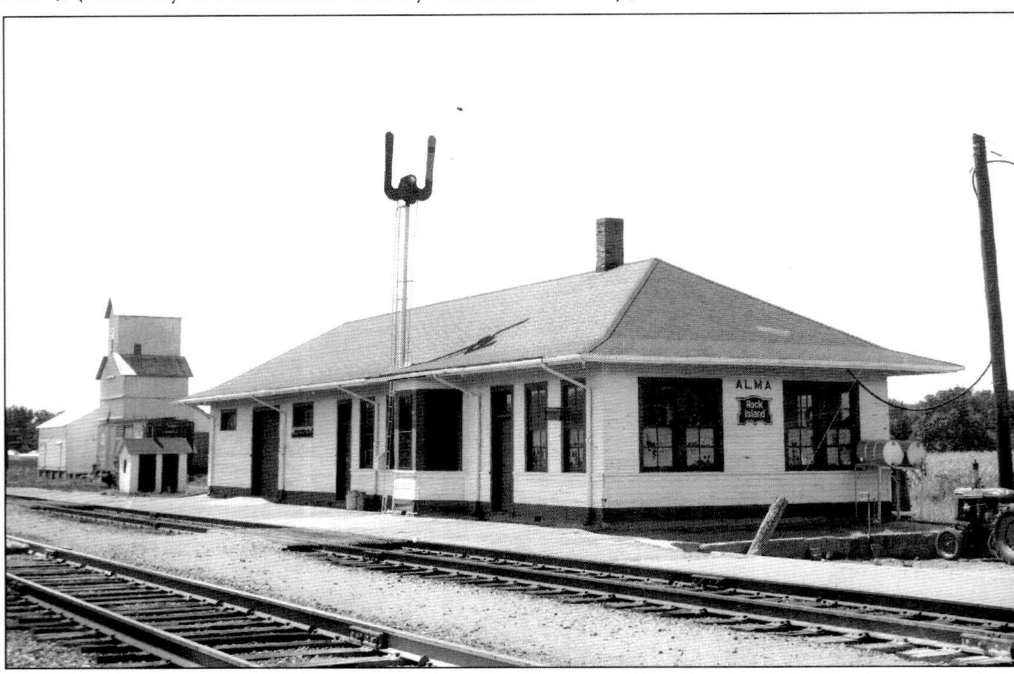

Above, the last Rock Island depot in Alma is seen in a 1950s photograph. The location of the depot can be seen in this photograph relative to the co-op elevators at the end of South Missouri Street to the west. (Courtesy of Kansas State Historical Society.)

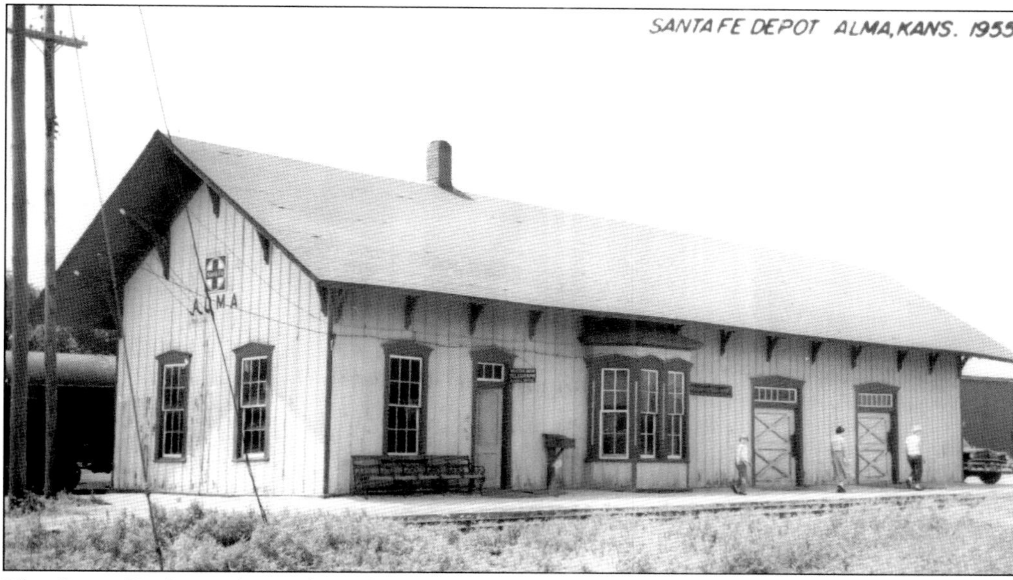

The Santa Fe depot, located on the east edge of Alma, was constructed in 1880 as the depot for the Manhattan, Alma and Burlingame Railroad, which was the first railroad in Wabaunsee County. The first vote for a $100,000 bond to bring rail service to Wabaunsee County in 1866 failed, and growth in the county was very slow. In 1879, a $140,000 bond for the Manhattan, Alma and Burlingame Railroad passed, bringing the first rail service to the county in 1880. This view is from 1955. (Courtesy of Paul Gronquist.)

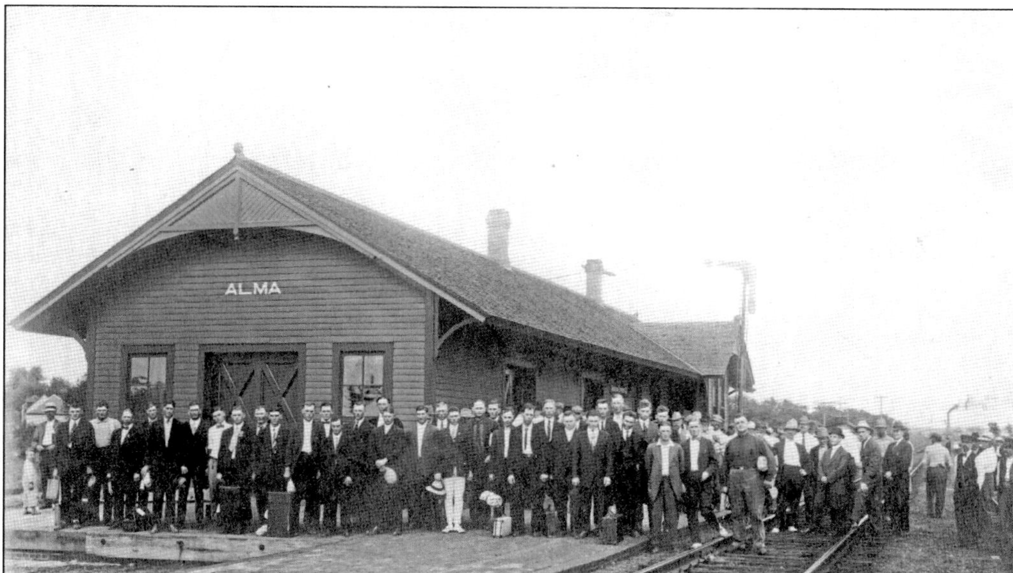

Wabaunsee County young men, drafted into World War I, gather at the Rock Island depot at Alma for transport to induction facilities. The depot was located at the south end of Missouri Street east of the co-op elevator. This is the third of four Rock Island depots that existed in Alma over the period of 80 years that the railroad operated there. Three were taken by fire, and the last was demolished. (Courtesy of Wabaunsee County Historical Society.)

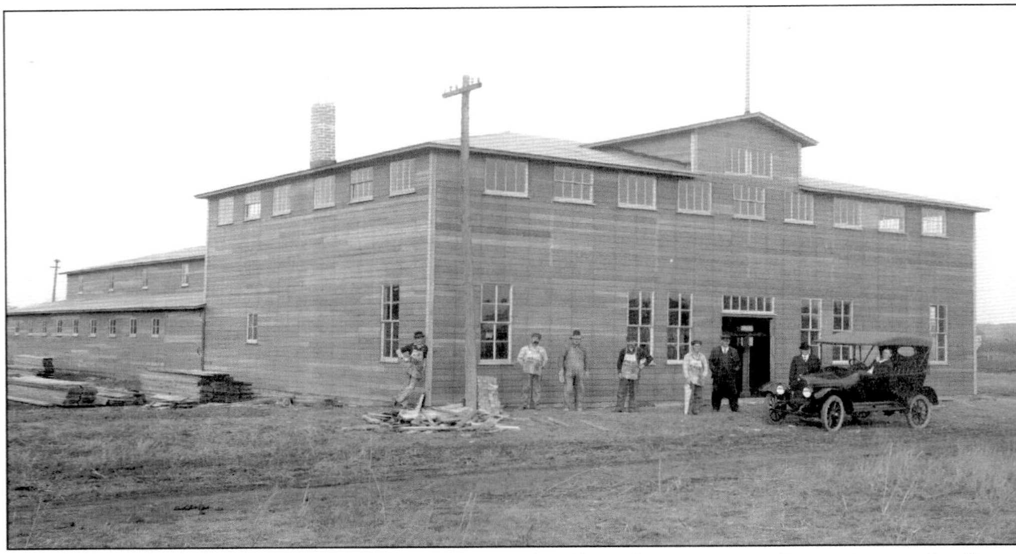

The Alma sales pavilion, construction just completed in this view, was located near the Santa Fe depot and stockyards in Alma. In later years before its demolition, the sales pavilion became known as the whey building for drying of the by-product of cheese manufacturing at the Dwight-Alma Dairy plant. (Courtesy of Wabaunsee County Historical Society.)

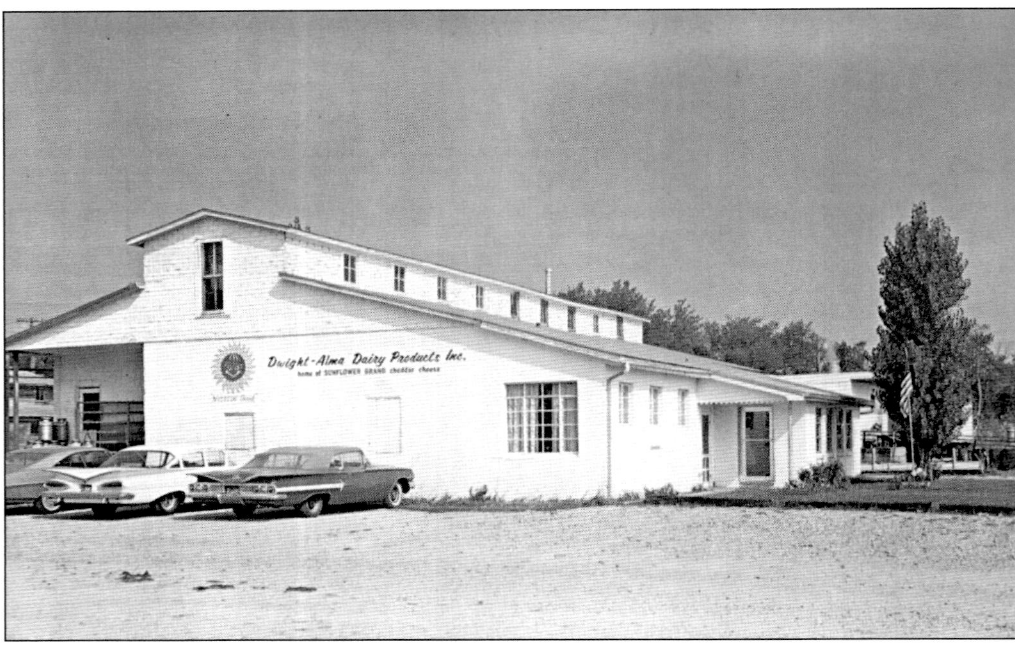

The Dwight Alma Dairy owned and operated the cheese plant in Alma in this 1960 real-photo postcard. The cheese plant, constructed in 1946, operates today as the Alma Creamery. (Courtesy of Paul Gronquist.)

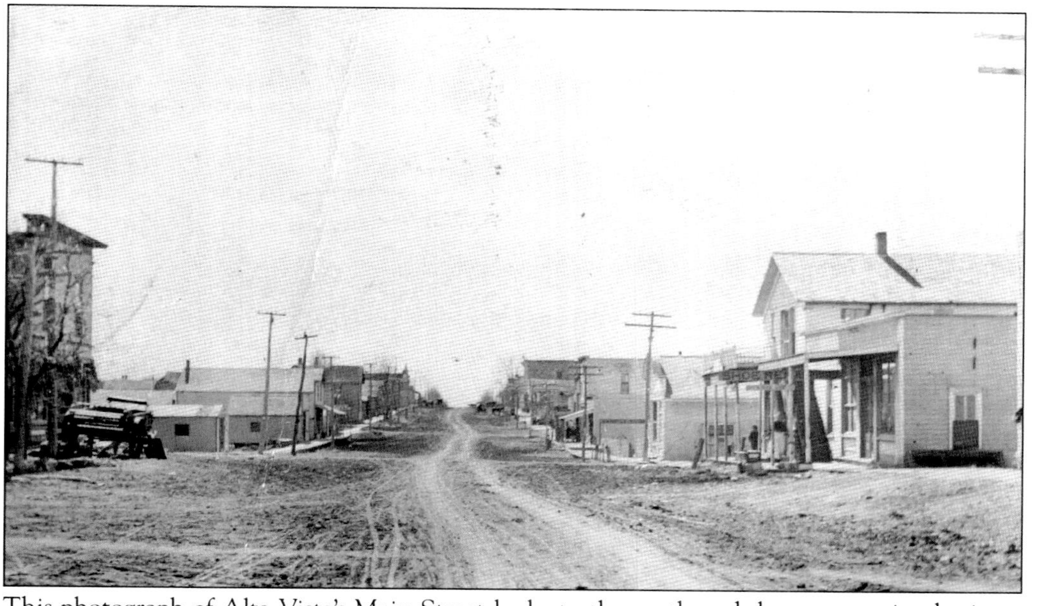

This photograph of Alta Vista's Main Street looks to the south and shows a growing business district. A business directory reveals five general stores, two hotels, two banks, two barbers, a furniture store, a lumberyard, two restaurants, a dentist, and a doctor all in Alta Vista in 1907. (Courtesy of Wabaunsee County Historical Society.)

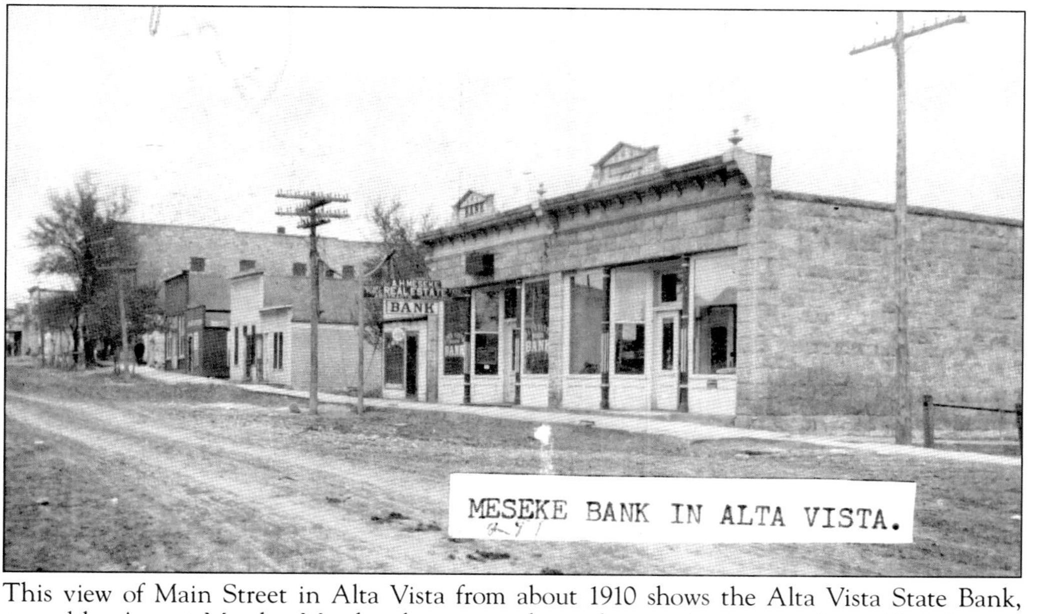

This view of Main Street in Alta Vista from about 1910 shows the Alta Vista State Bank, owned by August Meseke. Meseke also operated a real estate business and provided abstract and insurance services. To the right of the bank is the Bolton Dry Goods Store. (Courtesy of Wabaunsee County Historical Society.)

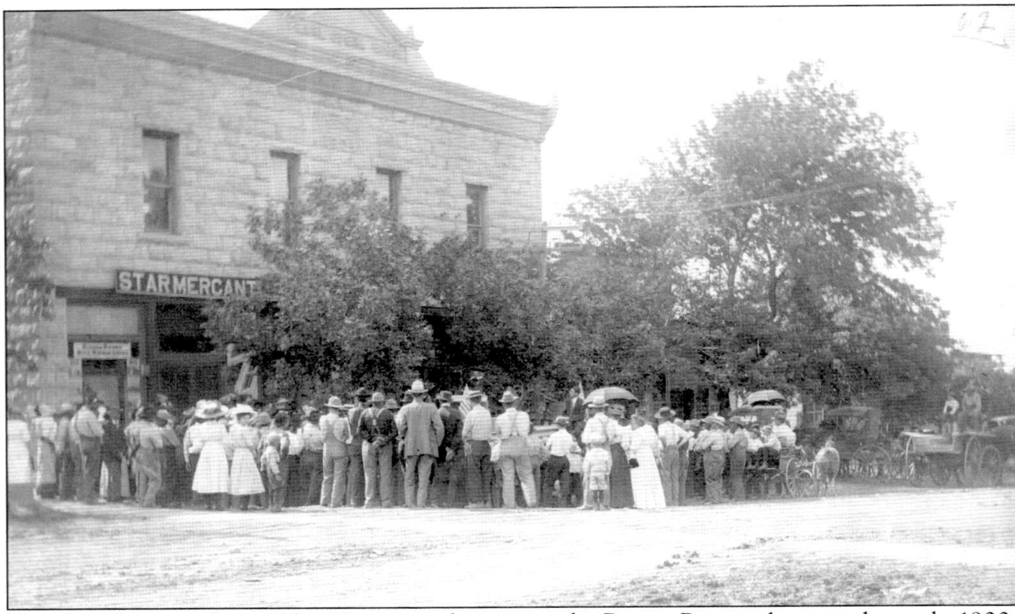

The Star Mercantile in Alta Vista was the scene of a Buster Brown show in the early 1900s. Brown Shoe Company purchased the rights to the comic character and from 1902 to 1930 hired small people to tour the United States, performing with a Boston terrier and depicting Buster Brown and his dog, Tige. (Courtesy of Wabaunsee County Historical Society.)

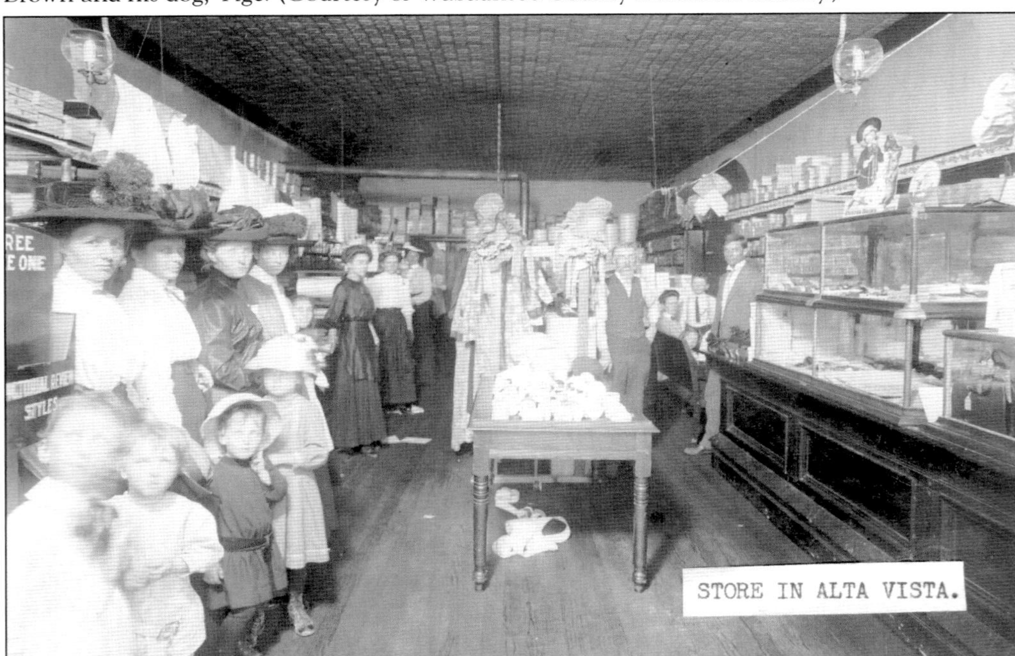

This interior view of the Star Mercantile in Alta Vista was taken in the late 1890s. Notice the gaslights hanging from the ceiling. Business buildings in the late 1800s were often unusually narrow and deep, allowing for two or more businesses in one structure, and it is noticeable in this view. (Courtesy of Wabaunsee County Historical Society.)

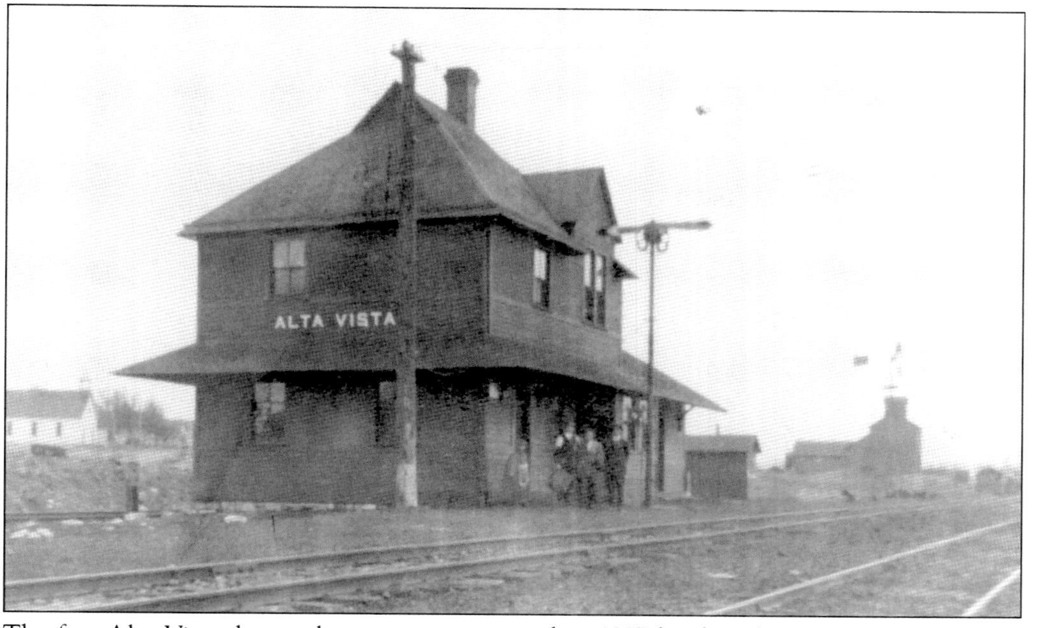

The first Alta Vista depot, above, was constructed in 1887 by the Chicago, Rock Island and Pacific Railroad. This depot burned on November 11, 1919. Mr. Jamison was the first depot agent. The interior of this depot can be seen on page 73. (Courtesy of Wabaunsee County Historical Society.)

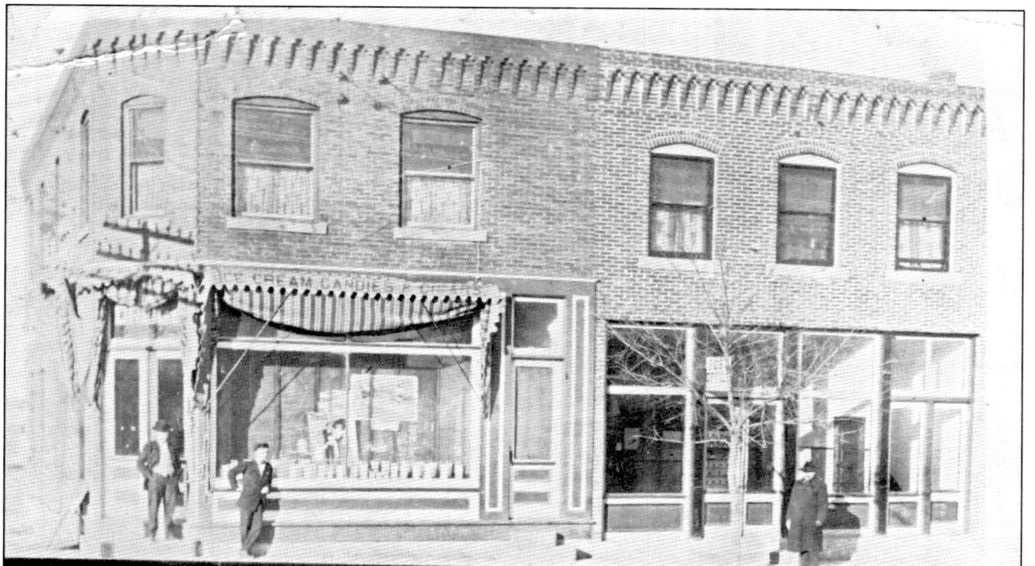

The brick building above, completed in 1911, housed Dr. Edgerton's corner drugstore, the post office, and the Journal office. It was struck by the 1912 tornado (see page 117). (Courtesy of Wabaunsee County Historical Society.)

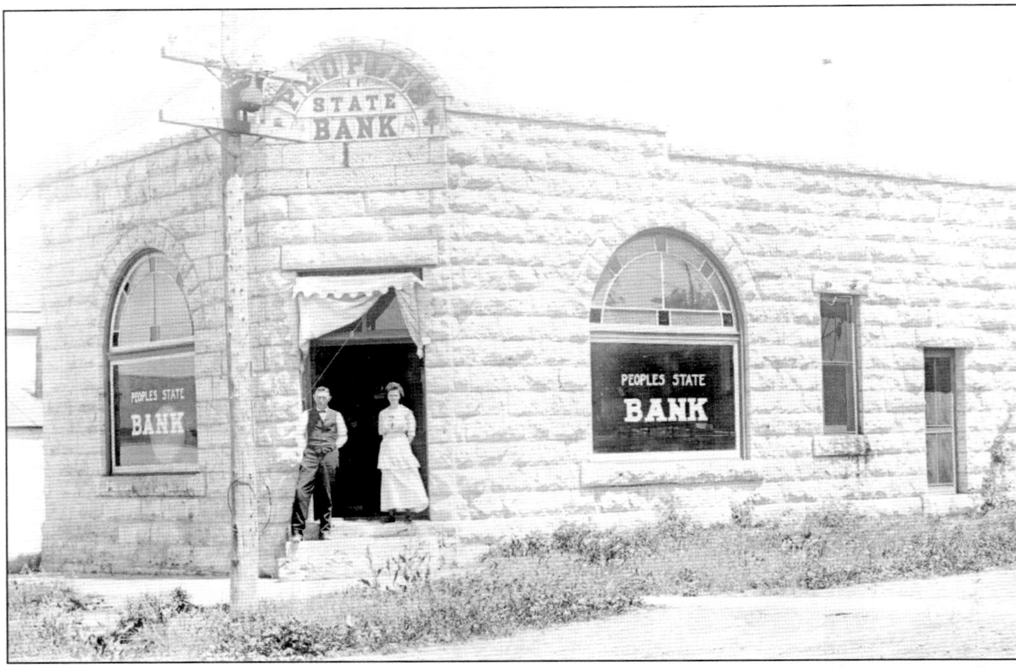

The Peoples State Bank of Alta Vista was chartered in 1906, with H. F. Dierking as president. The bank operated until its failure during the Depression in 1931. This photograph was taken around 1907. (Courtesy of Wabaunsee County Historical Society.)

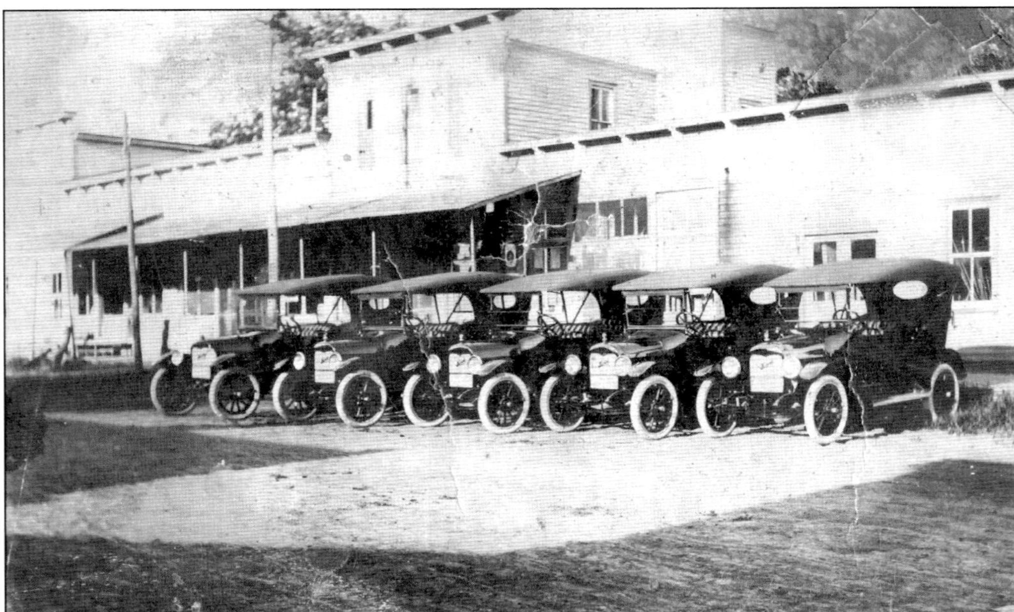

Five new Maxwell cars had been delivered to Otto Wolgast and Pete Holman in this 1914 Alta Vista photograph. Kistler and Arndt Hardware, Johnson Jewelry Store, and Wolgast Furniture and Undertaking can be seen in the background. (Courtesy of Wabaunsee County Historical Society.)

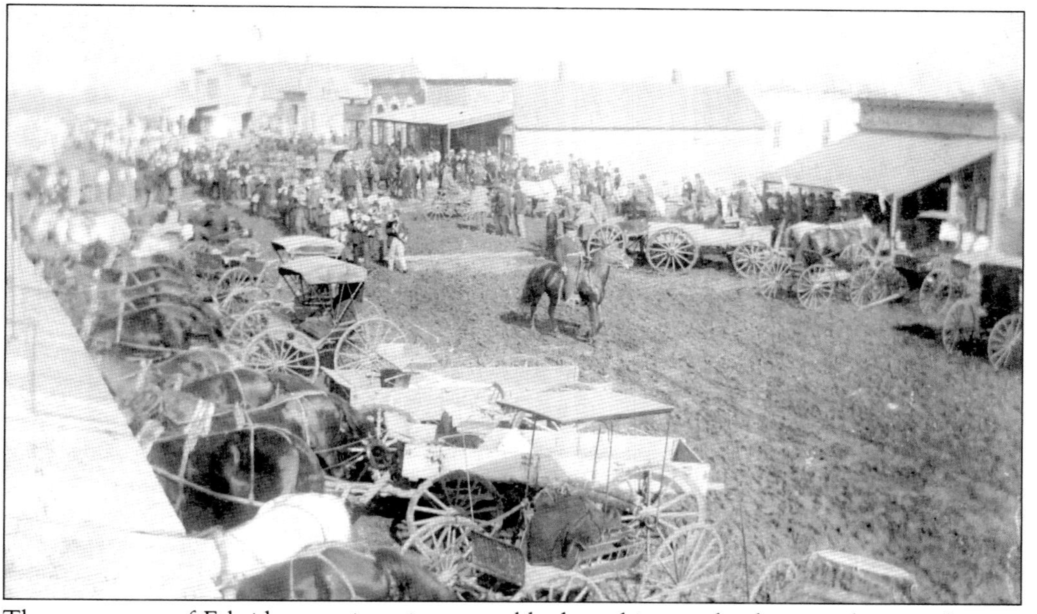

The new town of Eskridge was just six years old when this parade photograph was taken on July 4, 1886. The camera looks north at the east side of Main Street. Eskridge was platted by the Atchison, Topeka and Santa Fe Railway, and the streets are laid out relative to the rail line, as it came through town at somewhat of an angle. As a result, all the north streets in town are actually pointing 45 degrees northeast. (Courtesy of Wabaunsee County Historical Society.)

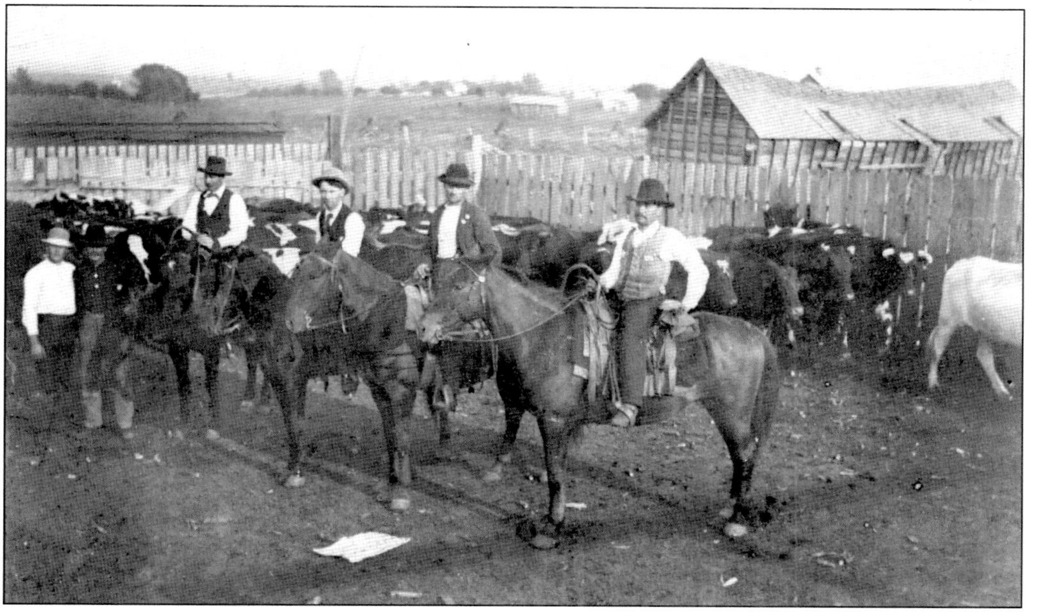

This group of cowboys was photographed at the Eskridge stockyards in the late 1880s. The stockyards were located where the senior citizen apartments are located on North Cedar Street today. The stockyards were located in close proximity to the railroad depot, as the train was the primary method of transporting cattle into and out of the Flint Hills. (Courtesy of Wabaunsee County Historical Society.)

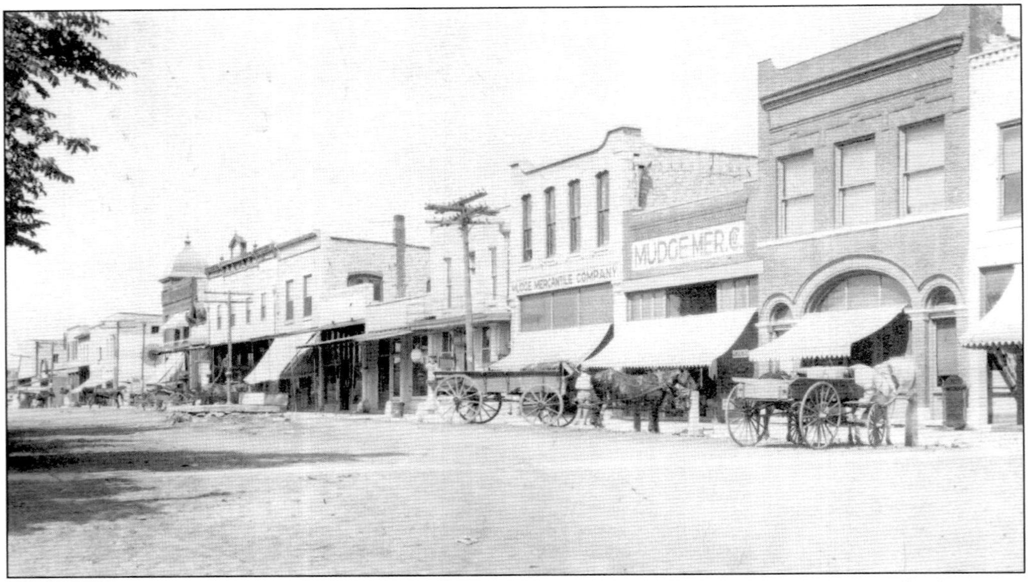

This view of the west side of Main Street in Eskridge, taken around 1910, shows the business district before the fire of 1913 when most of this block was destroyed. See photographs of the fire's destruction on page 114. (Courtesy of Wabaunsee County Historical Society.)

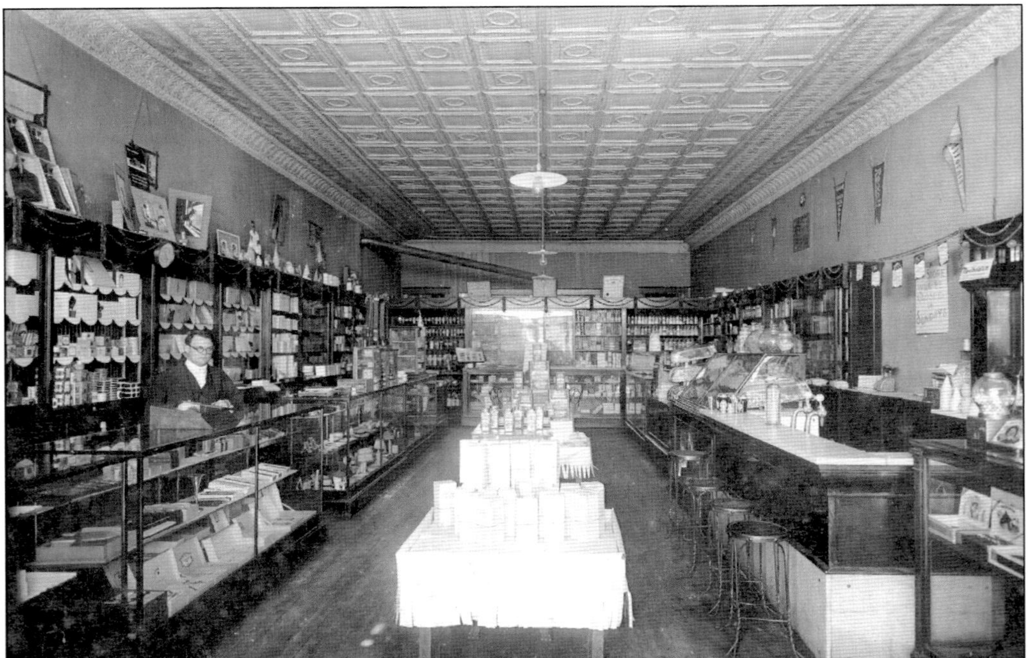

Preston Dunn stands behind the counter at his first drugstore on Main Street in Eskridge in the 1920s. Dunn moved to Eskridge in 1898 when he was five years old. He graduated from pharmacy school in 1915 and worked in a drugstore in Harveyville before being drafted into the army in 1918. After the war, he returned to Eskridge, where he operated a pharmacy for over 40 years. (Courtesy of Inez Dunn.)

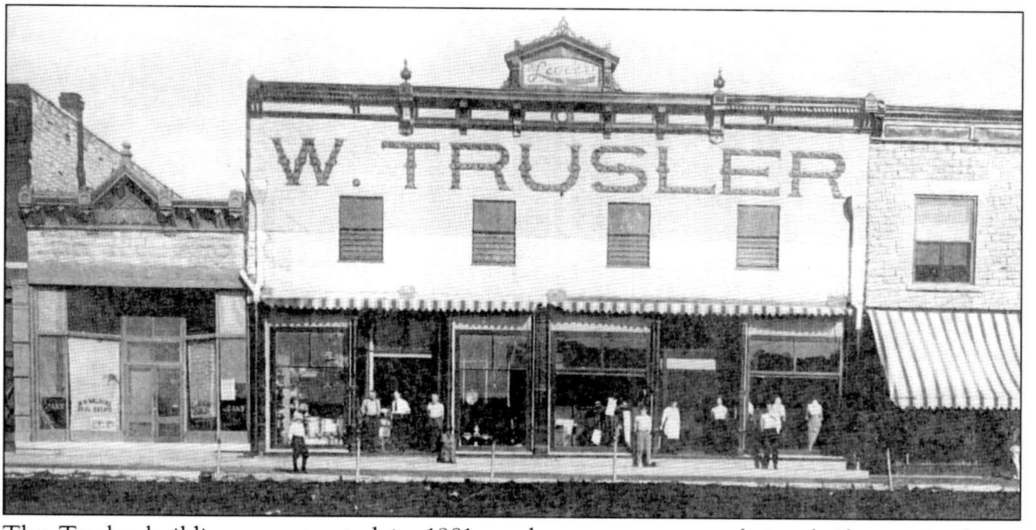

The Trusler building, constructed in 1881 as the new town was being built, survived two devastating fires on Main Street, one in 1890 and another in 1913. Both fires burned down the street to the Trusler building before being contained. William Trusler was one of the first merchants in the new town of Eskridge. (Courtesy of Inez Dunn.)

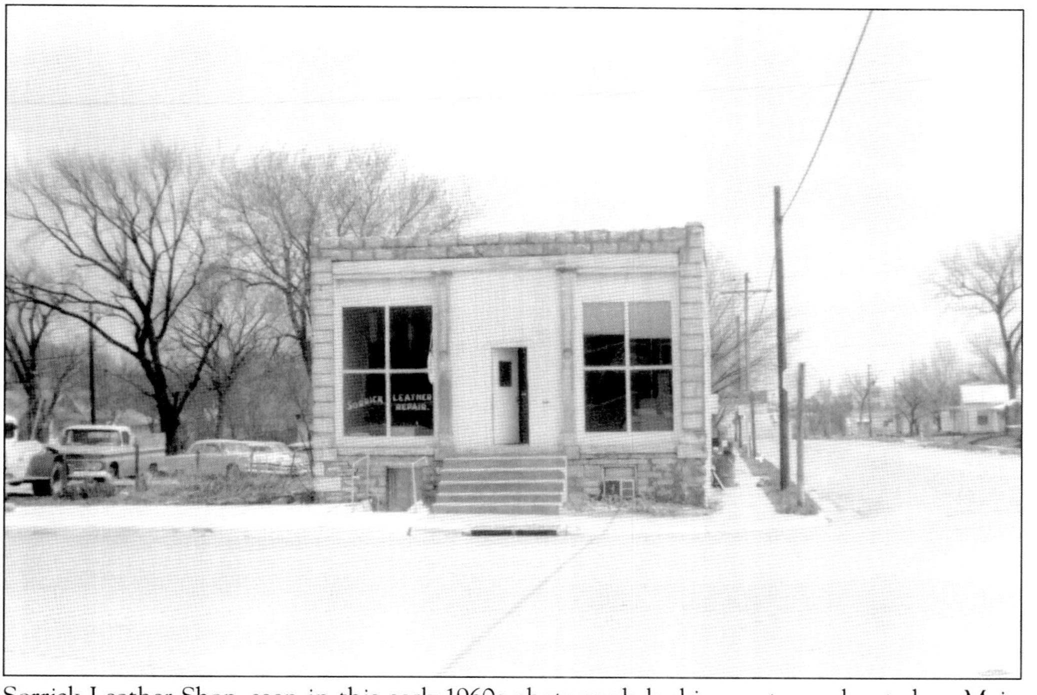

Sorrick Leather Shop, seen in this early-1960s photograph looking east, was located on Main Street in Eskridge at Third Avenue facing west. The building was demolished in the 1960s, and a gas station was built on the site facing south. That building is occupied today by the Rush In convenience store. (Courtesy of Inez Dunn.)

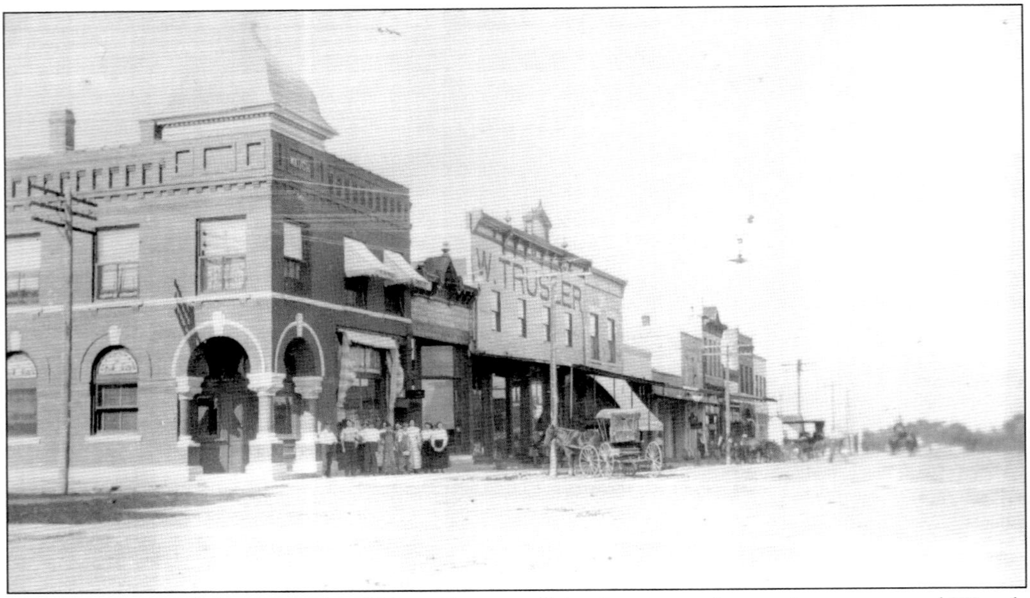

This 1908 view of the west side of Main Street in Eskridge shows the newly constructed Waugh building that housed the Security State Bank, the post office, and the offices of Dr. C. William Walker and Dr. A. H. Reynard. The next building north is the former Waugh bank building and then Trusler's hardware. (Courtesy of Kansas State Historical Society.)

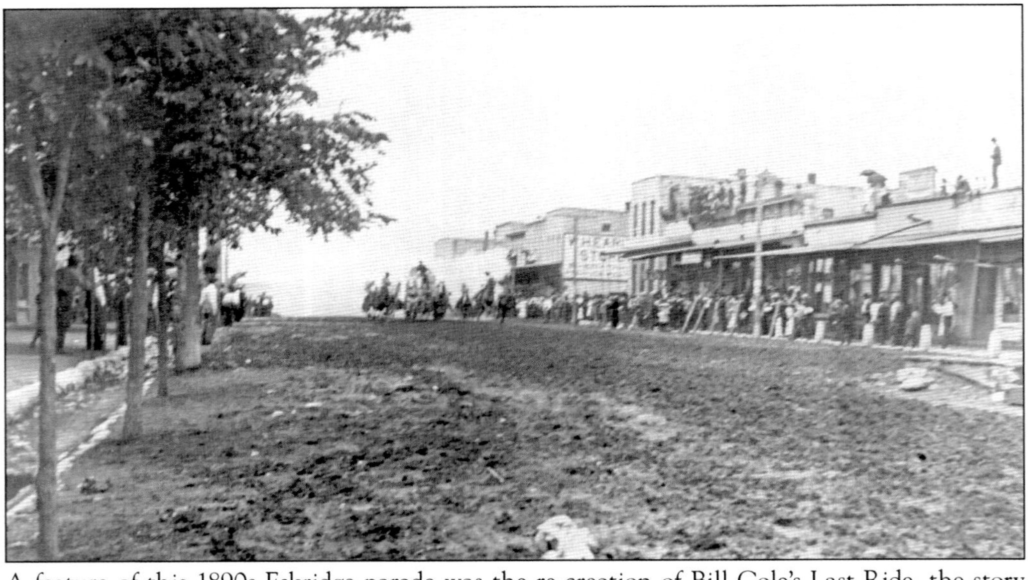

A feature of this 1890s Eskridge parade was the re-creation of Bill Cole's Last Ride, the story of an Overland Mail Company driver who, with the Smith brothers, was attacked by Kiowa warriors in western Kansas. Only Cole survived. Notice in this view that Trivett's general store was located where the Waugh building would be constructed after the store burned in January 1906. (Courtesy of Wabaunsee County Historical Society.)

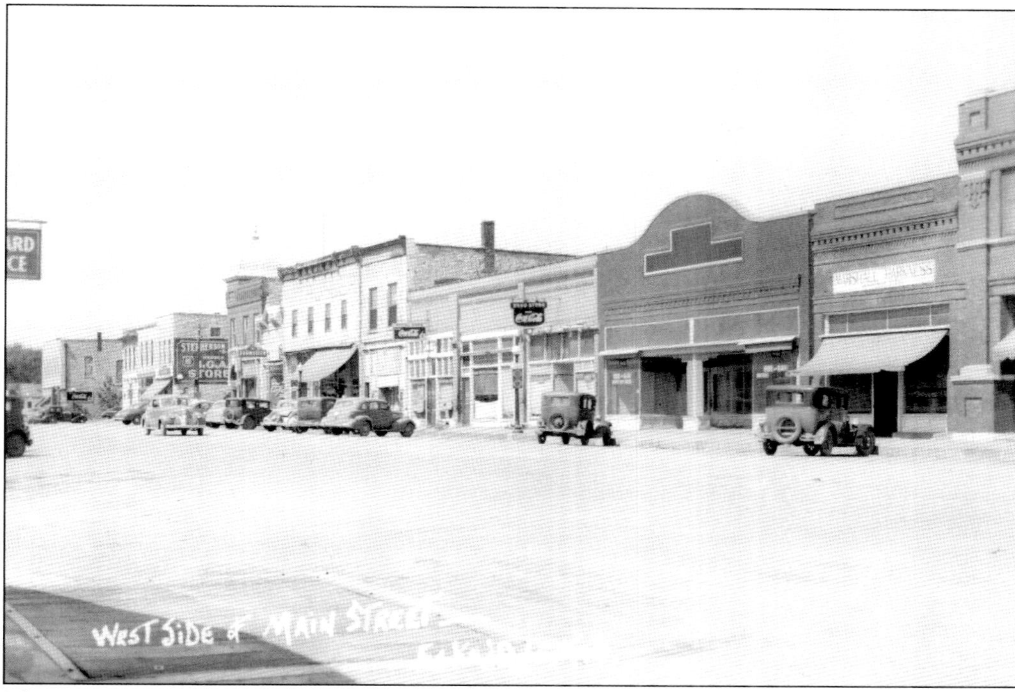

These two postcard views were taken around 1940, showing the business district of Eskridge looking south. In the above view, the buildings on the west side of the street are all still present today, with the exception of a structure at 205 Main Street two doors down from Stephenson's Grocery. On the east side, seen in the view below, all these buildings are intact, with the exception of the gas station at 122 Main Street, which was demolished to make way for the post office that was constructed in 1962. On both sides, the storefronts have been modernized, but amazingly, some 65 years after this photograph, all buildings except two are still standing. (Courtesy of Wabaunsee County Historical Society.)

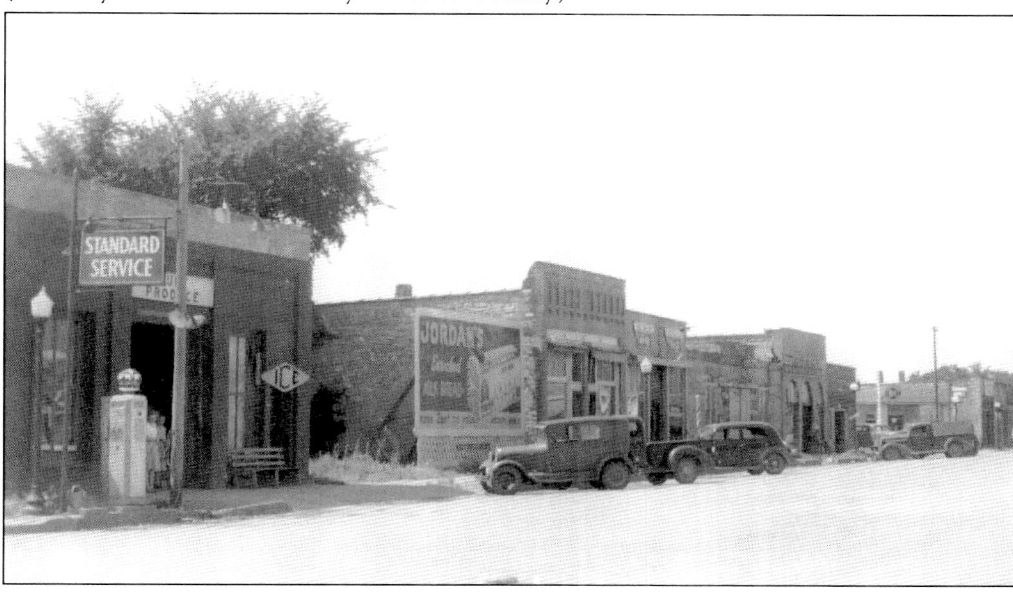

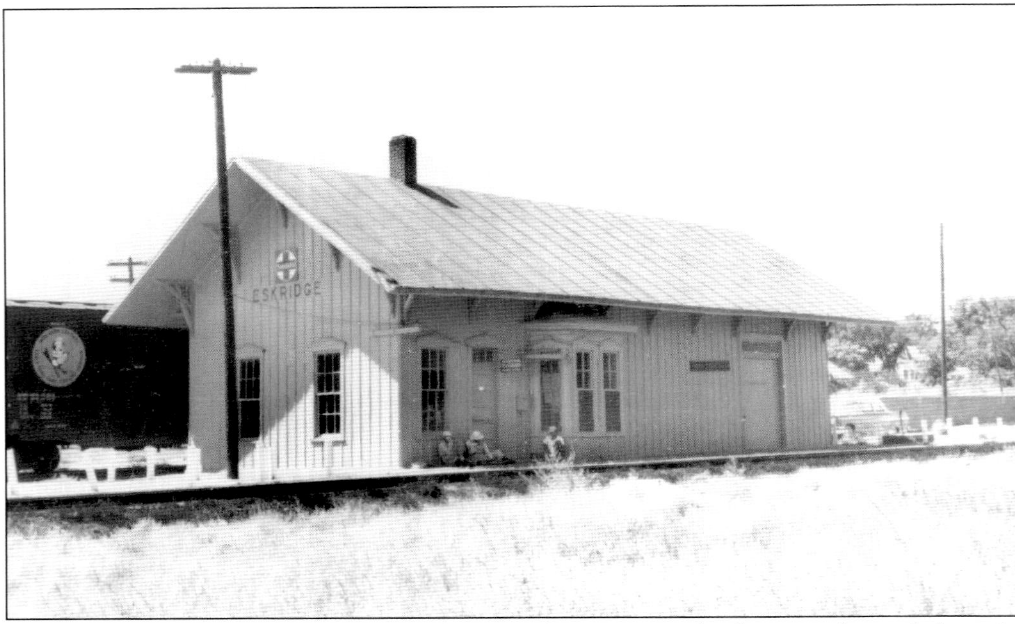

This view of the Santa Fe depot in Eskridge was taken in 1957. The depot was located along the tracks near where the Flint Hills Bank of Eskridge stands today. The stockyards were located just west of the depot, allowing for loading of cattle onto the railcars. There were cattle lanes leading from the Flint Hills pastures to the west, allowing cattle to be moved to and from the railhead. (Courtesy of Kansas State Historical Society.)

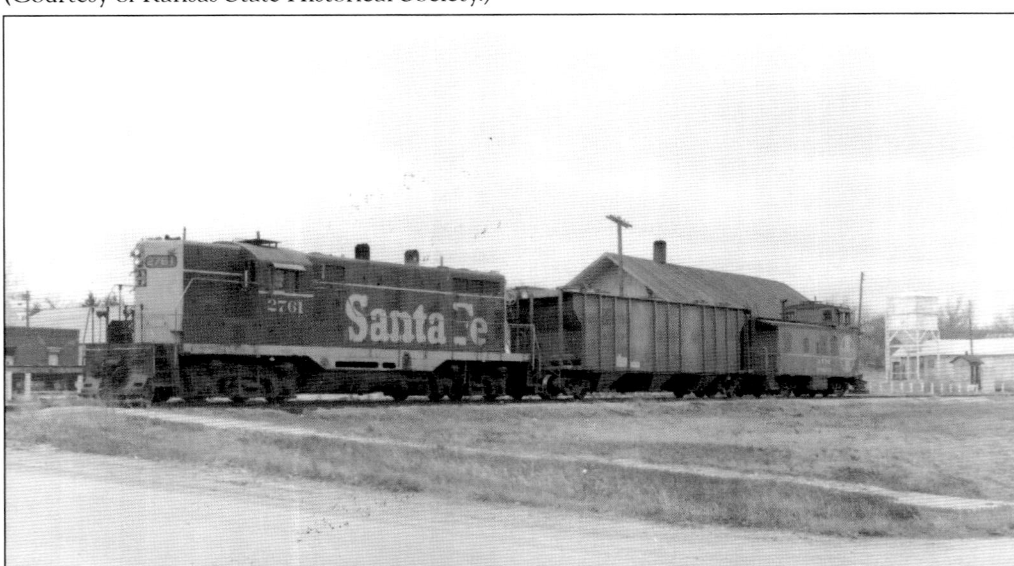

"Old Polly," the last train that departed Eskridge on the Atchison, Topeka and Santa Fe Railway line in 1972, was captured on film by Dean Dunn. Dunn was a longtime businessman in Eskridge as well as a camera enthusiast. He recorded many events of note in Eskridge and the surrounding area, including this train's departure. Just behind the train one can see the roof of the depot. (Courtesy of Inez Dunn.)

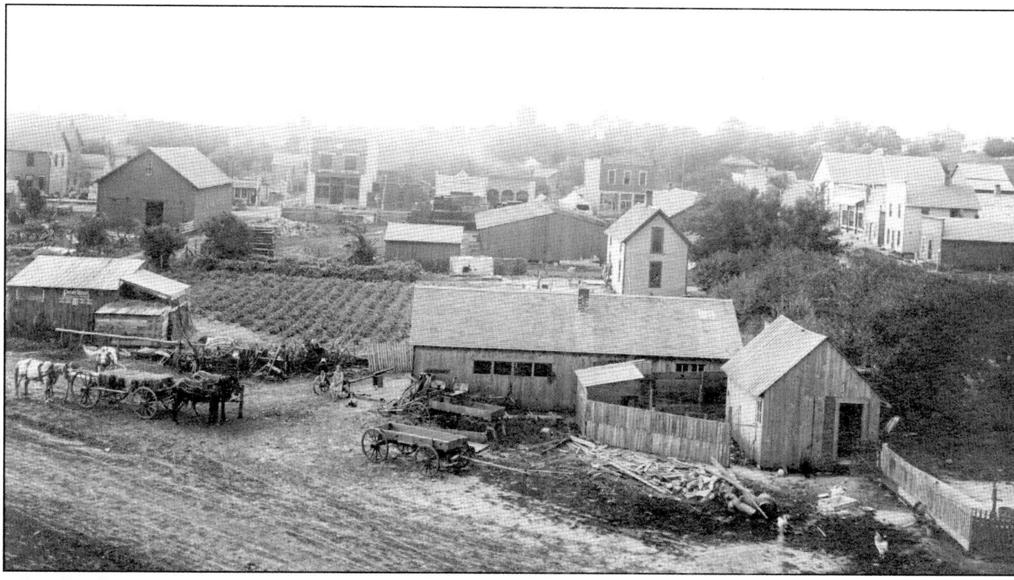

This bird's-eye view of Harveyville was taken from atop the co-op elevator. The photograph dates from the early 1900s, as J. S. May's General Merchandise store can be seen at center, a building constructed in 1904. Harveyville boasted three grocery stores, including May's at the dawn of the 20th century. The downtown also included a bank, a furniture store, two hardware stores, two restaurants, a doctor, a hotel, a creamery, a harness shop, a livery stable, two real estate offices, and a newspaper. (Courtesy of Wabaunsee County Historical Society.)

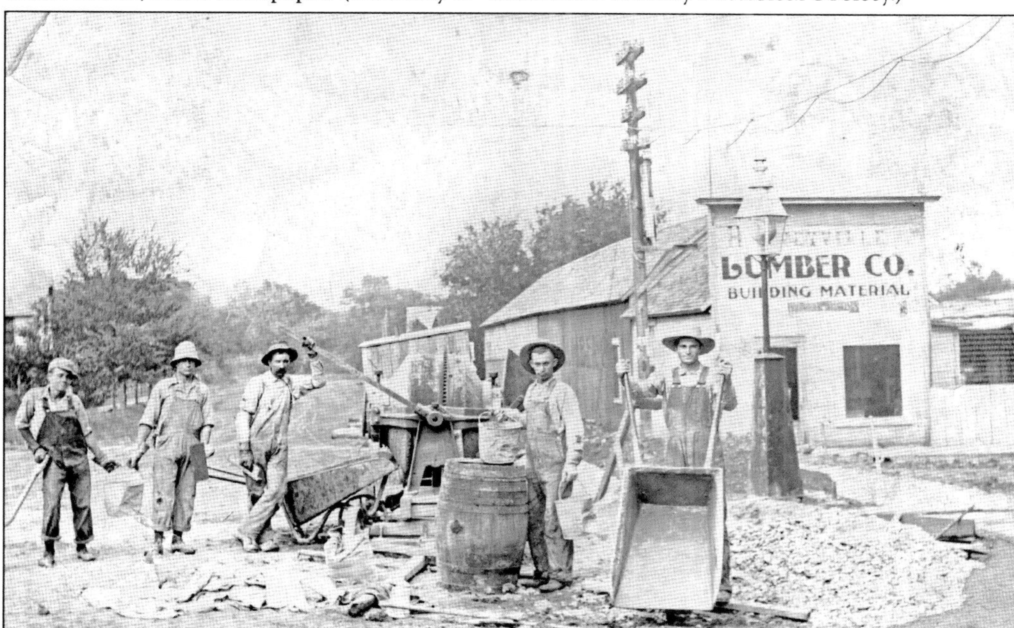

This crew of Harveyville men appears ready for work in this 1912 photograph. From left to right are Victor Grigsby, Walter Grigsby, C. L. Bogard, Reece Haller, and Ray Connley. Notice the Harveyville Lumber Company in the background. (Courtesy of Wabaunsee County Historical Society.)

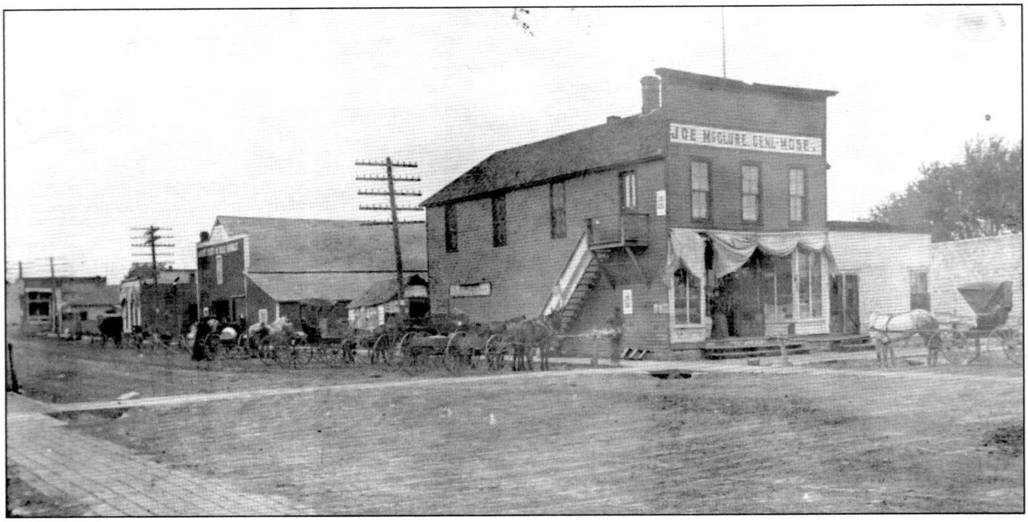

A few buggies are lined up outside Joe McClure's store in Harveyville in this late-1890s view. To the left, one can see the livery stable. Notice the wooden boardwalk sidewalks. (Courtesy of Wabaunsee County Historical Society.)

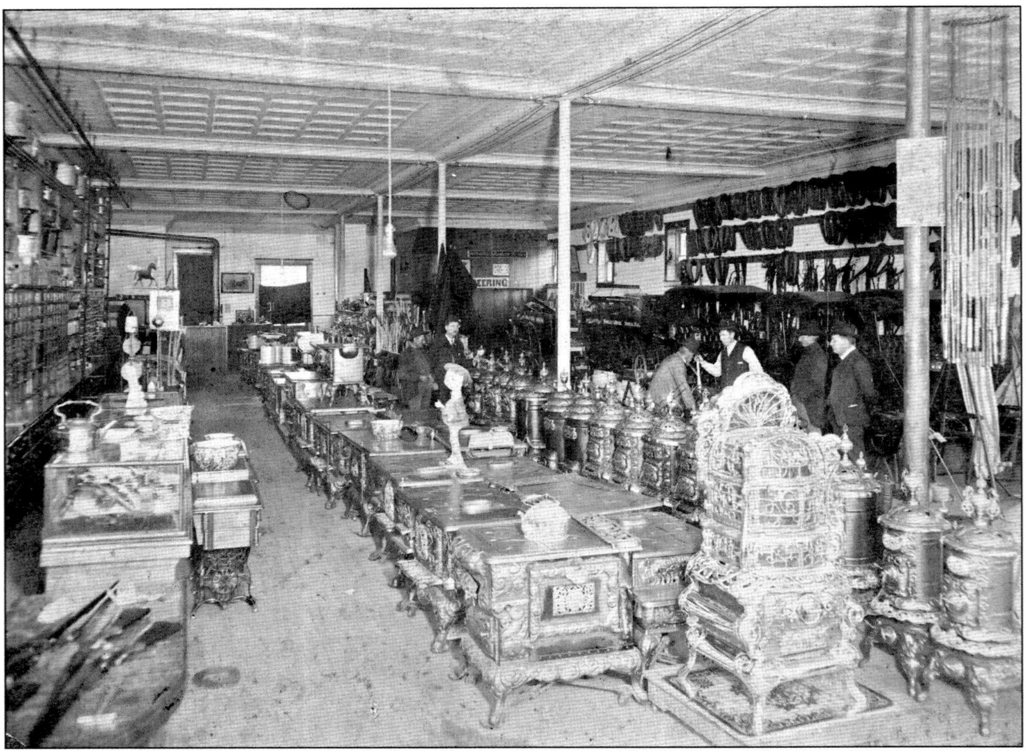

Thompson Hardware Company in Harveyville was prepared for the winter season with a wide variety of cooking stoves and coal and wood heating stoves. Thompson's offered a wide range of products; notice the buggies and harness equipment on the wall to the right. (Courtesy of Michael Stubbs.)

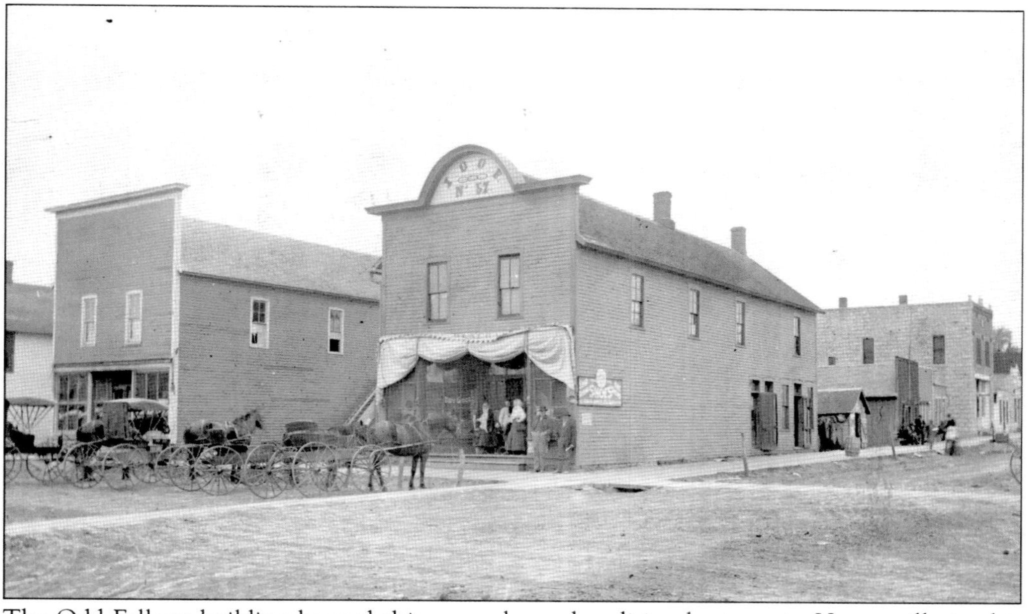

The Odd Fellows building housed this general merchandising business in Harveyville in this photograph from about 1900. Notice the abundance of frame buildings in the business district. The second small building to the right of the Odd Fellows building is the post office. (Courtesy of Michael Stubbs.)

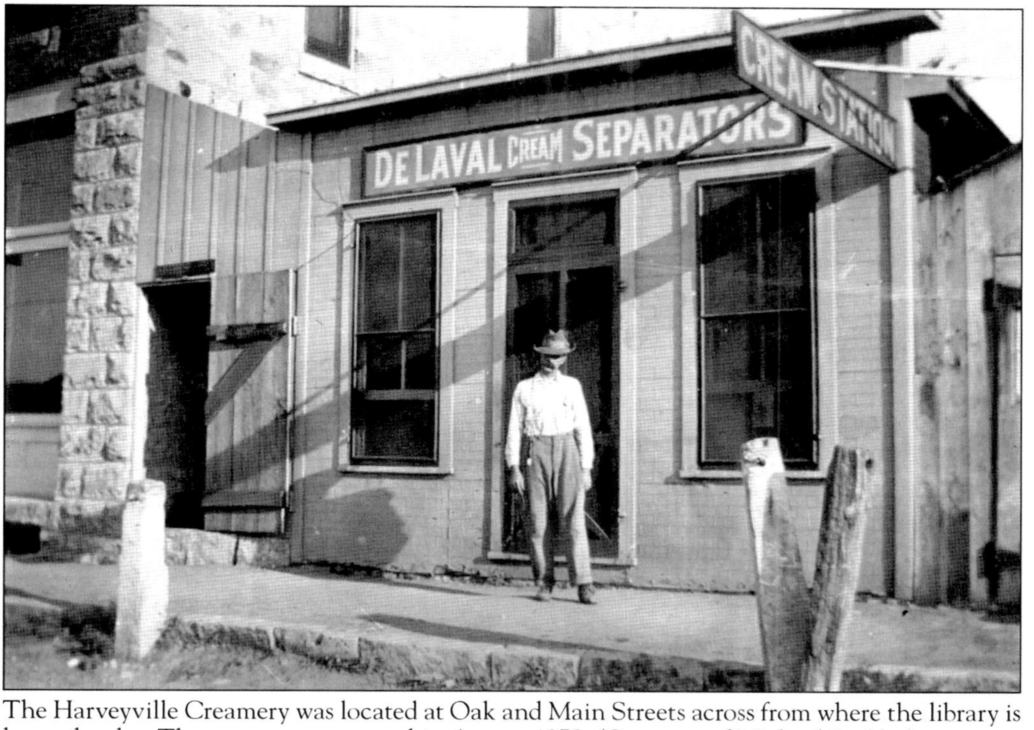

The Harveyville Creamery was located at Oak and Main Streets across from where the library is located today. The creamery was razed in August 1978. (Courtesy of Michael Stubbs.)

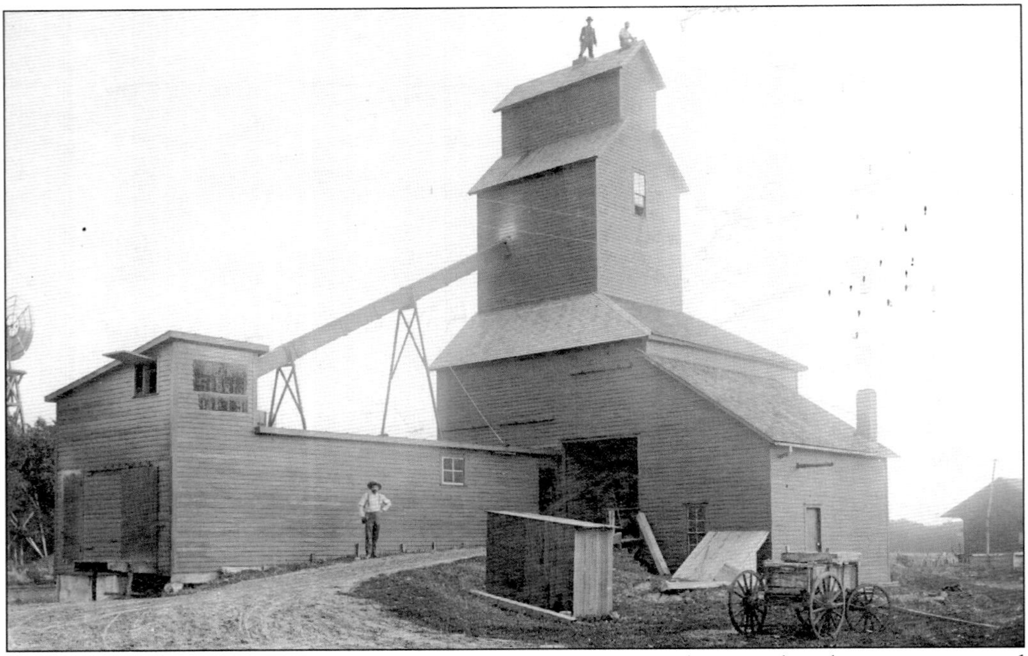

This is an early view of the co-op elevator at Harveyville around 1900. This elevator was owned by the Garinger-Farrell Elevator Company. The last of the Harveyville elevators was demolished on February 4, 2008. The photograph identifies the two men on top of the elevator as Bill Boatwright (left) and John Shrink. (Courtesy of Wabaunsee County Historical Society.)

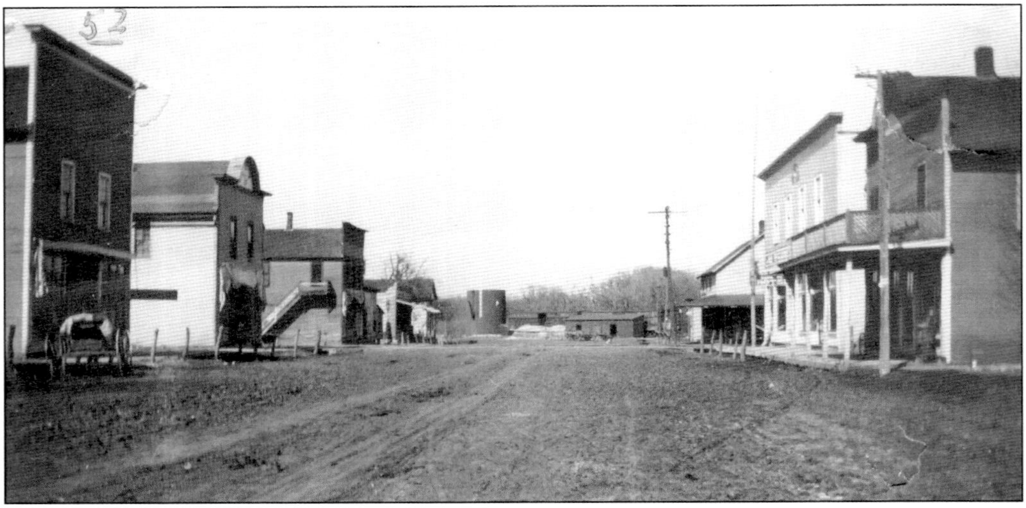

This view of Harveyville's Main Street is dated 1914. One can see the Santa Fe Hotel to the right as well as Joe McClure's store. In the center on the left side of the street, the Odd Fellows hall and the old McClure store are easily recognizable. These are the same buildings seen on the tops of pages 50 and 51. (Courtesy of Wabaunsee County Historical Society.)

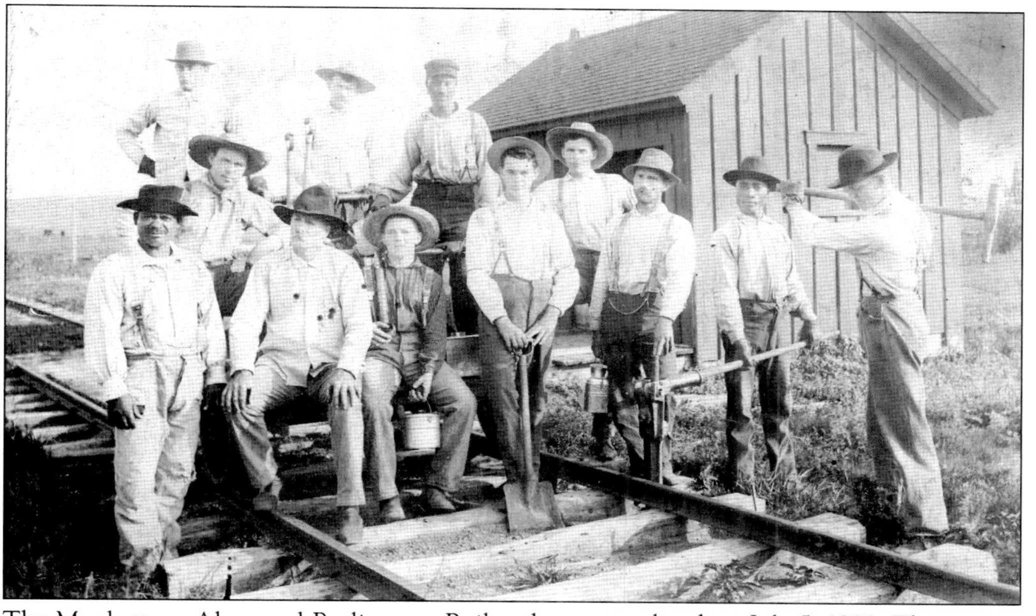

The Manhattan, Alma and Burlingame Railroad was completed on July 5, 1880. The section crew members at Harveyville are shown in front of the depot on that date, driving in the last spike. Soon after, Manhattan, Alma and Burlingame Railroad officially became part of the Atchison, Topeka and Santa Fe Railway. (Courtesy of Wabaunsee County Historical Society.)

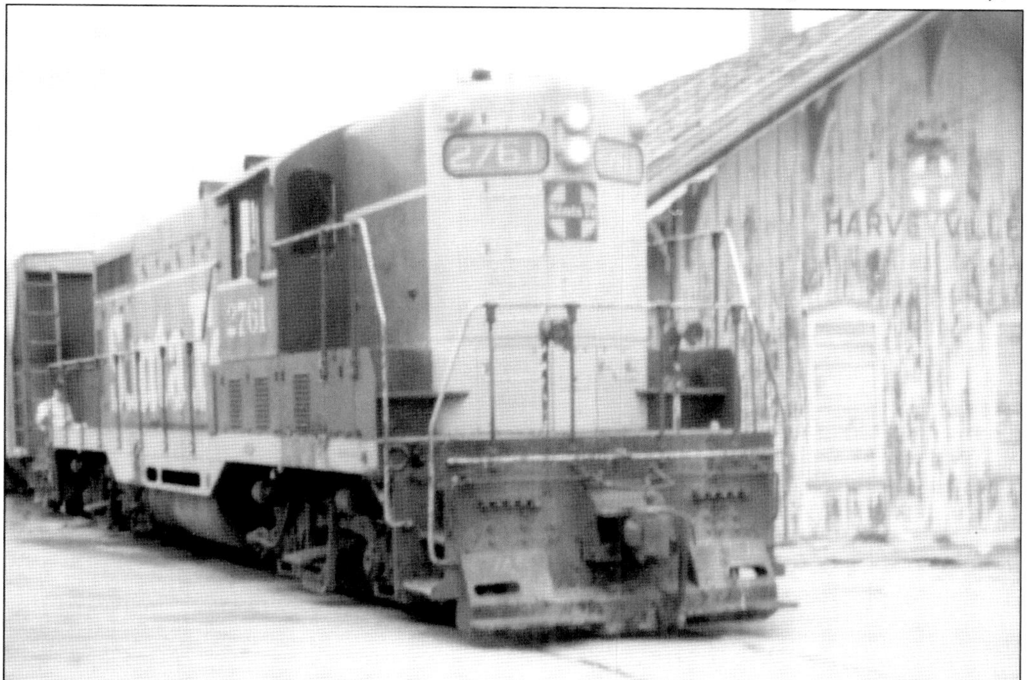

Santa Fe engine No. 2761, "Old Polly," is seen here on its last trip out of the Harveyville depot in 1972. Rail service had begun in Harveyville in 1880 and was responsible for the creation and growth of the town. (Courtesy of Wabaunsee County Historical Society.)

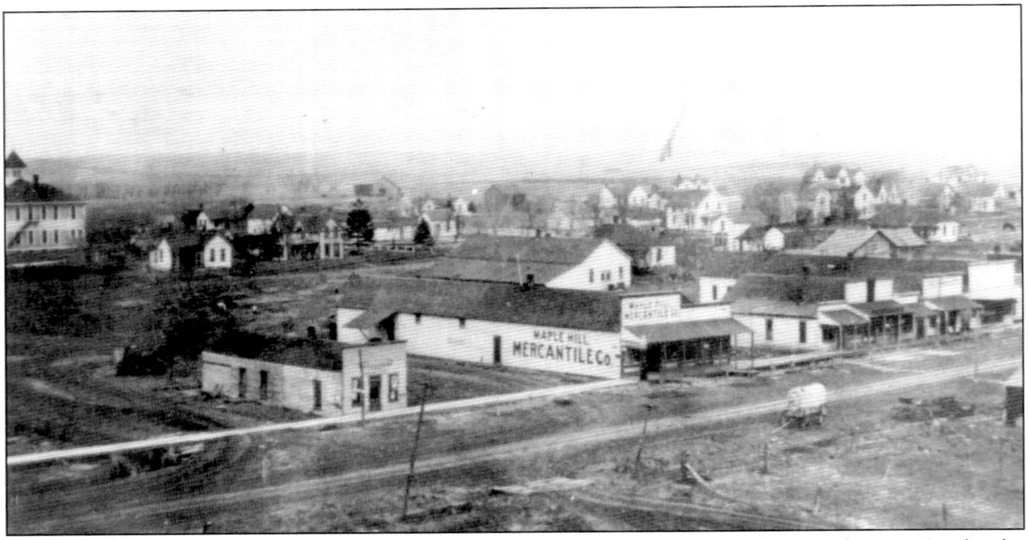

This view of Maple Hill, taken from atop the co-op elevator, looks to the northwest. At the far left one can see the old school building. Despite massive fires in the business district in 1900, 1901, and 1903, most of the buildings are still wooden in this photograph, taken around 1907. (Courtesy of Wabaunsee County Historical Society.)

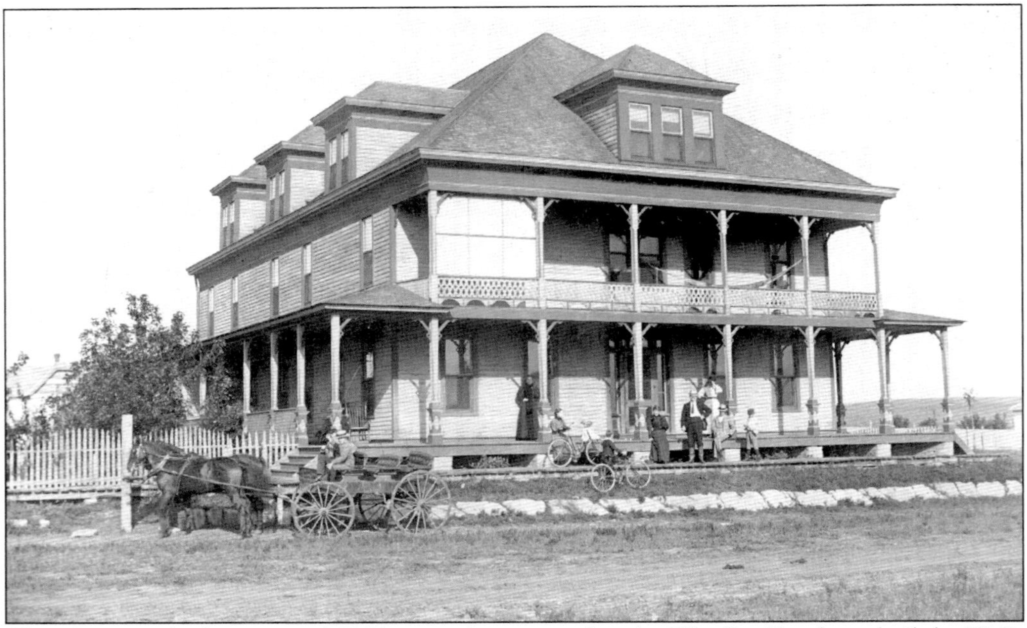
This photograph, from around 1890, was taken soon after the Windler Hotel was built by W. B. Small in Maple Hill. The hotel boasted gaslights and steam heat, both modern conveniences of the day. (Courtesy of Wabaunsee County Historical Society.)

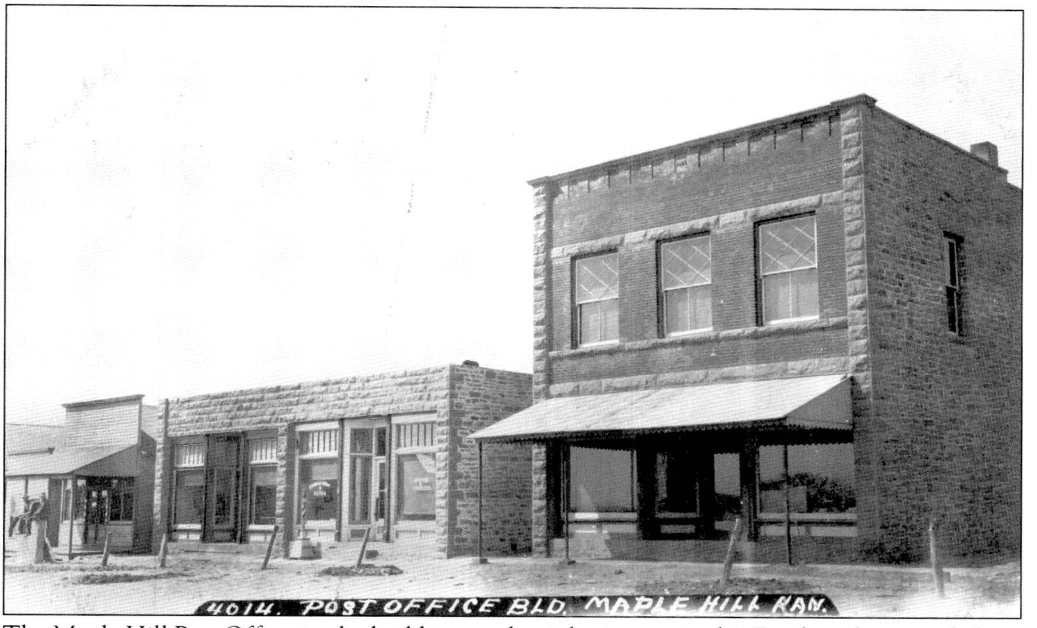

The Maple Hill Post Office, in the building on the right, is seen in this Zercher photograph from around 1907. To the left of the post office is a shop with advertising on the windows, "Barber Shop & Baths," and "Cigars and Tobacco." (Courtesy of Kansas State Historical Society.)

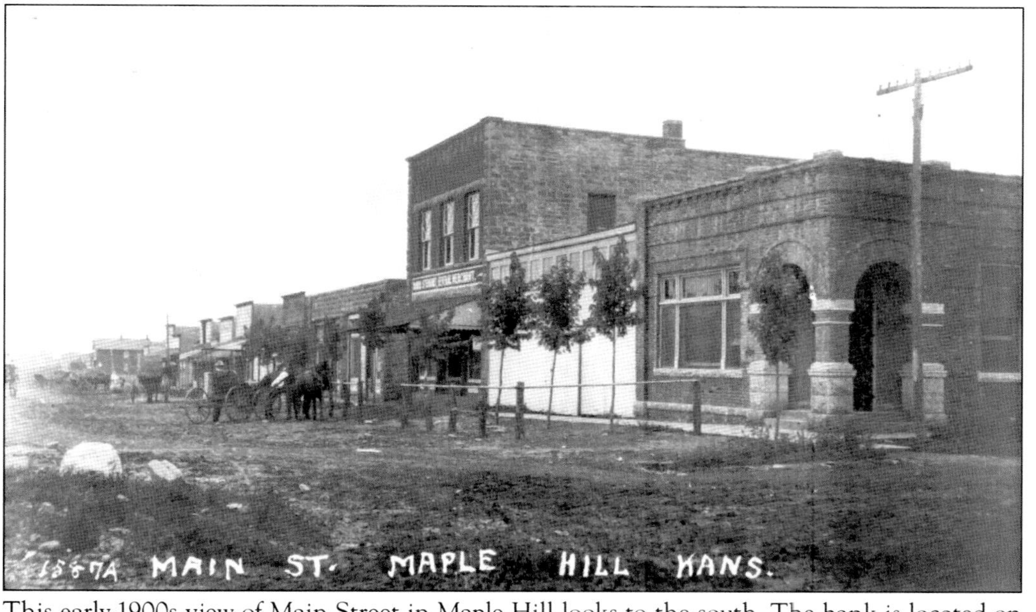

This early-1900s view of Main Street in Maple Hill looks to the south. The bank is located on the corner, where it is today. To the left of the bank is David Stewart General Mercantile, an early Maple Hill merchant. His business was burned in Main Street fires twice before he moved into this building after the 1903 fire. (Courtesy of Kansas State Historical Society.)

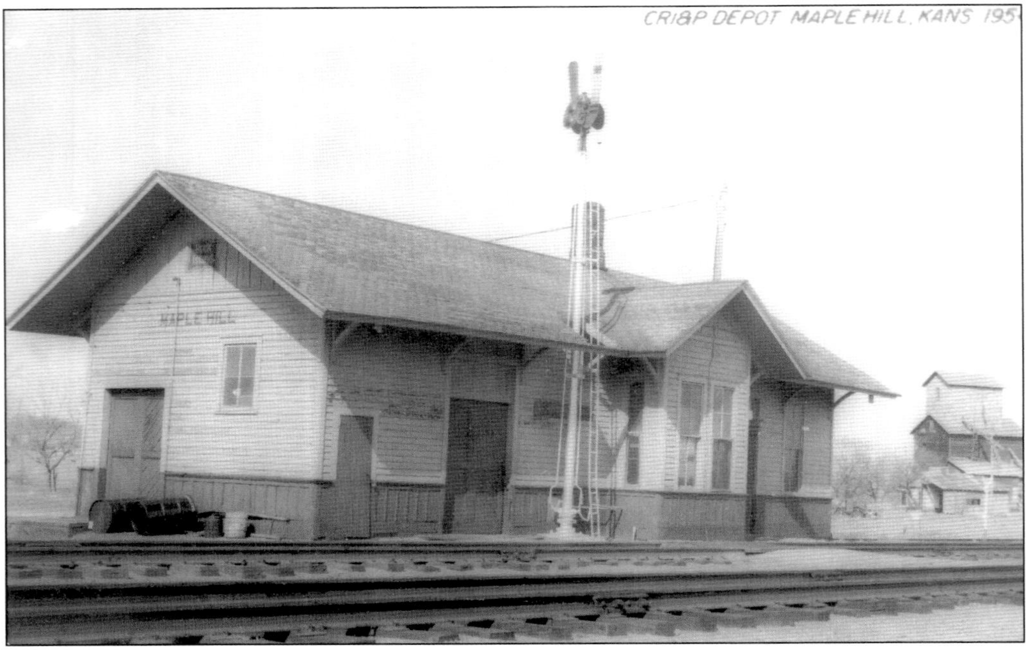

The Maple Hill depot was constructed in 1887 on the Chicago, Rock Island and Pacific Railroad line. This is a 1950s view of the depot, located on the south edge of town. Notice the co-op elevator to the right. (Courtesy of Kansas State Historical Society.)

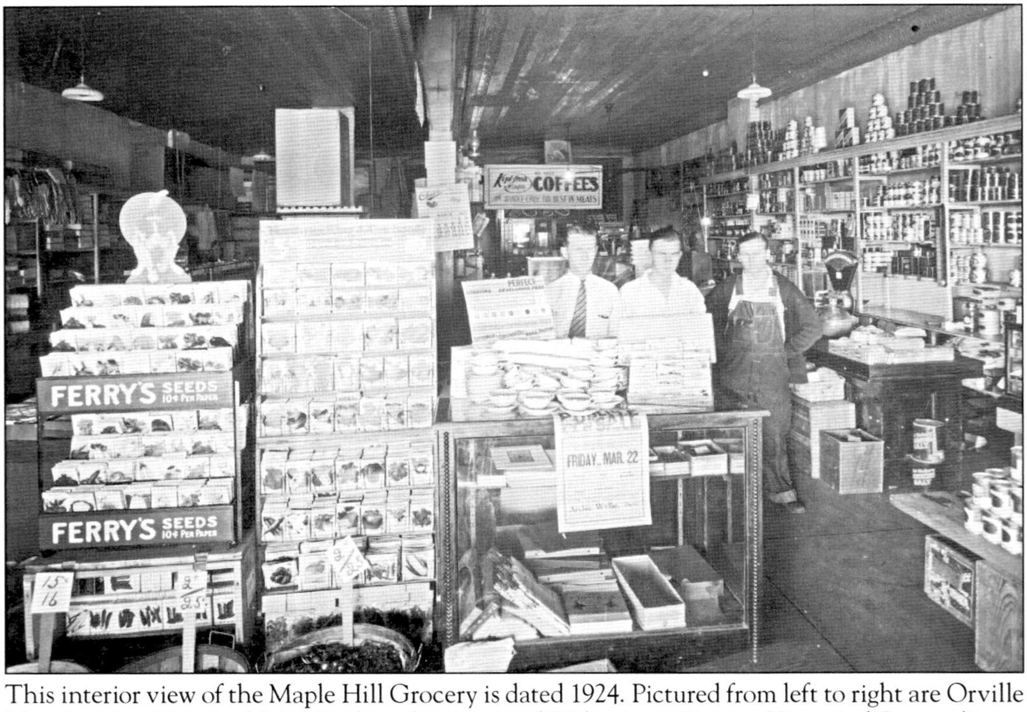

This interior view of the Maple Hill Grocery is dated 1924. Pictured from left to right are Orville Mee, Lynden Mee, and John Hedges. (Courtesy of Wabaunsee County Historical Society.)

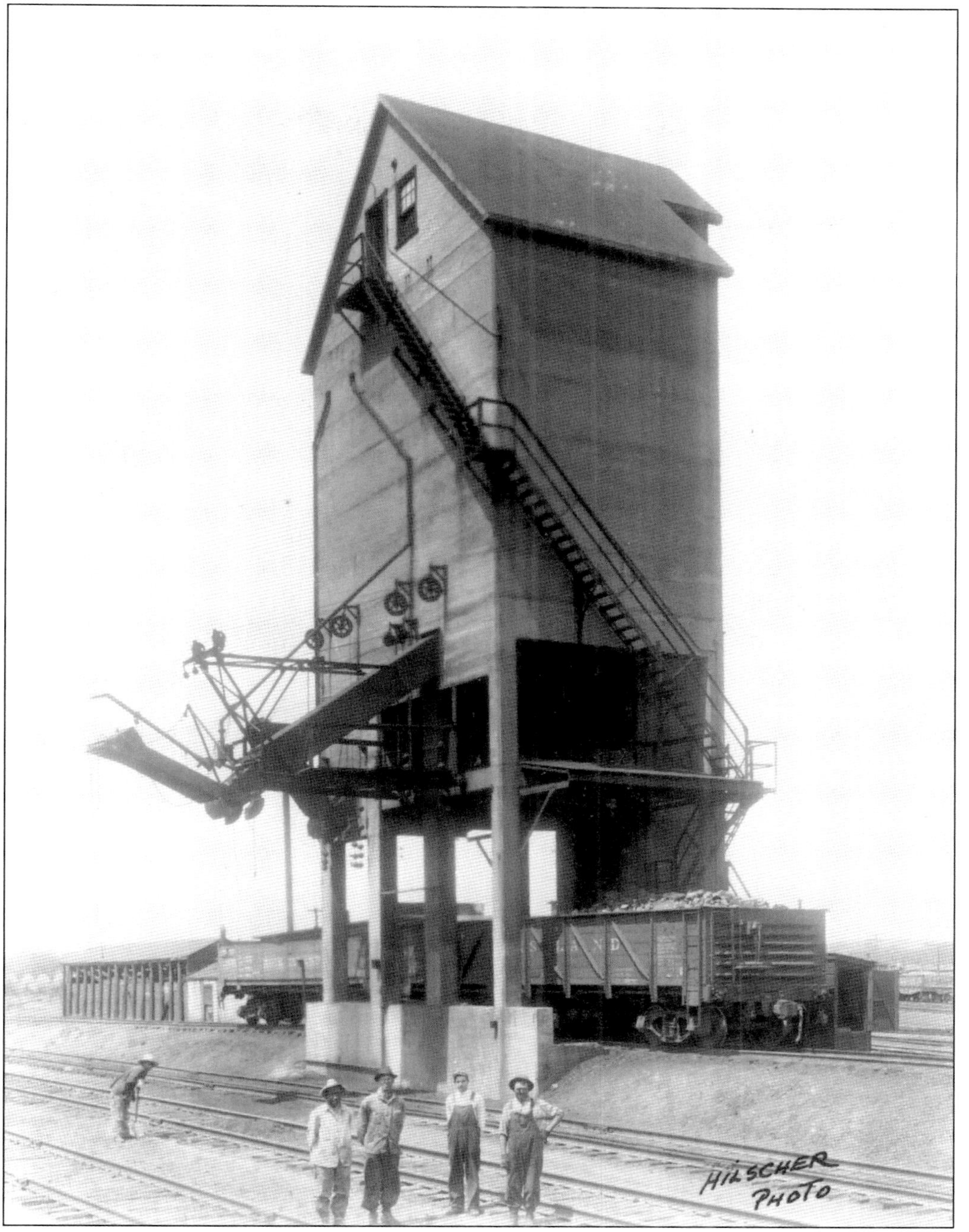

The McFarland coal chute was constructed by the Chicago, Rock Island and Pacific Railroad in 1922 at a cost of $30,000. Around 1930, the railroad began using oil to burn in the boilers of its steam locomotives, and the coal chute was abandoned. It was demolished by dynamiting on December 19, 1980. (Courtesy of Wabaunsee County Historical Society.)

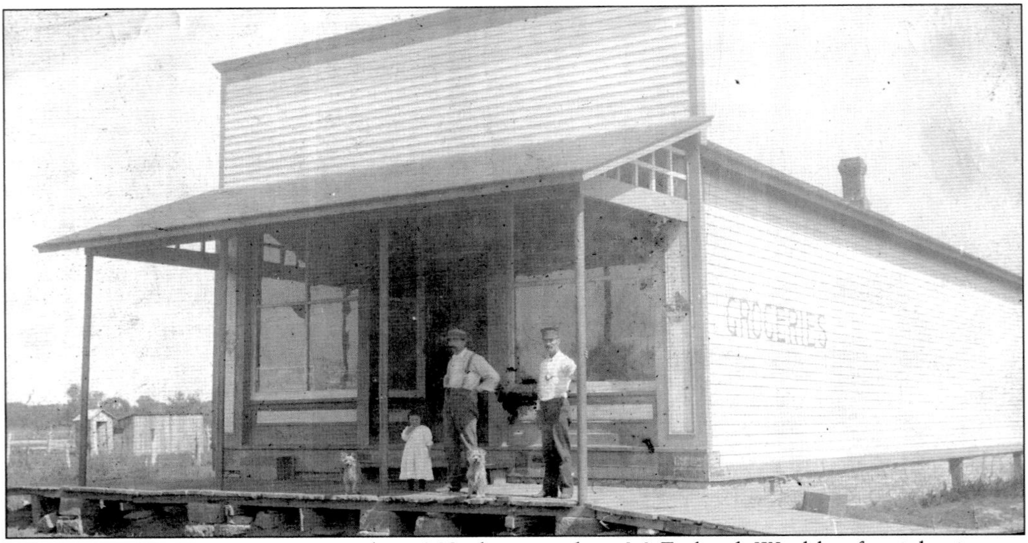

Arthur Winkler's store is seen in this 1903 photograph in McFarland. Winkler, far right, is seen here with McFarland mayor Dr. C. R. Silverthorne and Florence A. Winkler. The store was located 103 Main Street and faced west. In the 1920s, the building became a pool hall and remained so until it burned on May 2, 1979. (Courtesy of Wabaunsee County Historical Society.)

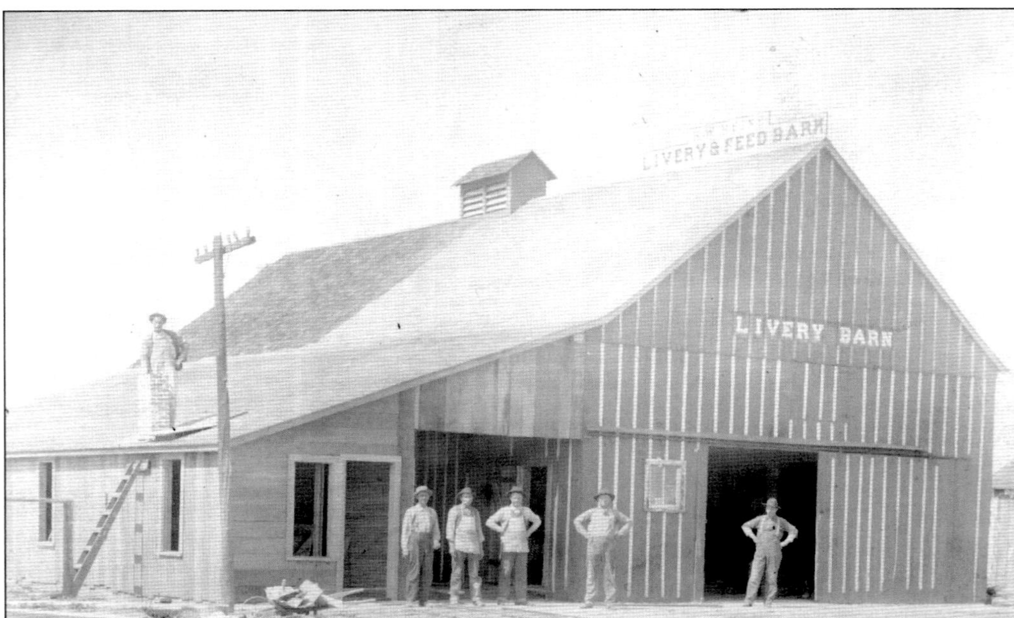

An addition to H. W. Heine's livery stable in McFarland was almost complete when workers and Heine posed for this photograph. The stable was located at 203 East Market Street. Bob and Ardyce Schrader demolished the livery for the lumber in 1958, using the lumber on their farm near Chalk. Ardyce recalls, "I couldn't stand to watch Bob up on top of those rafters taking them apart, it was too scary." (Courtesy of Wabaunsee County Historical Society.)

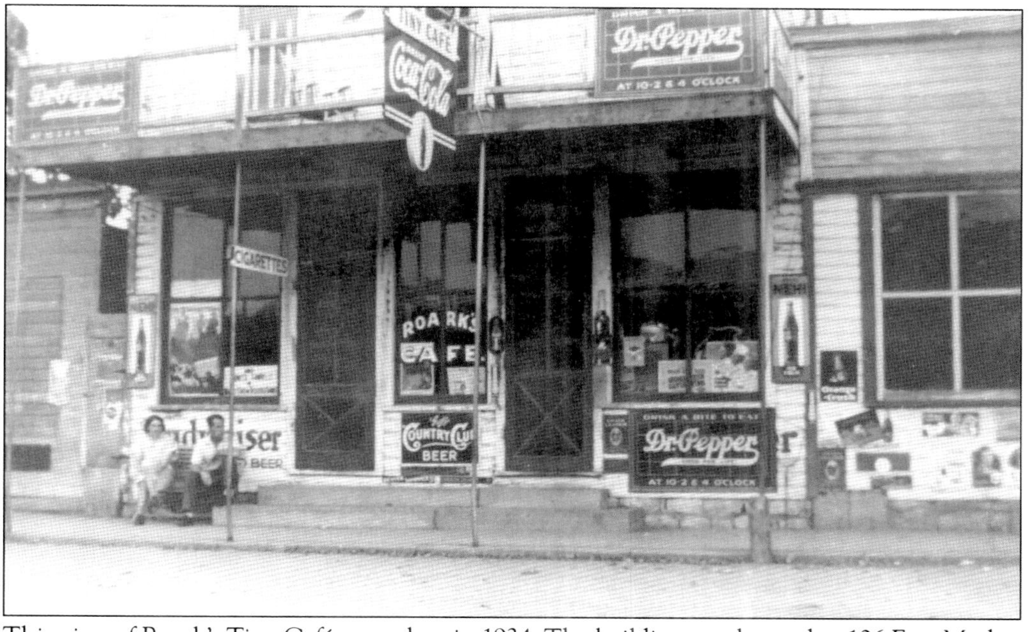

This view of Roark's Tiny Café was taken in 1934. The building was located at 106 East Market Street on the now-vacant lot next to the post office. The building was demolished in the early 1960s. (Courtesy of Wabaunsee County Historical Society.)

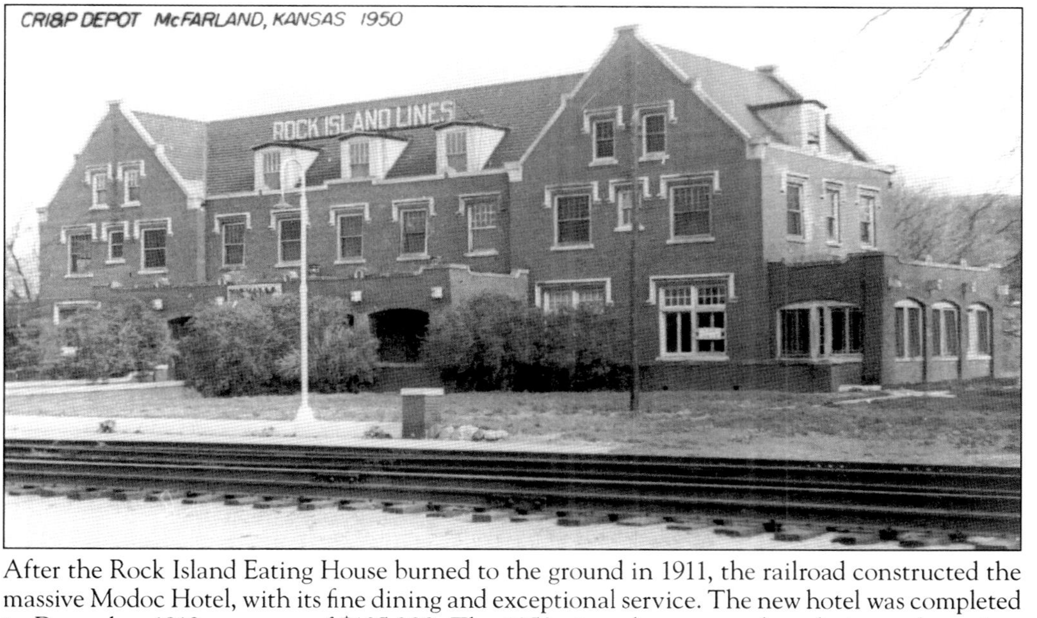

After the Rock Island Eating House burned to the ground in 1911, the railroad constructed the massive Modoc Hotel, with its fine dining and exceptional service. The new hotel was completed in December 1912 at a cost of $105,000. The 1950 view above was taken during a short time when there was no depot and the Modoc was serving that purpose as well. The Modoc was torn down for salvage in 1956. (Courtesy of McFarland Heritage Center.)

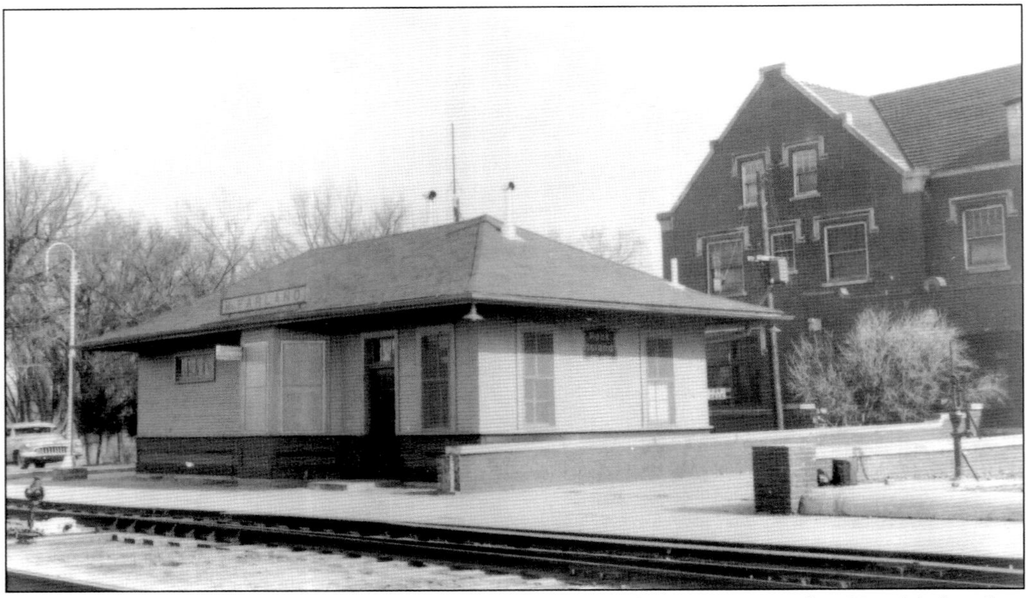

The last Rock Island depot at McFarland is dwarfed by the massive Modoc Hotel behind it. This depot was disassembled in Peck and moved to McFarland to serve as the depot in 1953. This building continued to be used by the railroad as a maintenance building after it closed as a depot. In 1987, the depot was sold to the City of McFarland for $1, and the building was restored and moved to the north end of town where it serves as city hall and the McFarland Heritage Center. (Courtesy of Kansas State Historical Society.)

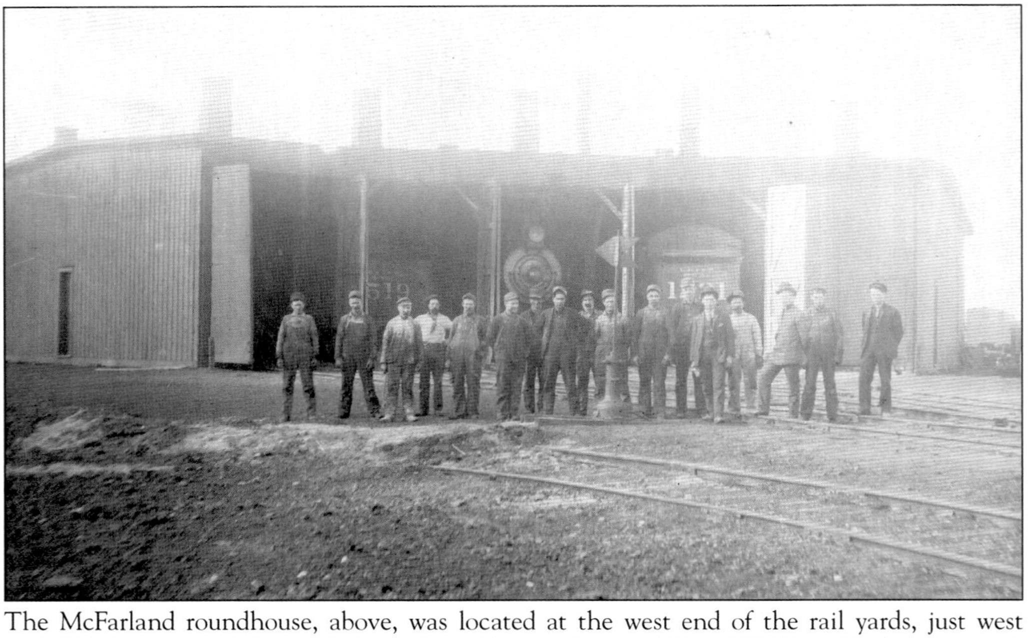

The McFarland roundhouse, above, was located at the west end of the rail yards, just west and slightly north of the coal chute. Its address today would be 500 West Market Street. It was replaced with a metal diesel maintenance building in 1953, which was in turn moved to Belleville in 1955. (Courtesy of Wabaunsee County Historical Society.)

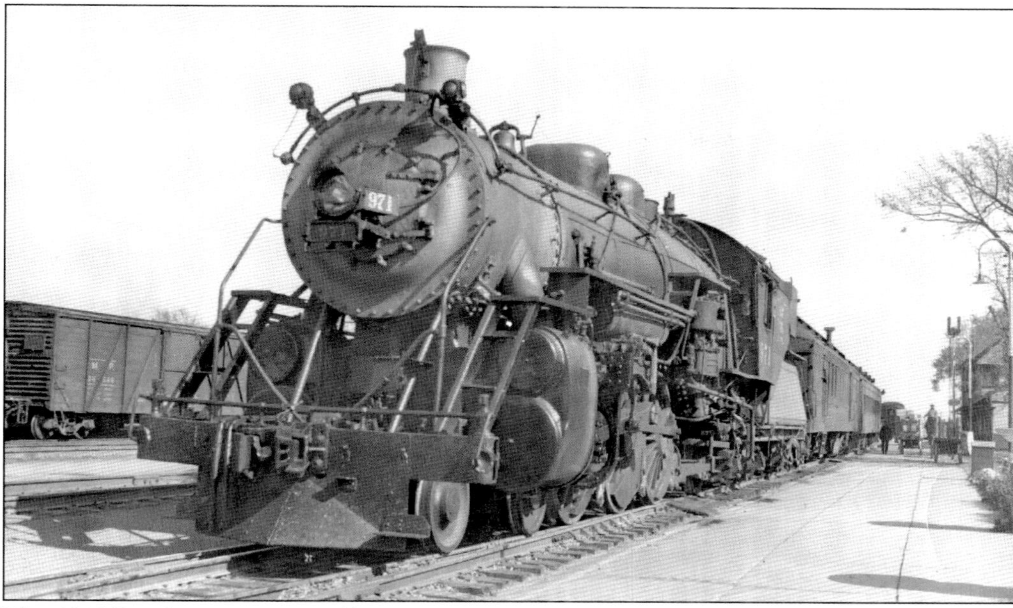

This 1913 Brooks engine was pulling a passenger train to Belleville, and it stopped for passengers in McFarland in this photograph from October 1946. One can see the eve of the old McFarland depot at the far right edge of the photograph. (Courtesy of McFarland Heritage Center, donated by the Harold K. Vollrath collection.)

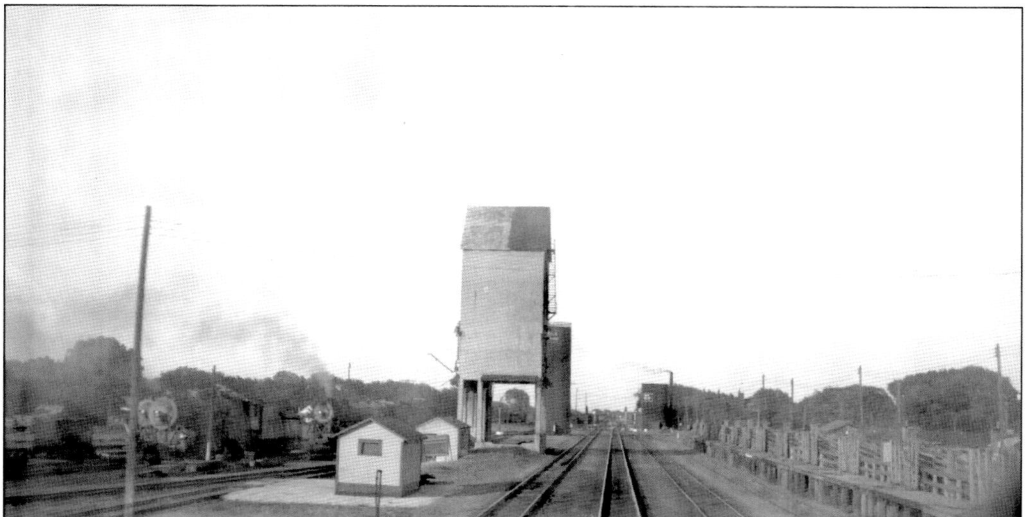

This photograph was taken from the engineer's cab of a diesel Rock Island Rocket, as it rolls down the double track through McFarland eastbound at 60 miles per hour. One can see the slower steam locomotives on the side tracks to the left, and the stockyards are to the right, while the coal chute stands in the middle of the yard. The date of this photograph is July 1947. (Courtesy of McFarland Heritage Center, donated by the Harold K. Vollrath collection.)

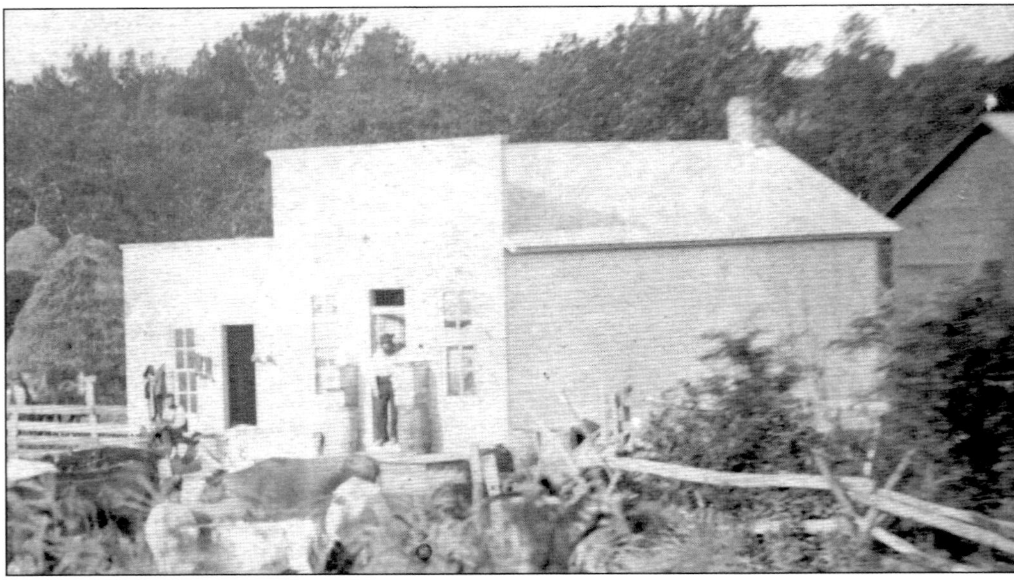

John Copp stands in the doorway of his store at the old Paxico town, located one mile east of the present town. The town was named Paxico after the Native American medicine man Pashqua, who owned the land prior to leaving for Indian Territory in 1870. Built in 1879 near Strowig's mill, the store contained the first Paxico Post Office. When the railroad created the new Paxico, Copp moved his store to the new town. Stores from Newbury were moved there as well. (Courtesy of Wabaunsee County Museum.)

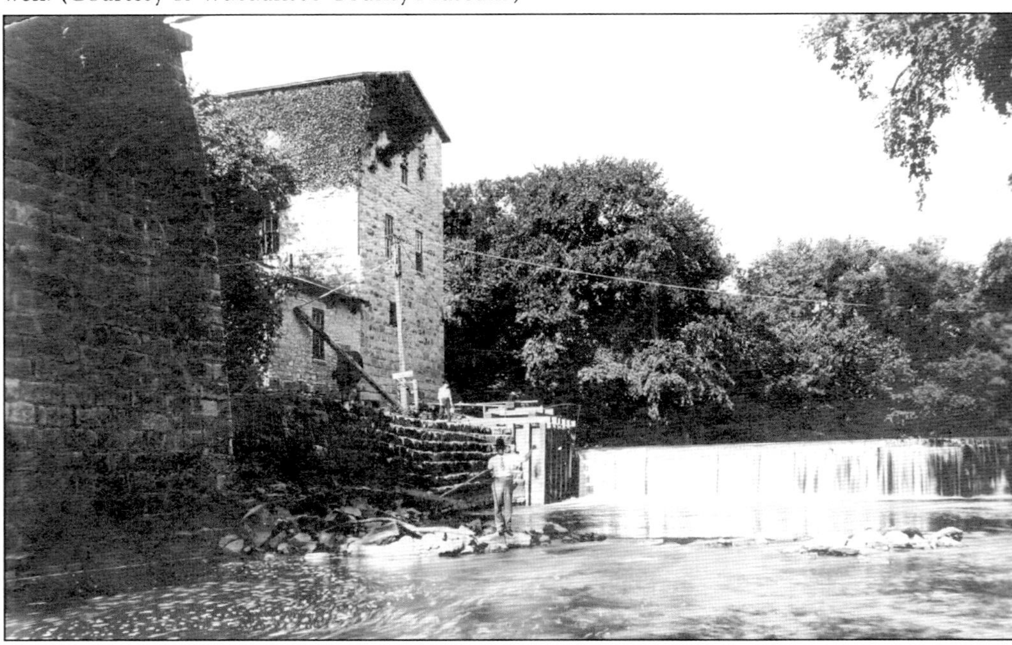

Robert and William Strowig built this mill in 1879 on Mill Creek at Snomoko Road. The brothers operated Paxico Milling Company on the site of the first Paxico town. In 1886, the Chicago, Rock Island and Pacific Railroad platted the town of Paxico one mile east of the old town to a location more suitable for the depot. (Courtesy of Wabaunsee County Historical Society.)

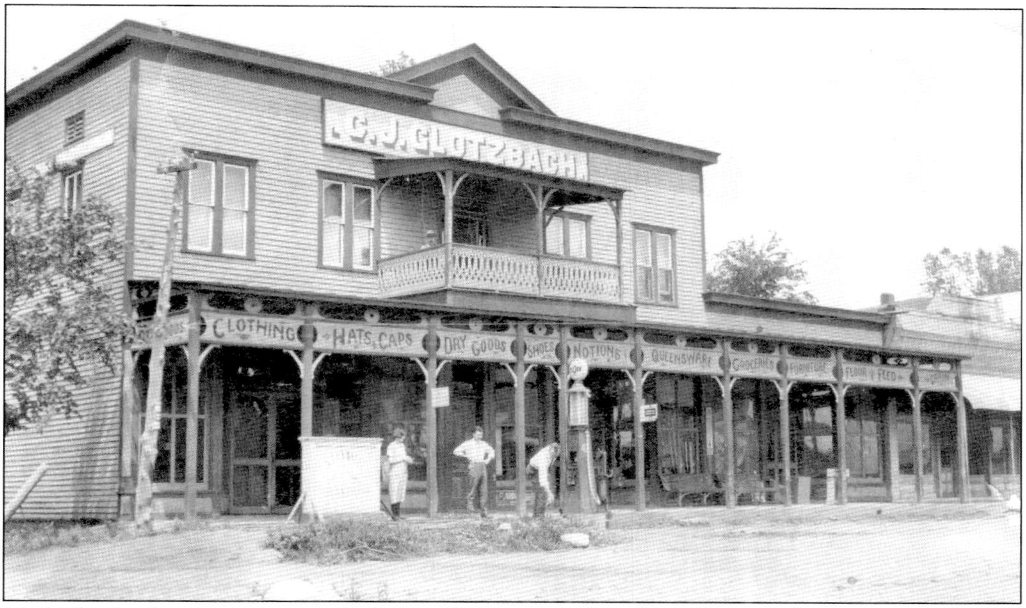

Carl Glotzbach, center, is seen in front of his store on Newbury Street in Paxico, around 1920. Glotzbach purchased the building from the Bolton brothers who had acquired the store from Anderson and Company. This structure is part of Paxico's historic antique district. (Courtesy of Wabaunsee County Historical Society.)

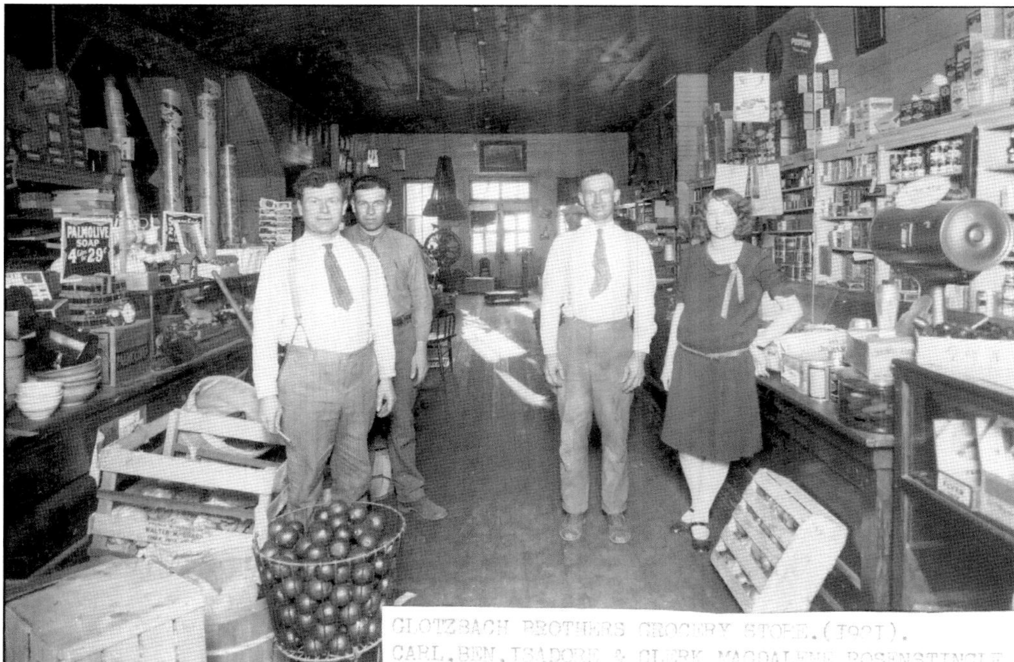

This interior view of the Glotzbach store is dated 1921. Written on the back of the photograph is, "Glotzbach Brothers Grocery Store 1921, Carl, Ben, Isadore and clerk, Magdalene Rosenstingle." (Courtesy of Wabaunsee County Historical Society.)

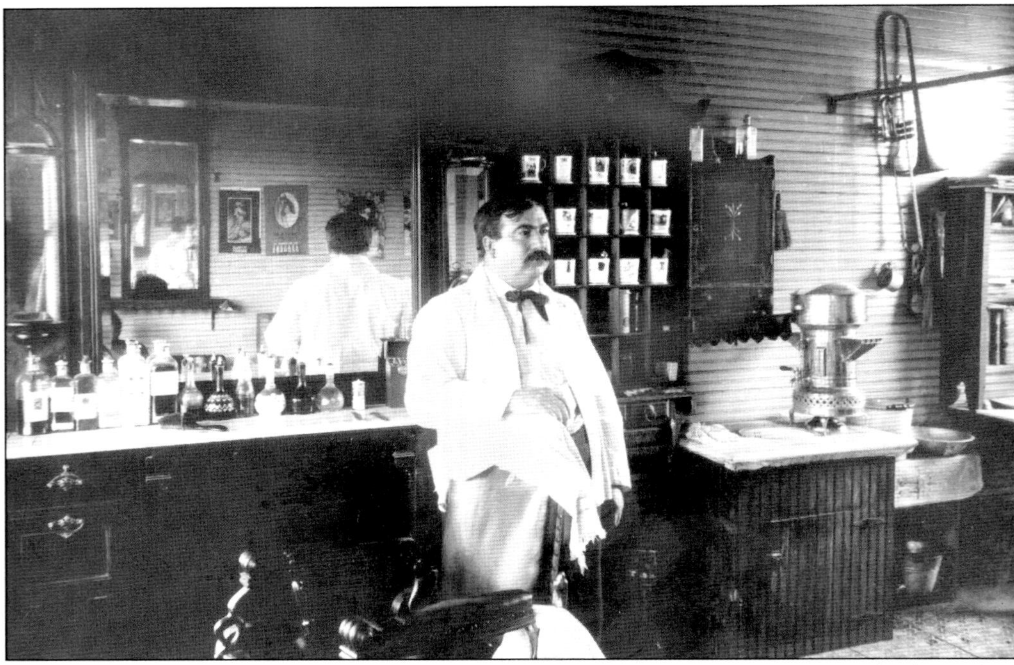

George Woody is seen in his barbershop in Paxico in this Gus Meier photograph, from about 1905. Meier operated a photograph studio one day a month in Paxico, and this photograph is one of his views from the state archives collection. (Courtesy of Kansas State Historical Society.)

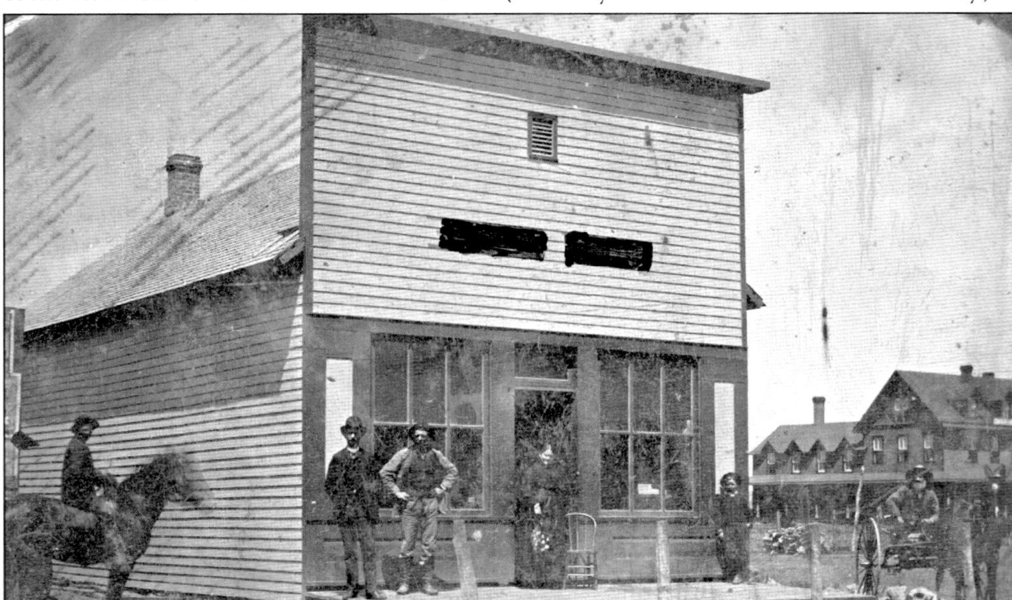

This rare image, made from a tintype, shows the old Paxico Saloon. This was the same building John Copp moved from the old Paxico town, seen on page 62. In addition to having housed a store, the building has been a saloon and later Werner Butcher Shop. In recent years, the building has been home to a bar and grill. It is located at 123 Newbury Street. (Courtesy of Wabaunsee County Historical Society.)

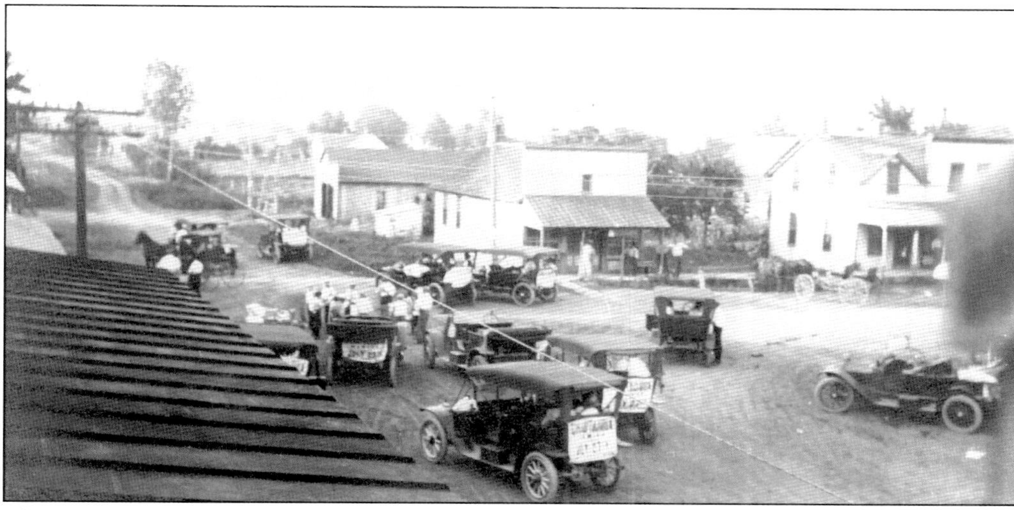

This view of the intersection of Main and Newbury Streets in Paxico is dated 1910. People from neighboring communities often visited towns advertising fairs and events. In this case, a July 27 chautauqua is being promoted. (Courtesy of Wabaunsee County Historical Society.)

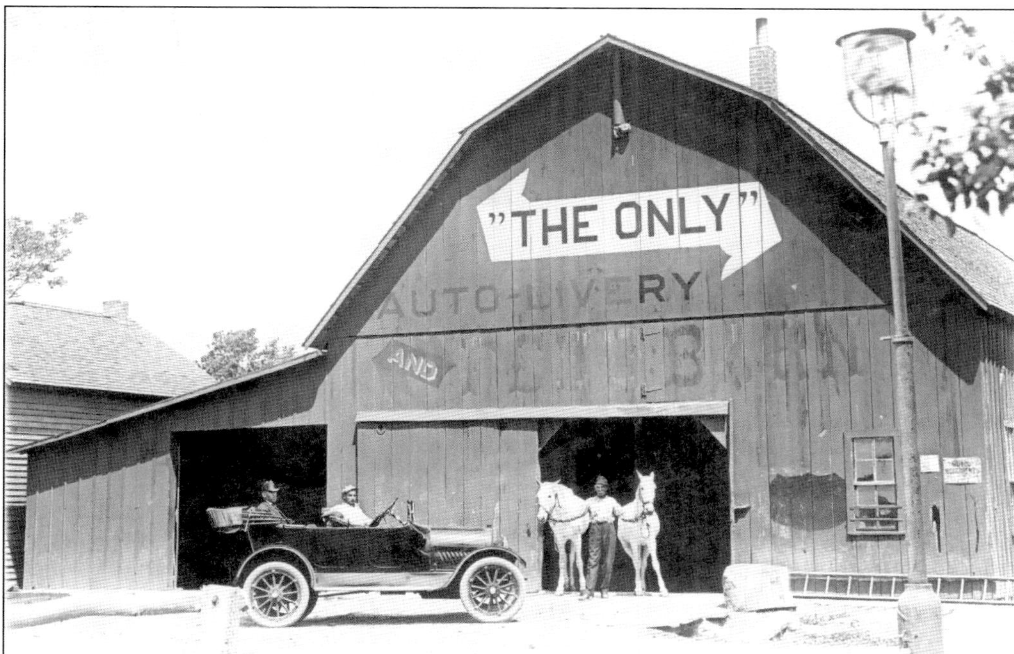

In 1878, Jack Pride set up a blacksmith shop in what became the first Paxico town site. He was a former slave from Nashville, Tennessee, who came to Kansas as part of the exodus from the South after the failure of Reconstruction. With the encouragement of Pride and J. H. Nuttman, this migration brought scores of freed slaves to Paxico. This photograph depicts the automobile livery business of O. J. Pride in the new Paxico in the early 1920s. (Courtesy of Wabaunsee County Museum.)

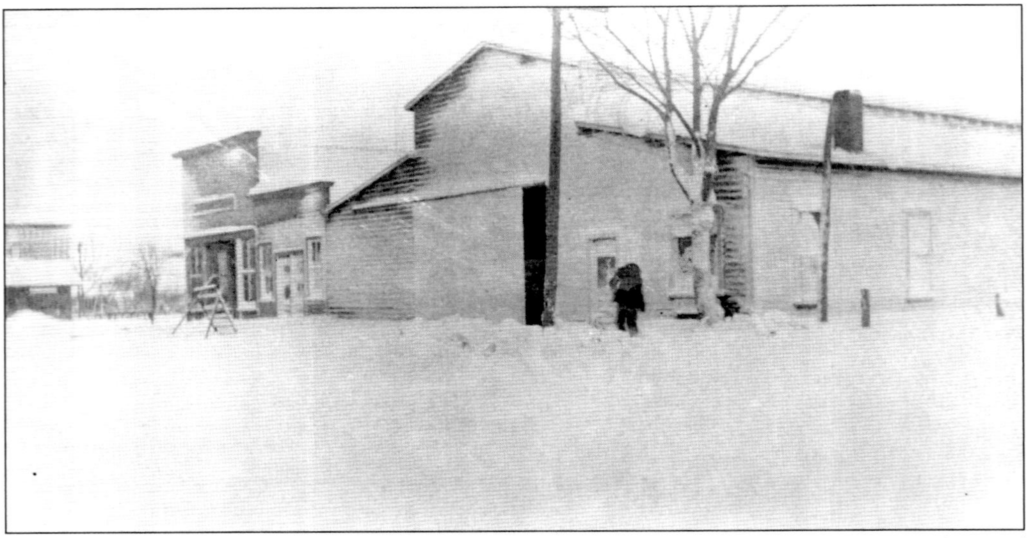

A man appears to be shoveling snow in front of the Paxico Lumber Company, right, and Muckenthaler Hardware, left, located on Main Street. This real-photo postcard was taken around 1910. (Courtesy of Wabaunsee County Historical Society.)

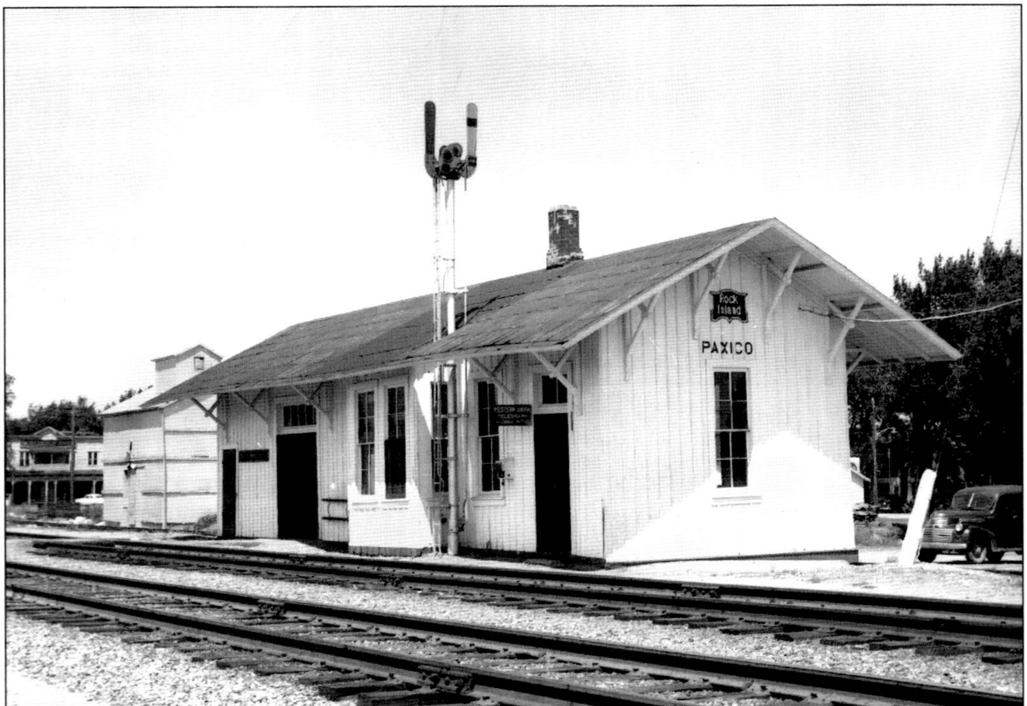

The Rock Island depot in Paxico is seen here in a 1940s view when the building was painted white. After the railroad closed, Paxico businessman Eddie Meinhardt purchased the depot and moved it to the west about a quarter of a mile down the railroad tracks to his campground. The depot is still located at the Mill Creek Campground in Paxico. (Courtesy of Kansas State Historical Society.)

Three

Wabaunsee County at Work

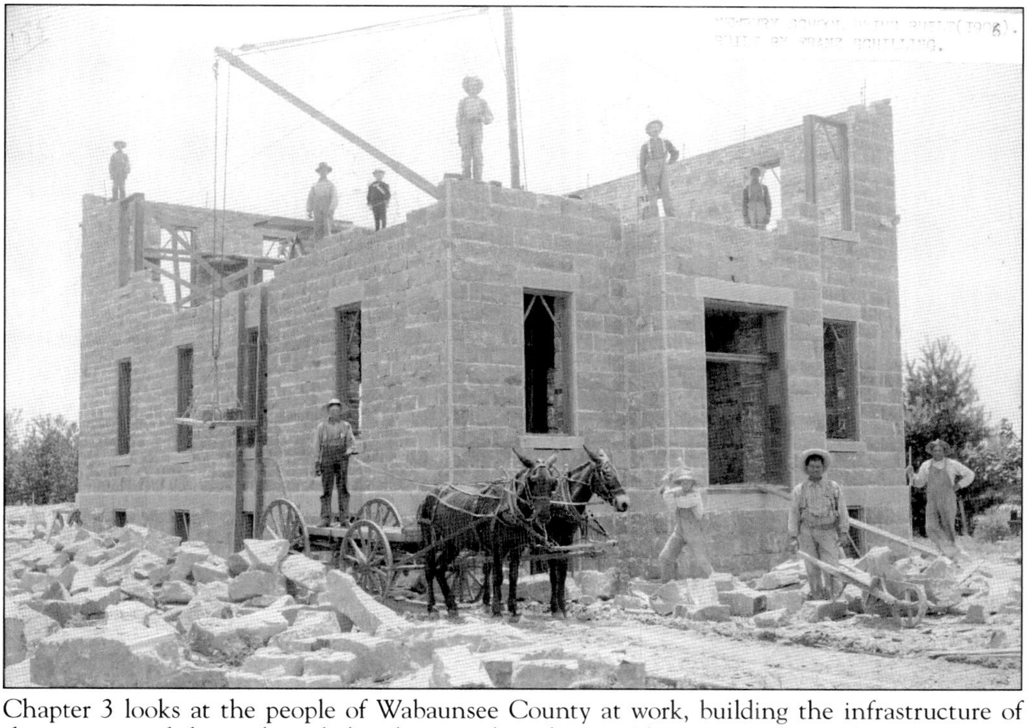

Chapter 3 looks at the people of Wabaunsee County at work, building the infrastructure of the county and doing their daily jobs to make a living. Above, 10 men can be seen cutting and laying stone during the 1905 construction of the Sacred Heart School in Newbury. Franz Schilling was the builder. The building is located at 22298 Newbury Road in Paxico. (Courtesy of Wabaunsee County Historical Society.)

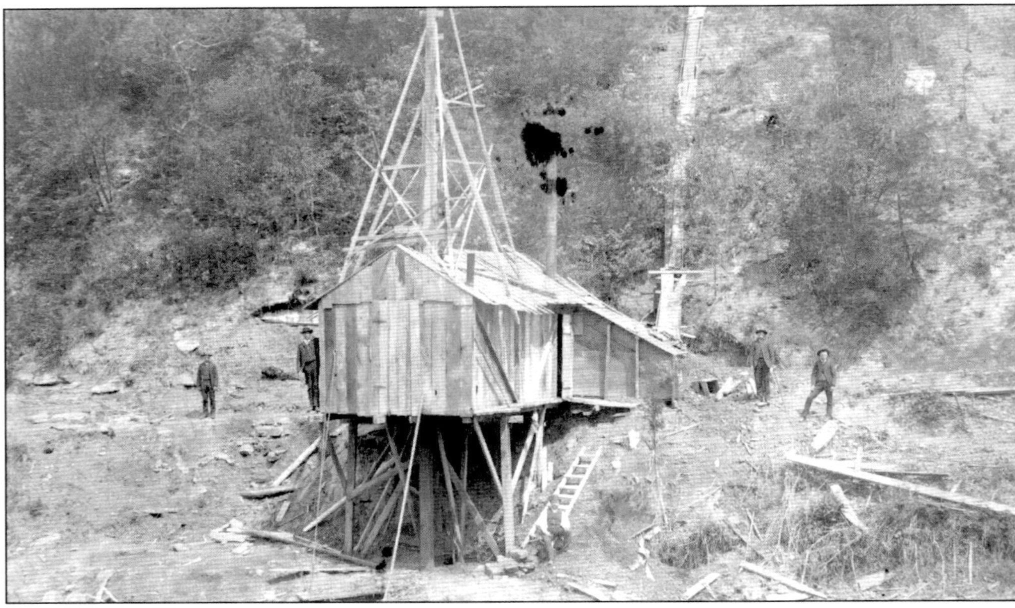

J. F. Limerick, a prominent Alma businessman, owned this coal-mining operation in Park Valley on the east edge of town. Henry Hutton was the engineer on the project. Limerick and his brother owned the First National Bank, located at 326 Missouri Street in the Limerick and Crafts building. The coal-mining business was one of many in which Limerick engaged before his financial collapse in 1890. (Courtesy of Wabaunsee County Historical Society.)

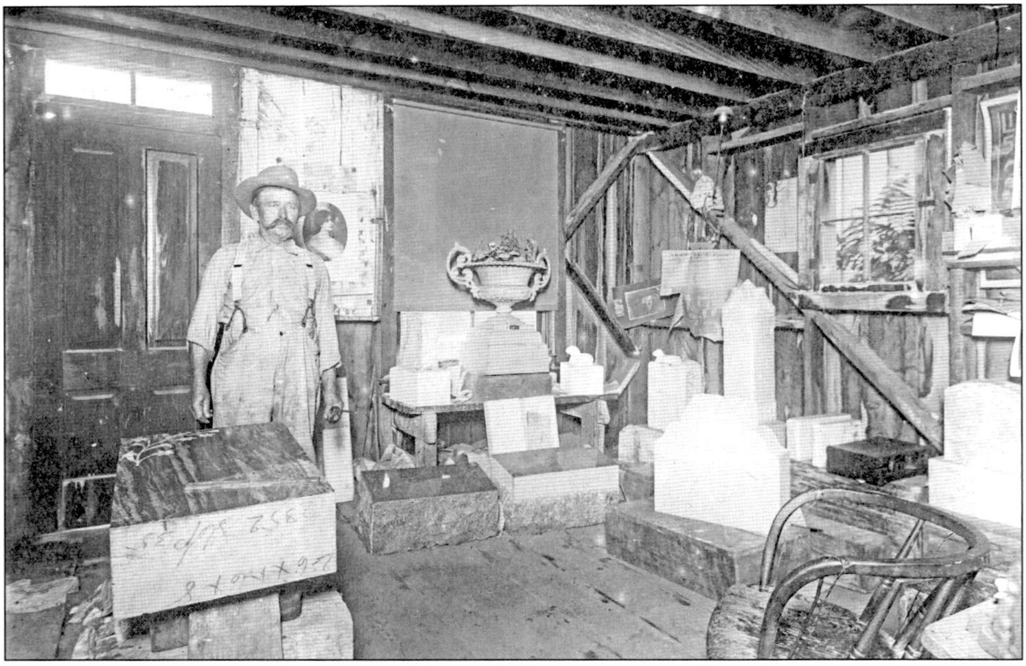

August Falk, above, owned Alma Marble Works, located next to the Falk Opera House on Main Street (West Third Street). Falk emigrated from Germany, moving directly to Alma in 1870, where he spent the rest of his life. (Courtesy of Wabaunsee County Historical Society.)

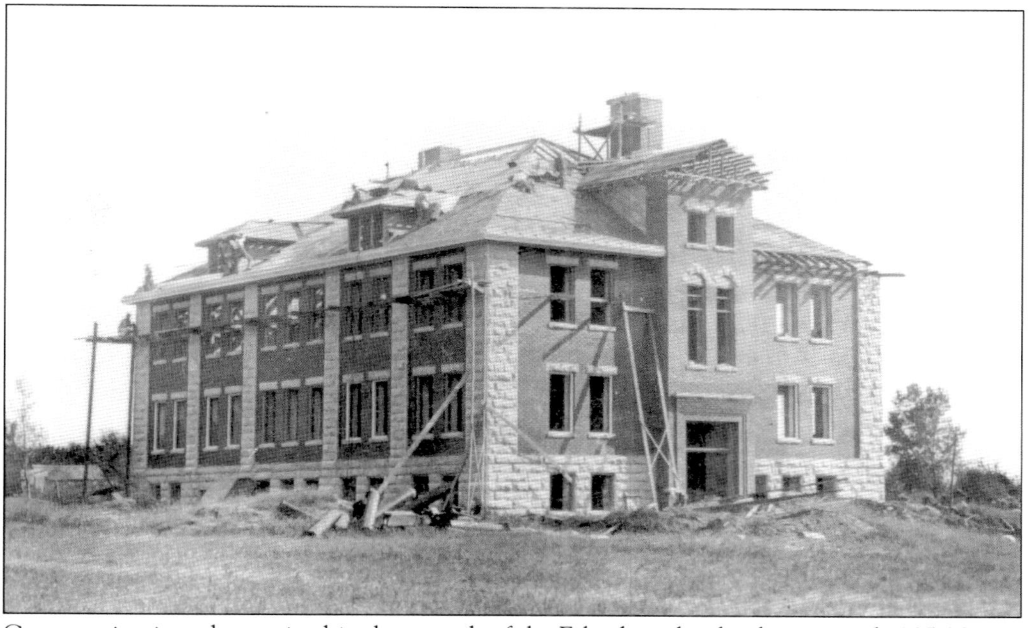

Construction is underway in this photograph of the Eskridge school, taken around 1905. Notice the workers on the roof. Grades 1 through 12 attended this school, which burned in 1920. (Courtesy Kansas State Historical Society.)

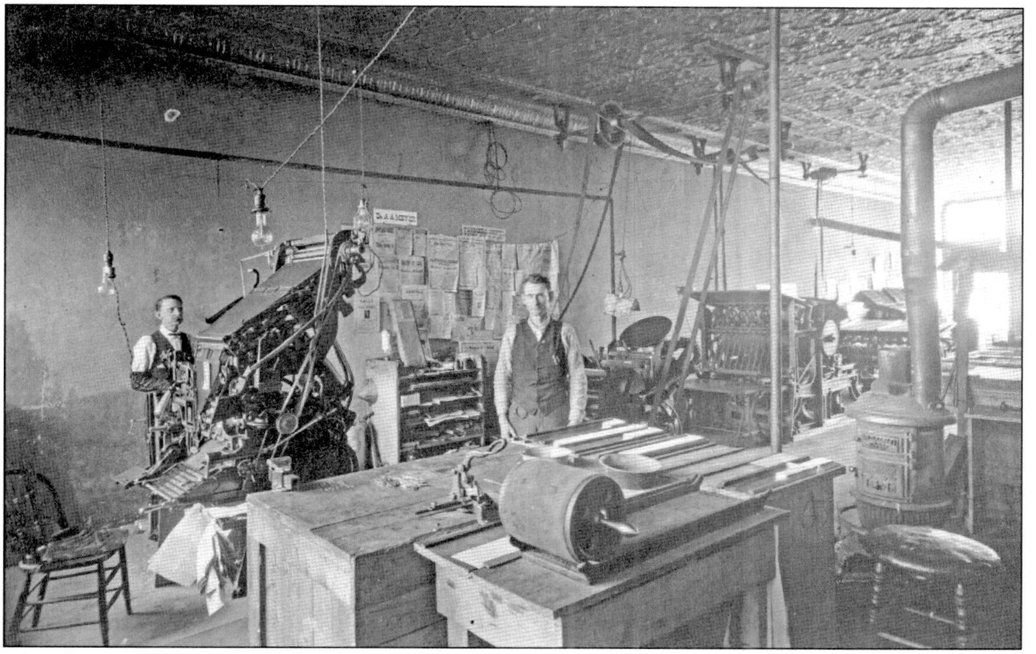

This is a 1923 photograph of the interior of the *Alma Enterprise* newspaper and job printing business, located at 319 Missouri Street. Frank Sage is at the left, and O. W. Little is to the right. At the beginning of the 20th century, two newspapers, the *Alma Enterprise* and the *Alma Signal*, operated in Alma simultaneously. A view of the exterior of both buildings can be seen on page 25. (Courtesy of Wabaunsee County Historical Society.)

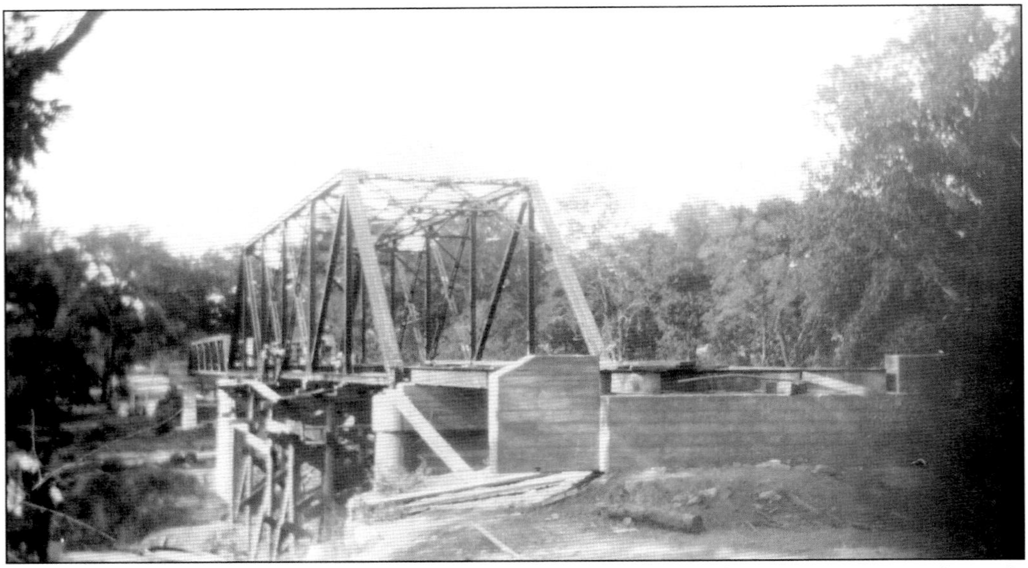

The steel bridge crossing Mill Creek on Vera Road is seen here under construction in the early 1920s. This bridge was replaced in 2004 with a modern concrete bridge. Today Wabaunsee County maintains 182 inspected bridges as well as many culverts, tubes, and low-water bridges not subject to inspection, yet still maintained. (Courtesy of Wabaunsee County Historical Society.)

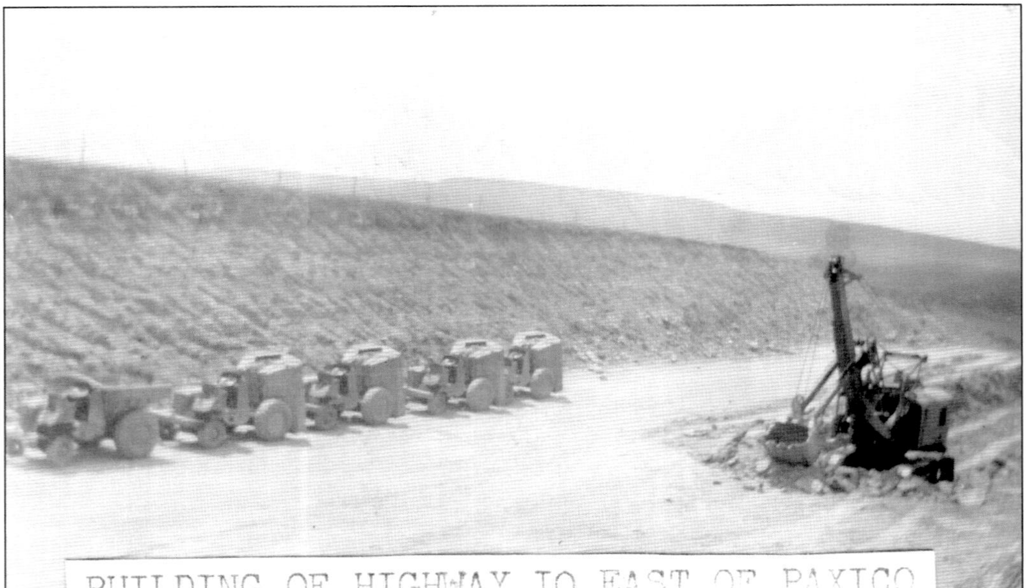

Labeled "Building of Highway 10 East of Paxico," a hoe can be seen in this view, cutting the roadbed. Highway 10 became a major east–west route through the county in the early 20th century; today it is a series of county gravel roads. Today Wabaunsee County maintains 220 miles of gravel road and 58 miles of chip and sealed paved road, while the various townships maintain 643 miles of gravel road. (Courtesy of Wabaunsee County Historical Society.)

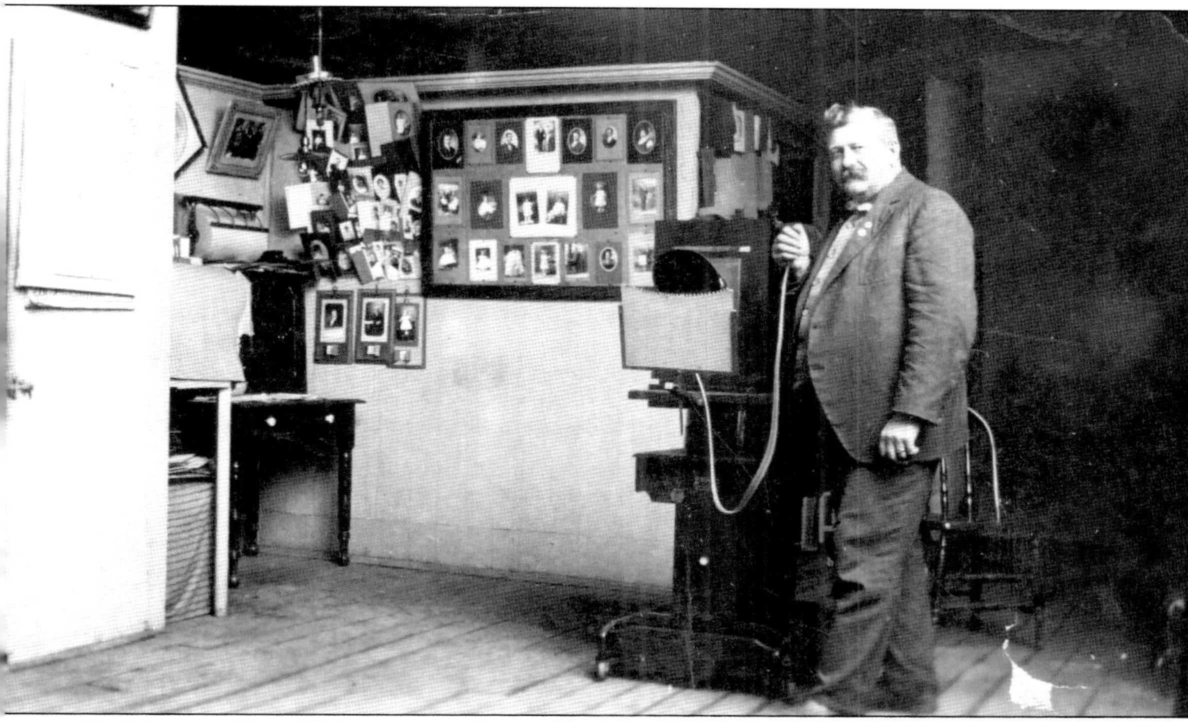

Gus Meier, a lifelong Wabaunsee County resident, was the most prolific professional photographer in the history of the county. Born on a farm near Bismark in 1865 as the son of German immigrant parents, Meier was educated at District 14, Halifax school, and then attended Kansas State Agriculture College in Manhattan before returning to Alma in 1887 to apprentice under Louis Palenske, a noted Alma professional photographer. He purchased Palenske's studio at 210 Missouri Street and established his photography business on the main floor, while residing with his wife, Mary, upstairs. He had a mobile photography studio on a wagon and traveled to Alta Vista on the first Saturday of the month and to Paxico on the third Saturday of the month. No other single individual recorded so much history of Wabaunsee County as Meier did. He was active from 1887 until his death in 1941. A number of Meier's "lost photographs" have been discovered at the state archives, which has generously allowed many of them to be printed in this book. (Courtesy of Wabaunsee County Historical Society.)

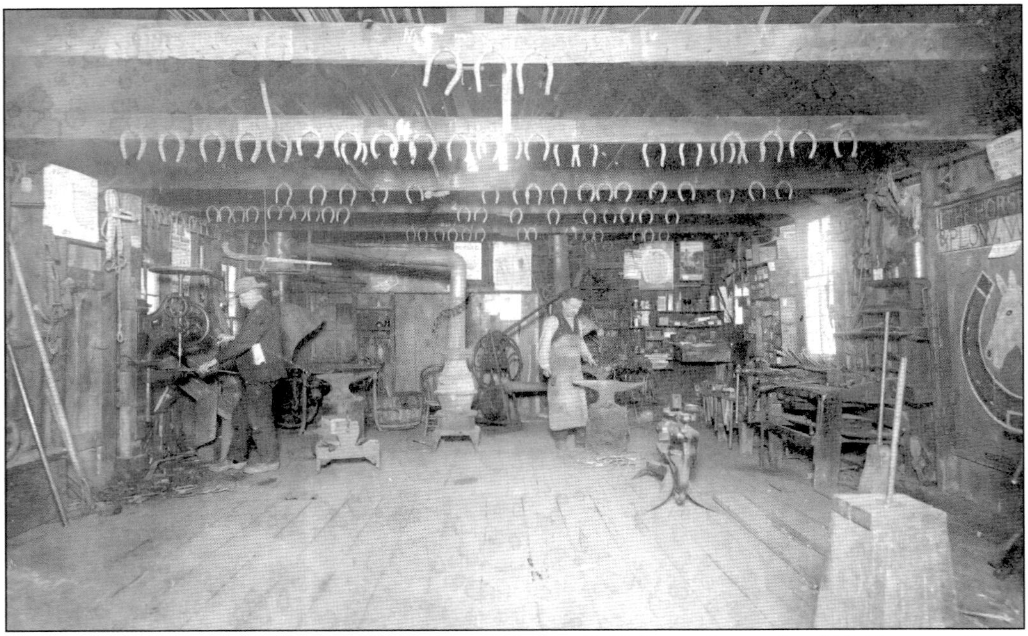

This interior view of the blacksmith shop operated by E. T. Linss, located at 329 Missouri Street in Alma, was taken in 1916. This small frame structure was located on the empty lot just north of the Hochhans building, which now houses Deb's Restaurant at 327 Missouri Street. (Courtesy of Wabaunsee County Historical Society.)

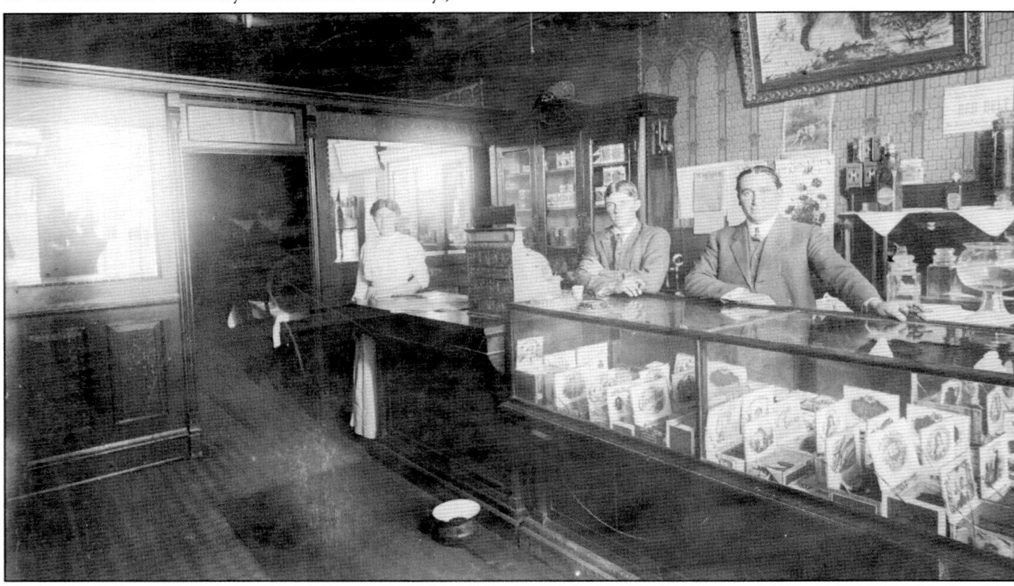

This late-1890s view of the interior of Hickory Jones's cigar store, located at 224 Missouri Street, was taken by Alma photographer Gus Meier. This photograph of (from left to right) Mrs. Hickory Jones, her brother Charlie Loehr, and Hickory Jones shows the depth of Meier's recording of life in Alma on film. His works include street scenes, interior views of businesses, and shots of new construction, as well as thousands of portraits of Wabaunsee County residents. (Courtesy of Wabaunsee County Historical Society.)

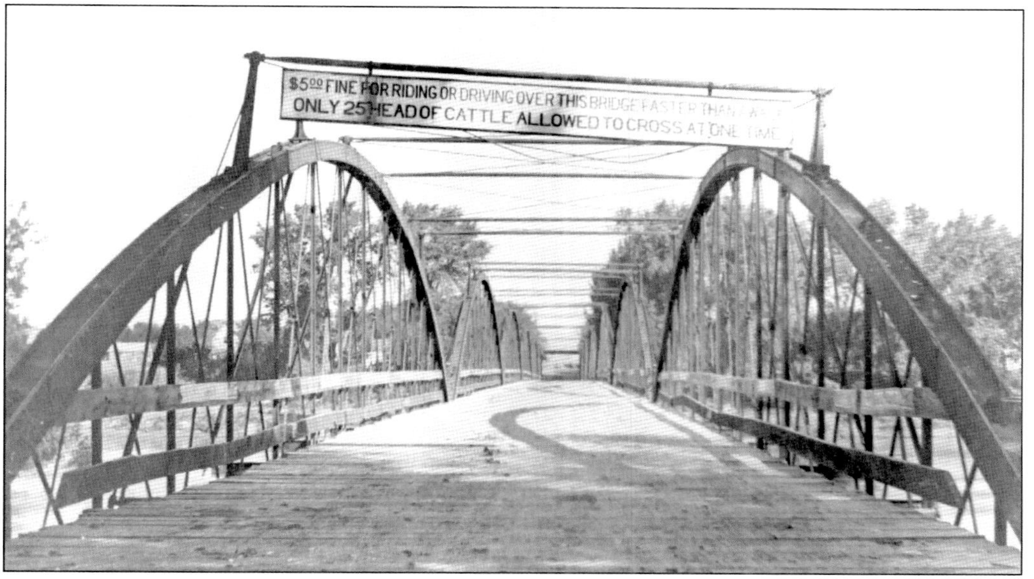

In June 1872, the bridge over the Kansas River at Wamego north of Alma was completed. A similar bridge north of Maple Hill was completed in February of that year. These bridges signaled an end to the ferry business across the river that had operated with marginal reliability for about 15 years. The construction of these river bridges and the many on streams throughout the county marked the government's role in building the infrastructure. (Courtesy of Wabaunsee County Historical Society.)

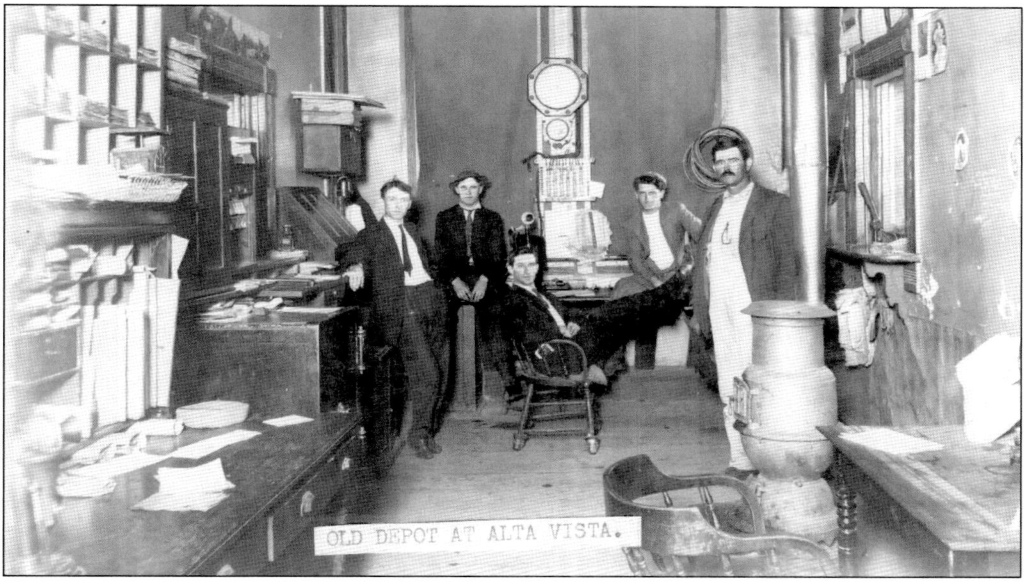

Workers pose for this early interior view of the Alta Vista Rock Island depot. In every town, the depot was an important cornerstone. Goods for virtually every merchant came by rail. Likewise, the railroad was the primary method of transportation for people traveling to and from Wabaunsee County during its first 100 years. The telegraph office, an important communications center before the advent of the telephone, was located at the depot. (Courtesy of Wabaunsee County Historical Society.)

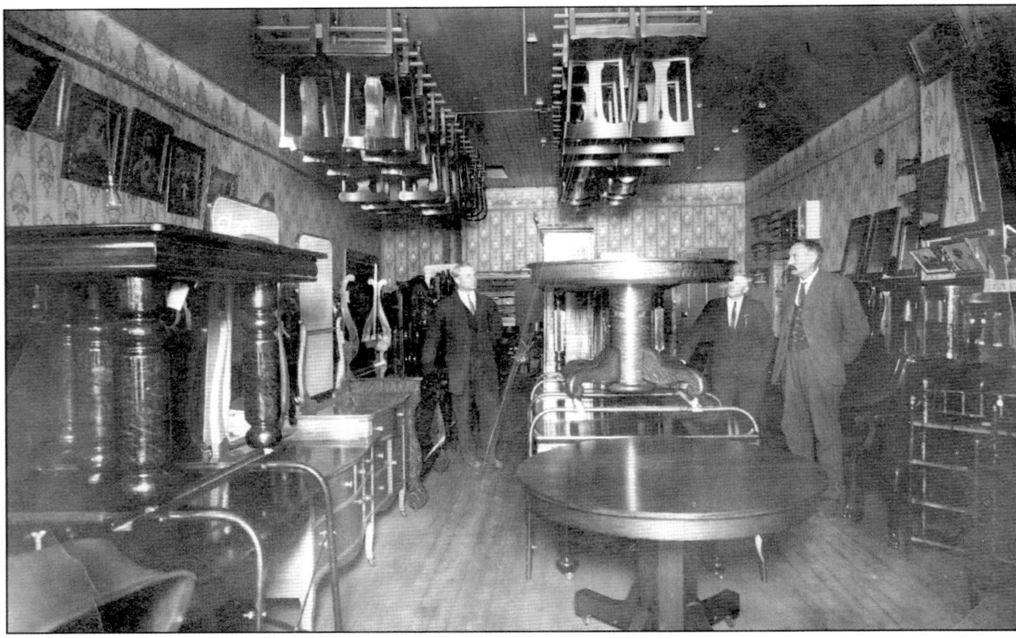

This interior view of Hasenbank Furniture Store, located at 204 Missouri Street, was taken in 1910 before the business moved to 324 Missouri Street in 1915. The exterior of this store can be seen on page 30. From left to right are W. C. Hasenbank, Herman Hasenbank, and Dick Thoes. (Courtesy of Wabaunsee County Historical Society.)

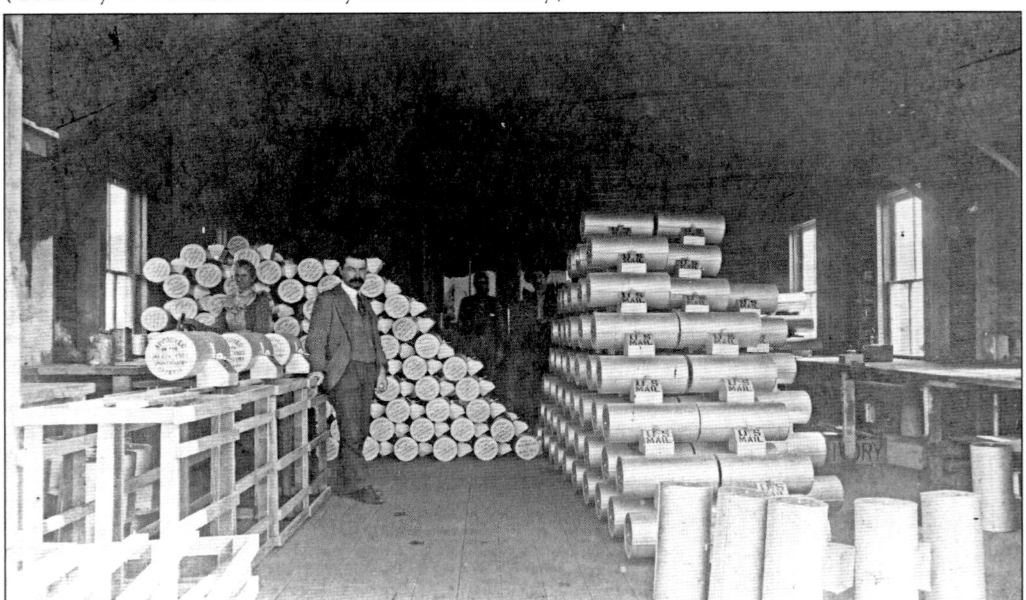

After obtaining a patent in 1902 for a cylindrical mailbox, Maple Hill Manufacturing Company operated for less than two years. H. R. Williams, front, partnered with J. N. Dolley, W. S. Isham, and P. C. Chamberlin in the venture, producing 10,000 boxes in the first year before the business faltered and closed in 1903. All assets were purchased by Isham. (Courtesy of Wabaunsee County Historical Society.)

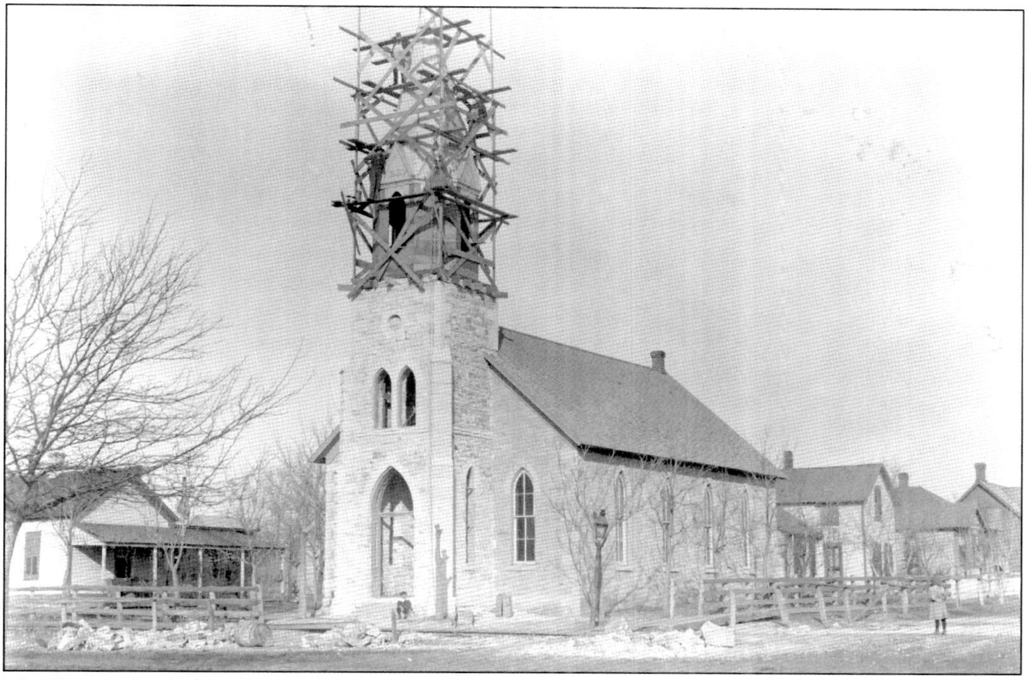

The Evangelical church was dedicated on May 14, 1882. The church was originally built without a spire. This photograph shows construction of the spire that was completed in 1899. The church stands today, known as the Peace United Church of Christ, located at 401 Grand Street. (Courtesy of Wabaunsee County Historical Society.)

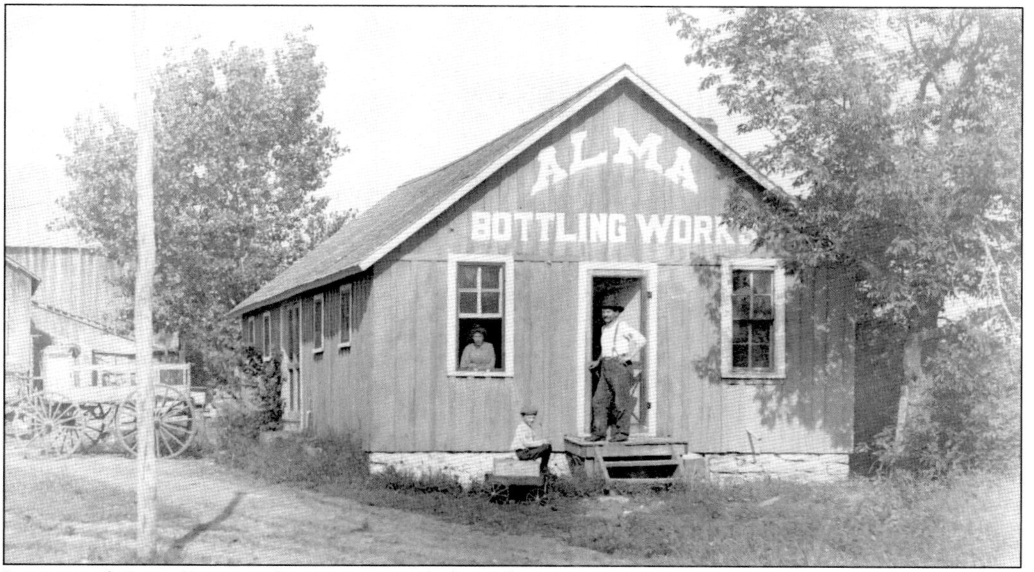

James and Dora Barger, above, operated the Alma Bottling Works. Their business was located behind the residence at 1021 Ohio Street in Alma. Arnold and Iris Schimtz purchased the residence after World War II. Arnold tore the bottling works building apart and constructed a chicken house on the site. He recalled hauling load after load of old Alma pop bottles to the dump. This view is from about 1908. (Courtesy of Wabaunsee County Historical Society.)

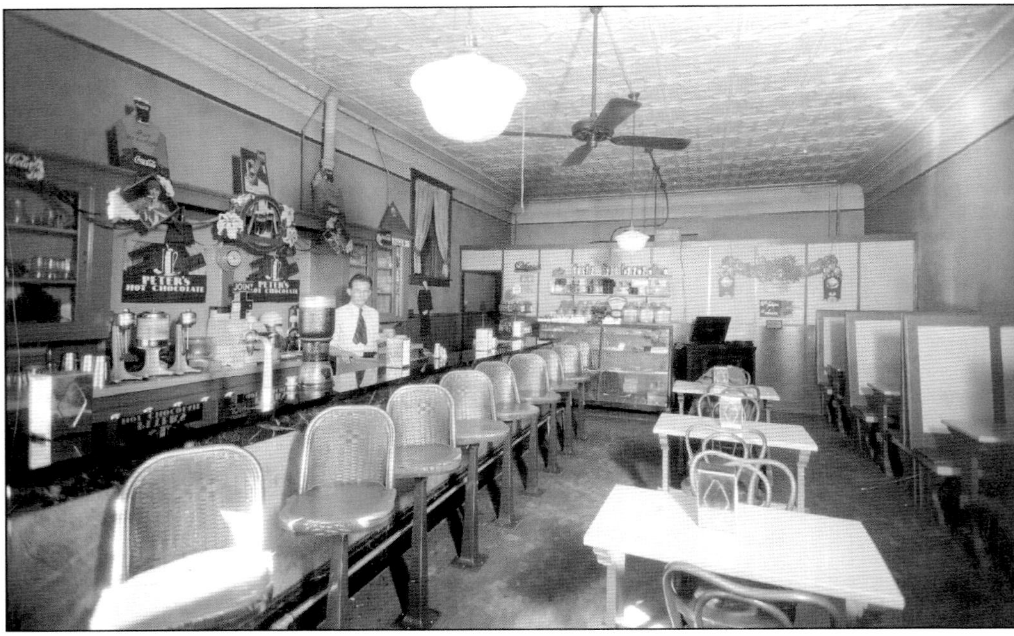

This Alma soda fountain is unidentified but is believed to be Meyer and Johnson's drugstore in the building that now houses the Wabaunsee County Museum. (Courtesy of Wabaunsee County Historical Society.)

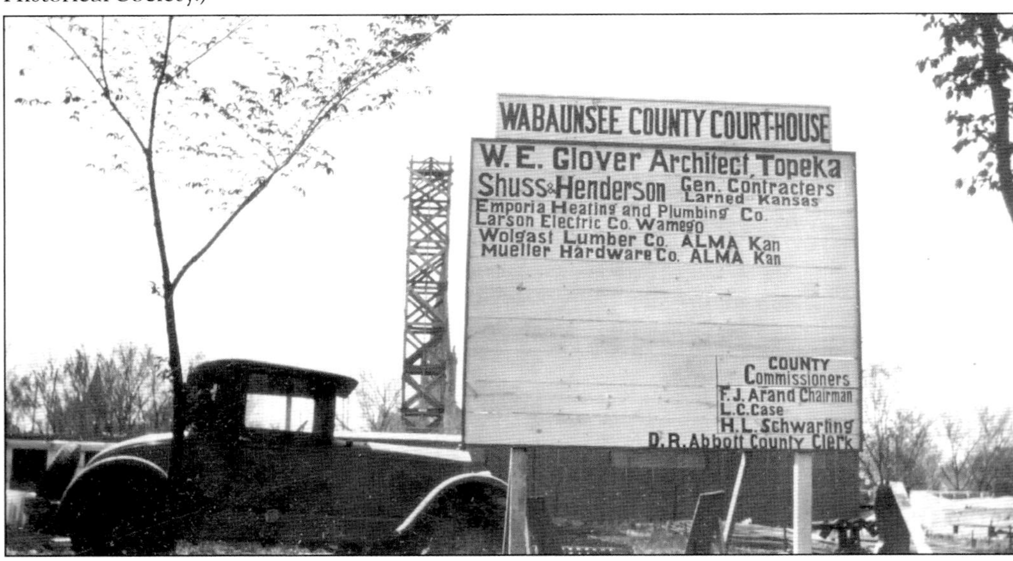

In 1931, construction of a new Wabaunsee County Courthouse began on the block where the old courthouse stood at the corner of Third and Kansas Streets. The project was funded by the county in the depths of the Depression before most federal public works projects had yet begun. The project employed many area men at a time when jobs were scarce. More than a dozen photographs of the construction were taken by Alma resident Arthur Vobach, who worked on the project. When renovations were done a few years ago at the courthouse, workers found a two-by-four that Vobach had signed and dated, which is now on display at the museum. (Courtesy of Jay Dee Miller.)

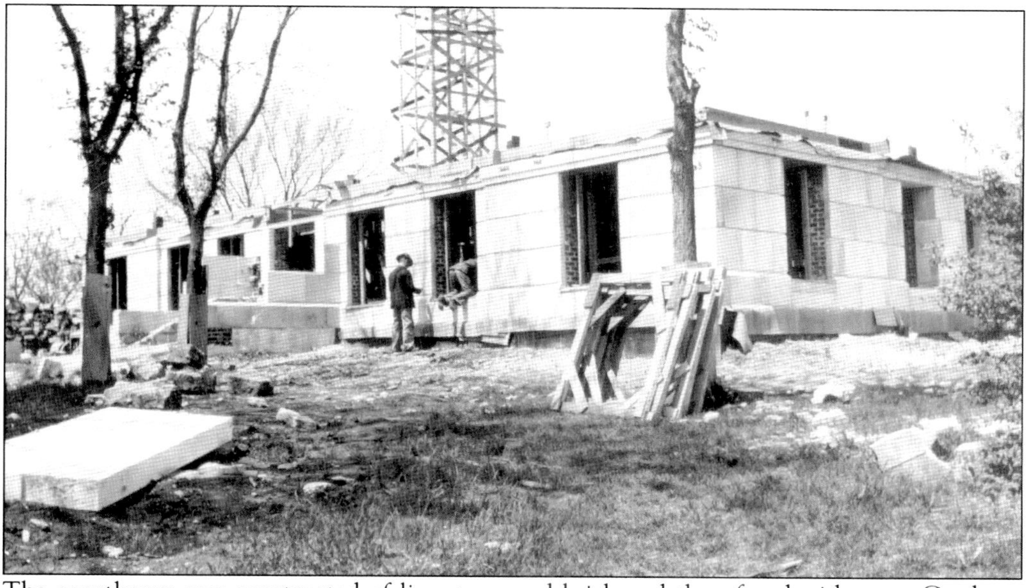

The courthouse was constructed of limestone and brick and then faced with sawn Carthage stone. Workers erected a derrick to lift the timbers, stone, and mortar during construction. Here they can be seen working on the basement level of the structure. After the new courthouse was occupied, the old courthouse was demolished in May 1932. (Courtesy of Jay Dee Miller.)

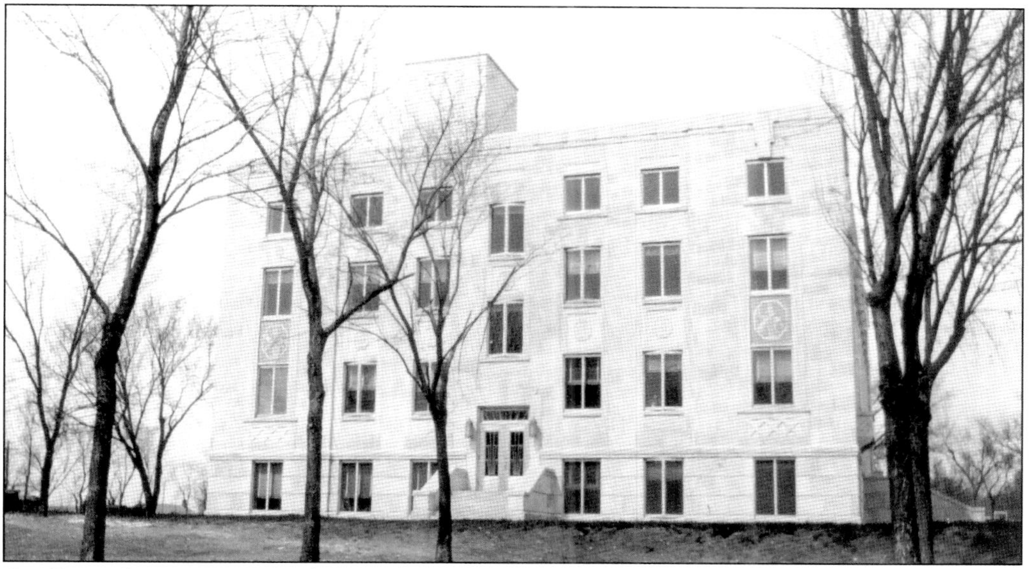

On December 10, 1931, Wabaunsee County commissioners received the completed building from the general contractor, and in four days, all the offices had moved into the new building. The building cost $148,357.57; however, no indebtedness was incurred by the taxpayers, as a one mill property tax had been levied beginning in 1928 to pay for the building, thus it was debt free upon its completion. In this late-1931 view by Vobach, notice that the sidewalks were not yet constructed. (Courtesy of Jay Dee Miller.)

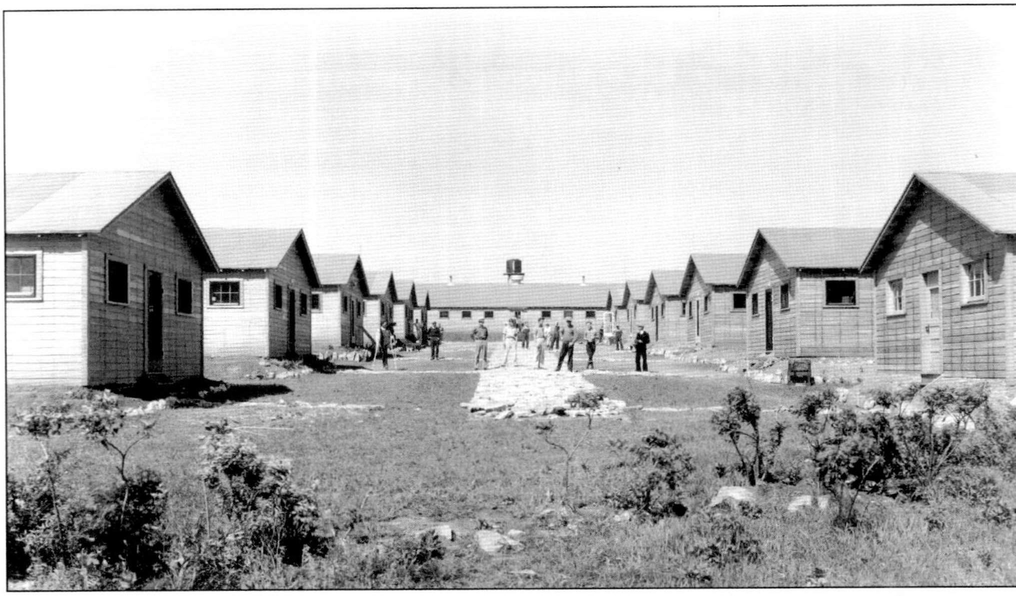

In 1934, after five years of promotion by local leaders, the State of Kansas created a transient camp four miles west of Eskridge to build Lake Wabaunsee. Workers at the Kansas Economic Relief Committee's Lake Wabaunsee project are seen in this 1935 Harold Wolfe photograph of the first barracks complex. The Lake Wabaunsee Corporation sold lots on the lake to finance the purchase of the 500 acres of land required for the lake park. (Courtesy of Wabaunsee County Historical Society.)

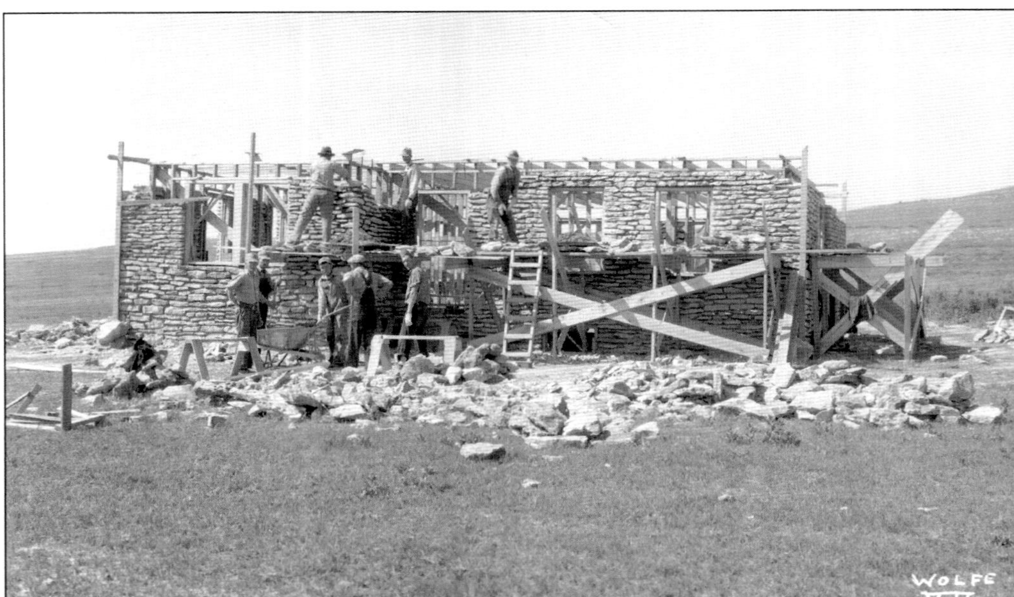

In this 1935 Wolfe photograph, Kansas Economic Relief Committee workers lay stone for the caretaker's cabin at the east end of the dam at Lake Wabaunsee. This was the first structure built at the camp by transient labor. This caretaker's cabin burned in December 1936 before the lake was ever completed. (Courtesy of Wabaunsee County Historical Society.)

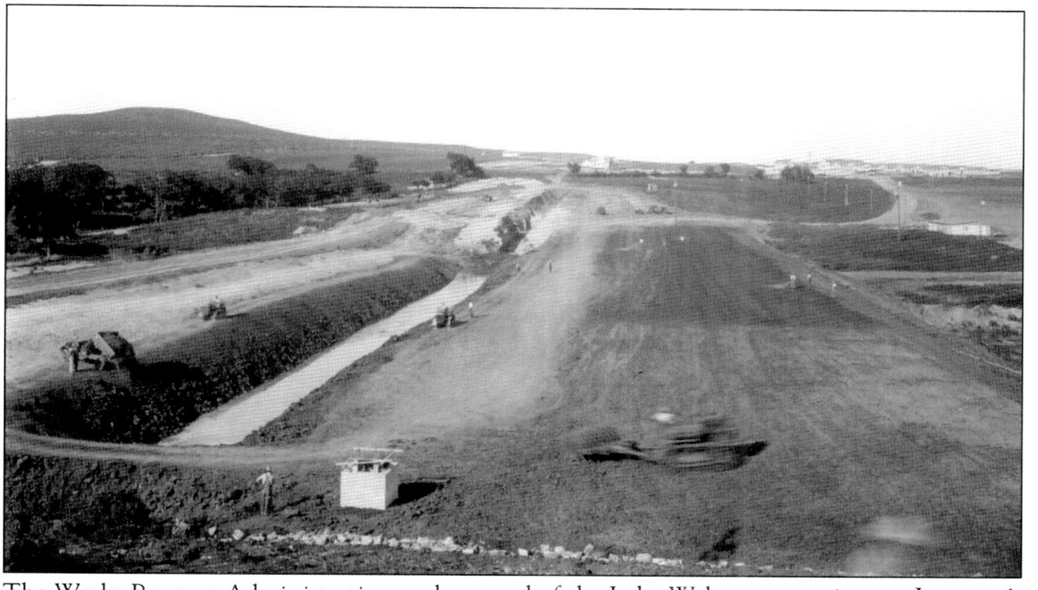

The Works Progress Administration took control of the Lake Wabaunsee project on January 1, 1936, and dam construction is fully underway in this Gus Meier photograph. The dam was completed on December 31, 1936. The lake promoters had been unable to sell enough lots to pay for the park property, so in March 1937, citizens of Eskridge passed an $11,000 bond election to pay for the remaining land, and the city became owner of the lake and park property except for lots sold on the south and west shores. (Courtesy of Kansas State Historical Society.)

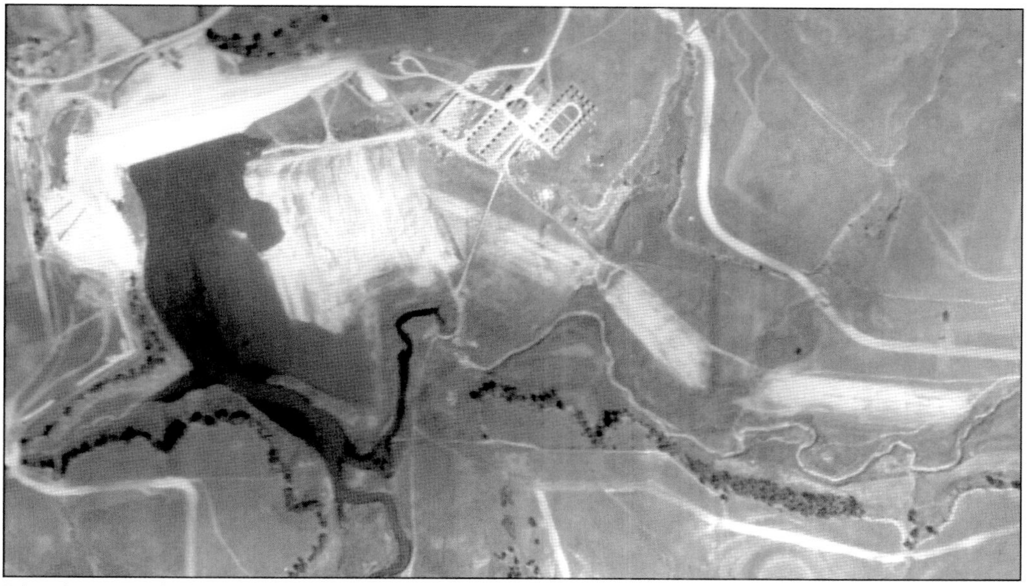

The first aerial photograph ever taken of Lake Wabaunsee is dated September 11, 1937, just weeks after the gate valve was closed on the dam. The arms of the lake had not filled; in fact, water had not even made its way to the barracks. This photograph belonged to Homer Reppart, a longtime lake resident and former Works Progress Administration engineer on the Lake Wabaunsee project. Lake resident Bruce Taylor purchased Reppart's house, and the framed lake photograph came with the deal. (Courtesy of Bruce Taylor.)

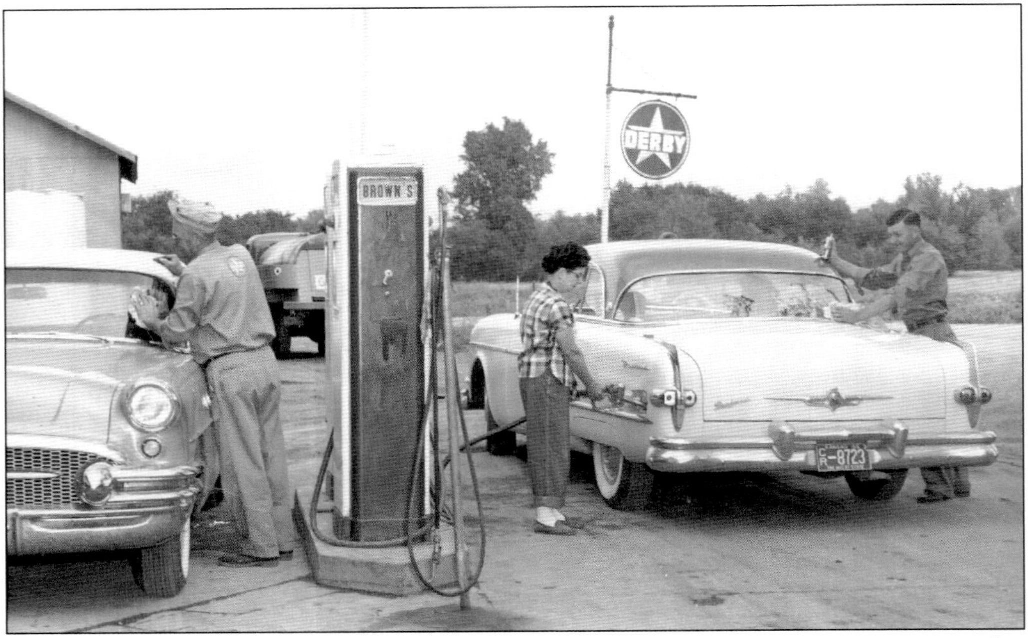

The Brown family's Derby gas station in Harveyville provides real service to customers in this October 30, 1955, photograph. From left to right, Ross, Marie, and Paul Brown are seen fueling and servicing cars. Ross opened this station on October 25, 1941. (Courtesy of Wabaunsee County Historical Society.)

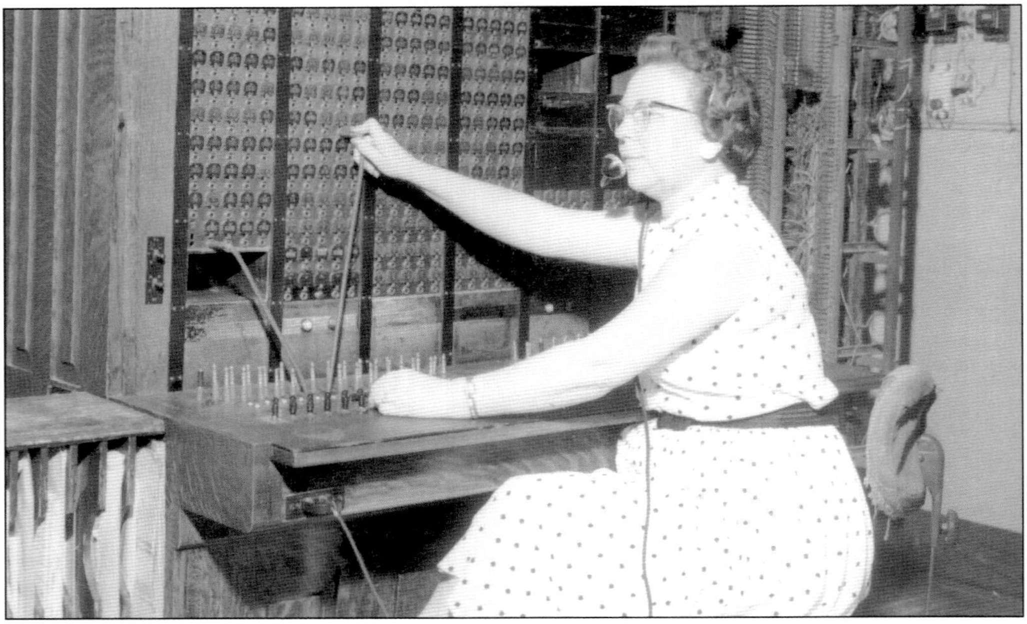

Nola Conrad, above, worked for many years as the switchboard operator in Eskridge. The telephone switchboard was located in the building at 208 South Main Street where the senior citizens center is located today. This photograph was taken around 1960. (Courtesy of Kansas State Historical Society.)

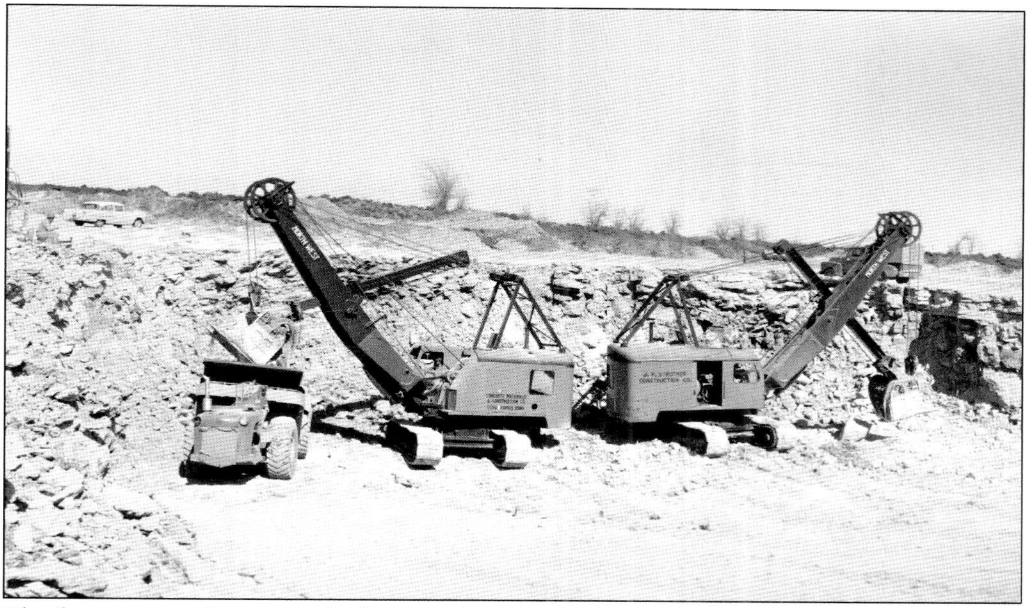

The first section of interstate highway in America was completed on November 14, 1956, and spanned nine miles, beginning at mile marker 341 in Wabaunsee County and extending four miles into Shawnee County to mile marker 350. The company that is now Koss Construction, Topeka, was located in Cedar Rapids, Iowa, when it landed the contracts for the first two sections of interstate highway in the country. Above, two hoes cut though rock ledges in Wabaunsee County during construction of the first section of Interstate 70. (Courtesy of Inez Dunn.)

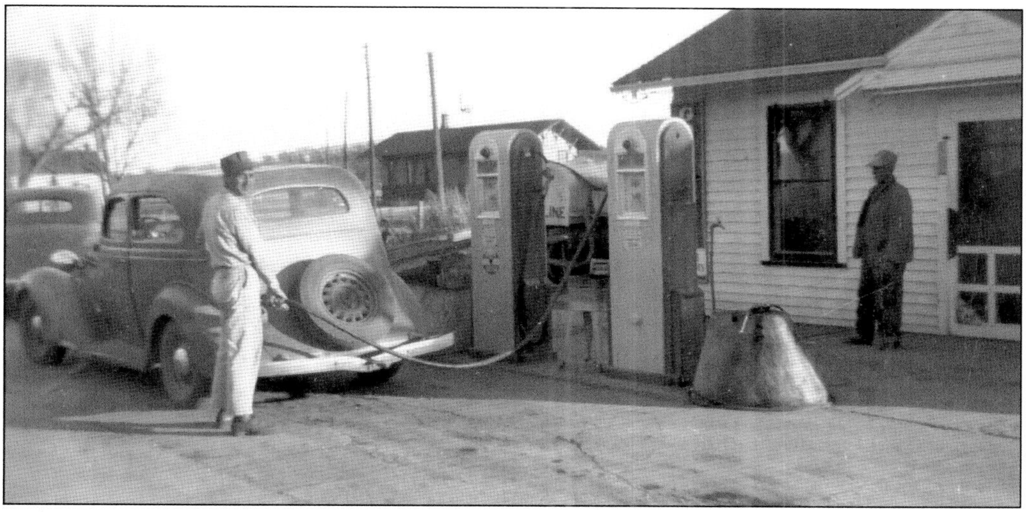

Wabaunsee County native Eddie Meinhardt, above, is seen at his first gas station in Paxico in 1956. Meinhardt spent nearly a half a century as a leading businessman in Paxico, operating his gas stations, antique stores, and a campground. One can see the Paxico depot in the background. Ironically, Meinhardt purchased this depot 40 years after this photograph was taken and moved it to his Mill Creek Campground. (Courtesy of the Eddie Meinhardt family.)

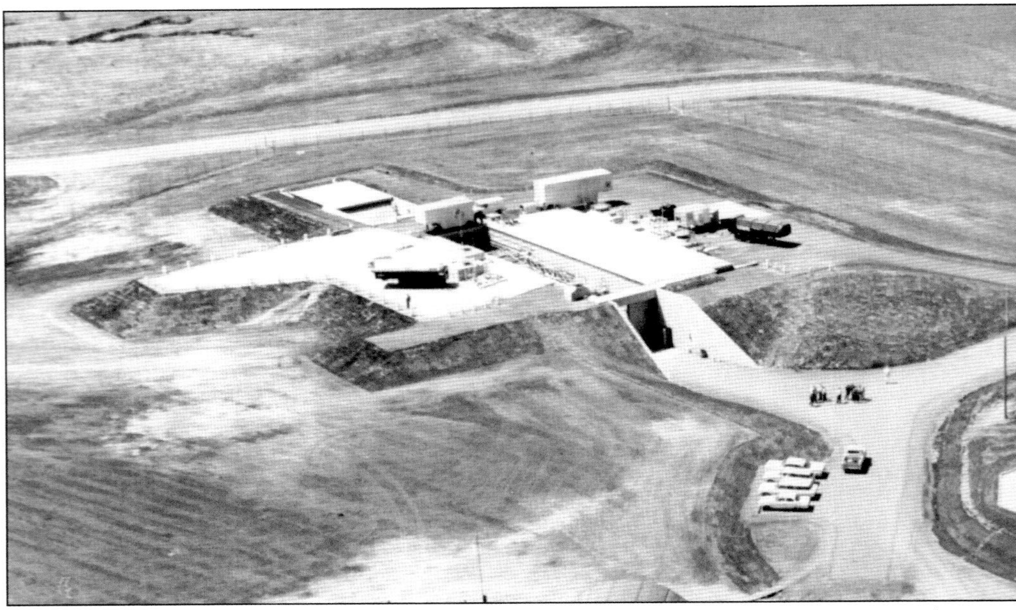

The Atlas missile launcher at Keene is seen here in late 1961 as the base was turned over to the air force by civilian contractors. The missile, armed with a nuclear warhead, rested in a horizontal position in the missile bay and was lifted vertically before fueling and launching. The missile base was located at 15513 Missile Base Road, and it is now a private residence. (Courtesy of Ed Peden.)

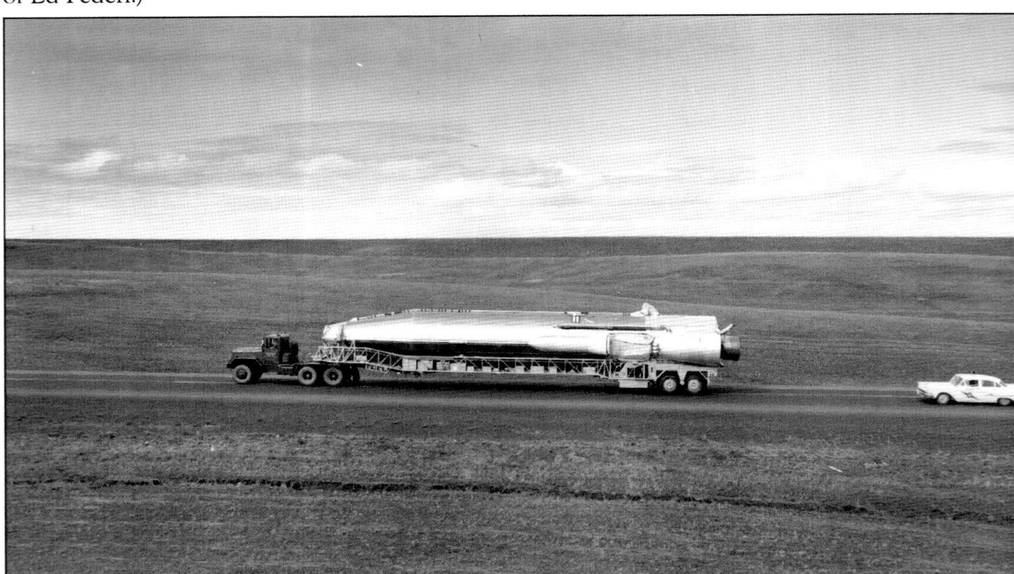

An Atlas E missile from Forbes Field in Topeka is shown here being towed down Interstate 70, west of Topeka. One crew member rode in a compartment forward of the rear trailer wheels, maintaining air pressure inside the missile body, which was empty of its liquid fuel and would collapse if not pressurized. The air force installed the intercontinental ballistic missiles in July 1961, and they remained operational until their decommissioning in January 1965. (Courtesy of Ed Peden.)

Four

Community Affairs

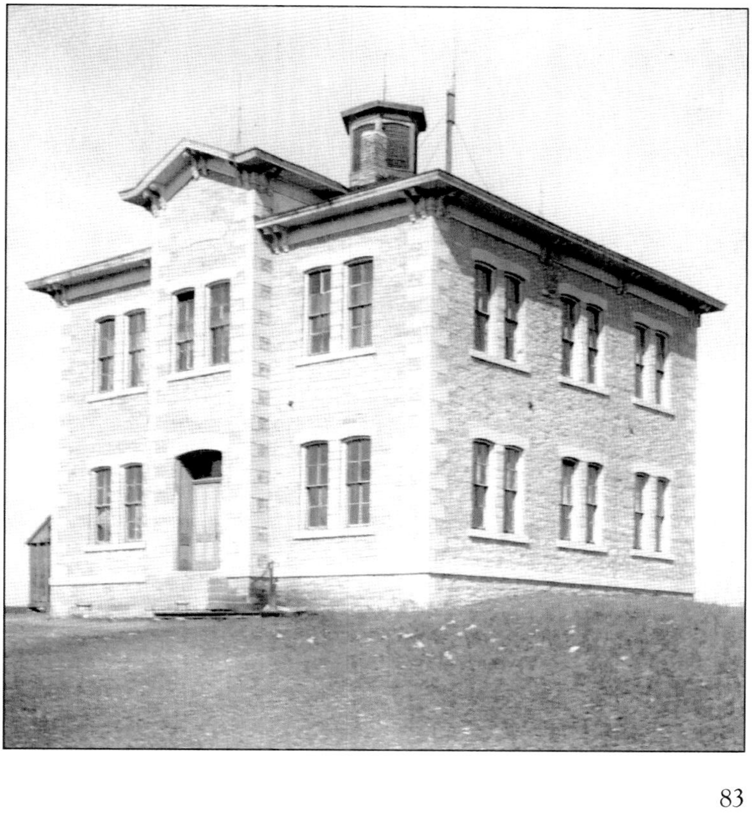

Chapter 4 examines the schools, churches, and organizations of Wabaunsee County's past. At right, the first Alma city school was opened on January 18, 1875. Known as the "School on the Hill," it was located on the hill in the northwest end of Alma where the water towers stand today. (Courtesy of Wabaunsee County Historical Society.)

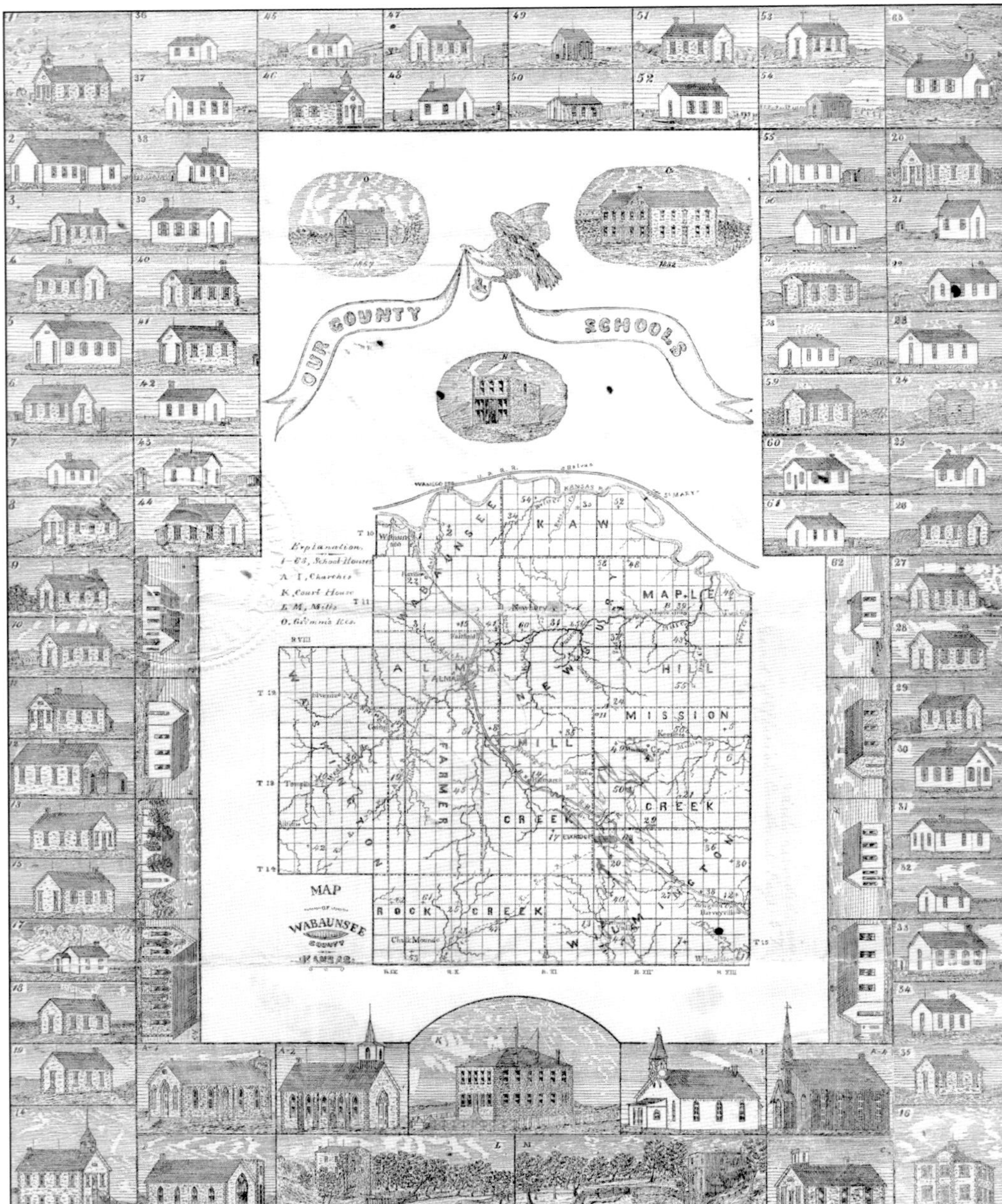

Alma Signal owner Matt Thomson, author of the book *Early History of Wabaunsee County, Kansas, with Stories of Pioneer Days and Glimpses of Our Western Border*, created this 1882 etching showing the schools in the county along with a map showing each school's location. Every school had one of these etchings on display. (Courtesy of Wabaunsee County Historical Society.)

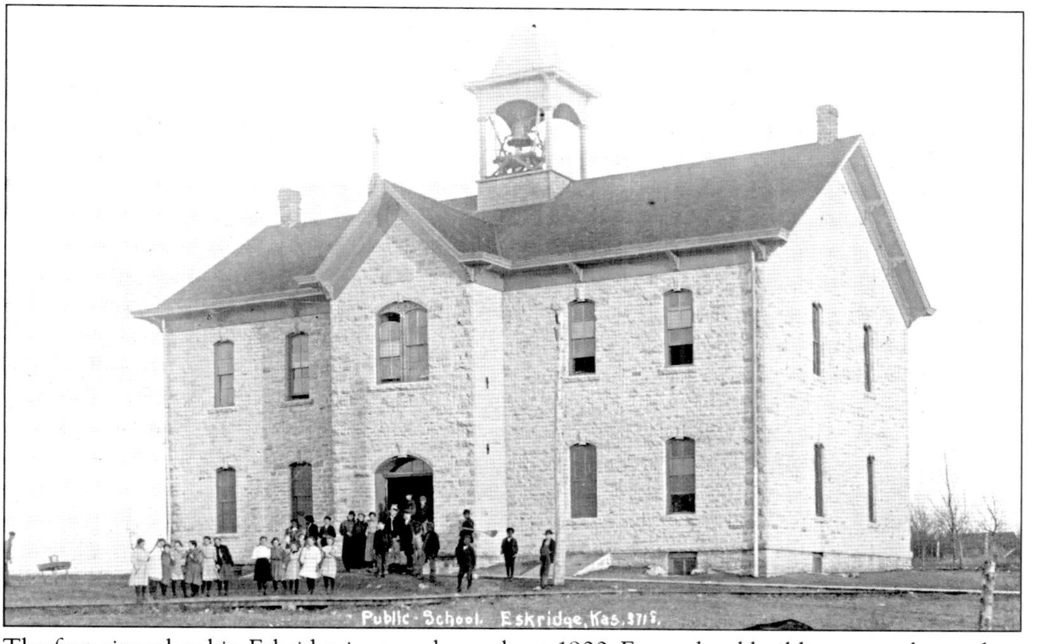

The first city school in Eskridge is seen above about 1900. Four school buildings were located on this same site in the 400 block of West Second Avenue over a period of 125 years. (Courtesy of Wabaunsee County Historical Society.)

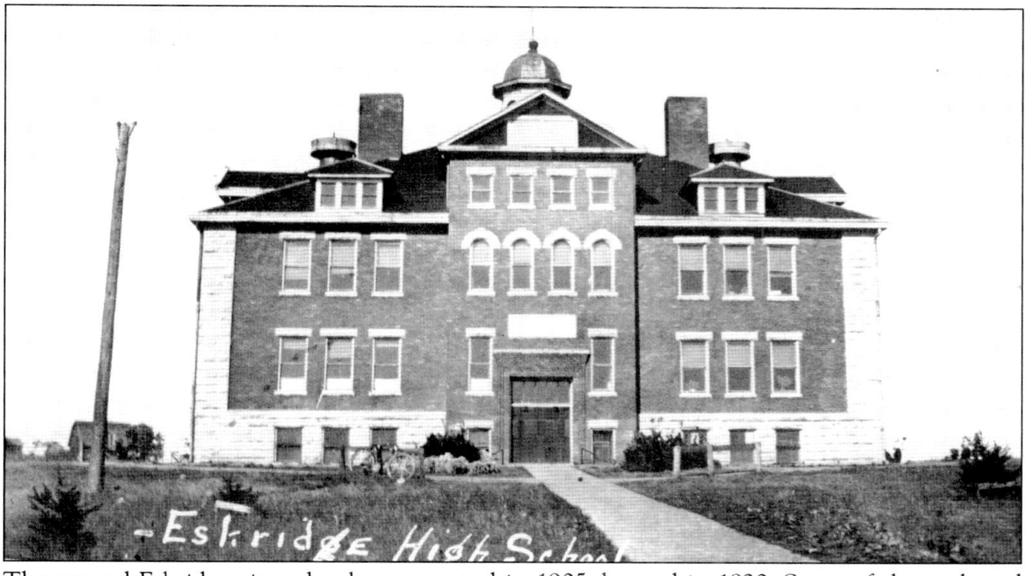

The second Eskridge city school, constructed in 1905, burned in 1920. Some of the rock and cornerstones were salvaged and used in the construction of the two buildings that were erected in 1921 to replace this structure. (Courtesy of Inez Dunn.)

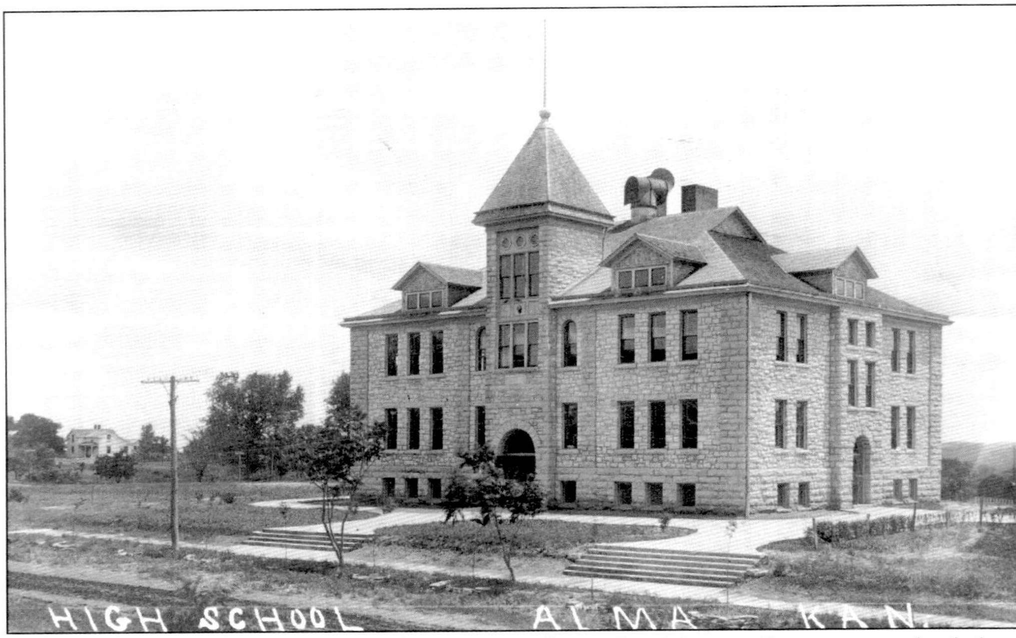

The second Alma school, constructed in 1906, was located on Missouri Street just south of where the high school stands today. This building was razed in 1957, and a gymnasium and tennis courts were built on the site in 1960. (Courtesy of Wabaunsee County Historical Society.)

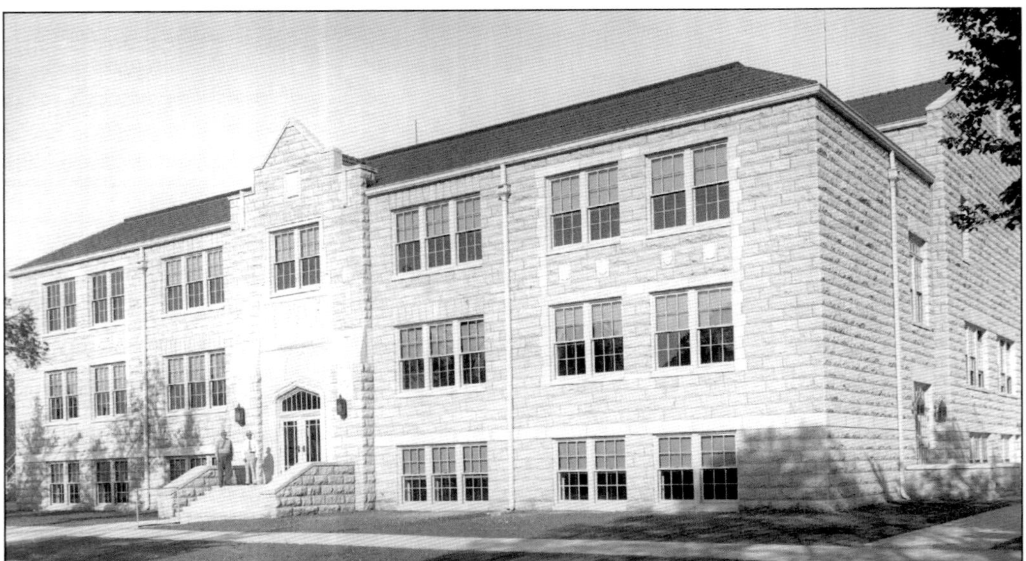

The new Alma school, designated project 1027-D by the Works Progress Administration, was completed in 1937. Federal works projects constructed thousands of public buildings and recreational facilities across America. The Alma school and Lake Wabaunsee were the two public works construction projects in Wabaunsee County. (Courtesy of Wabaunsee County Historical Society.)

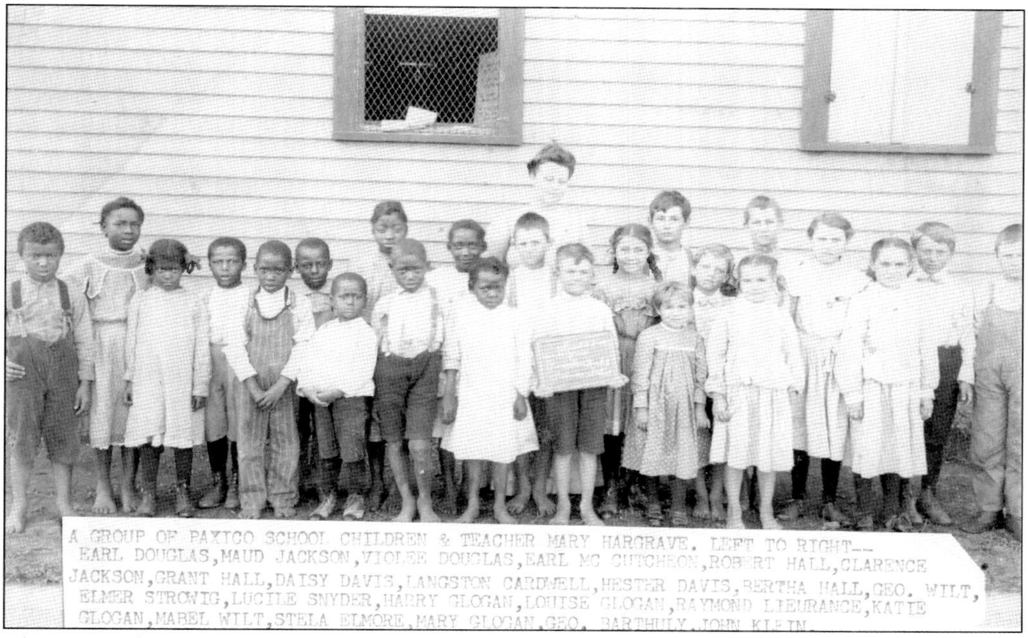

This view of a Paxico elementary school class from 1905 reveals that half the class was black. Segregation was never practiced in Wabaunsee County schools, and some areas of the county had large black populations. Notice that more than half the kids in the class had no shoes to wear to school. (Courtesy of Wabaunsee County Historical Society.)

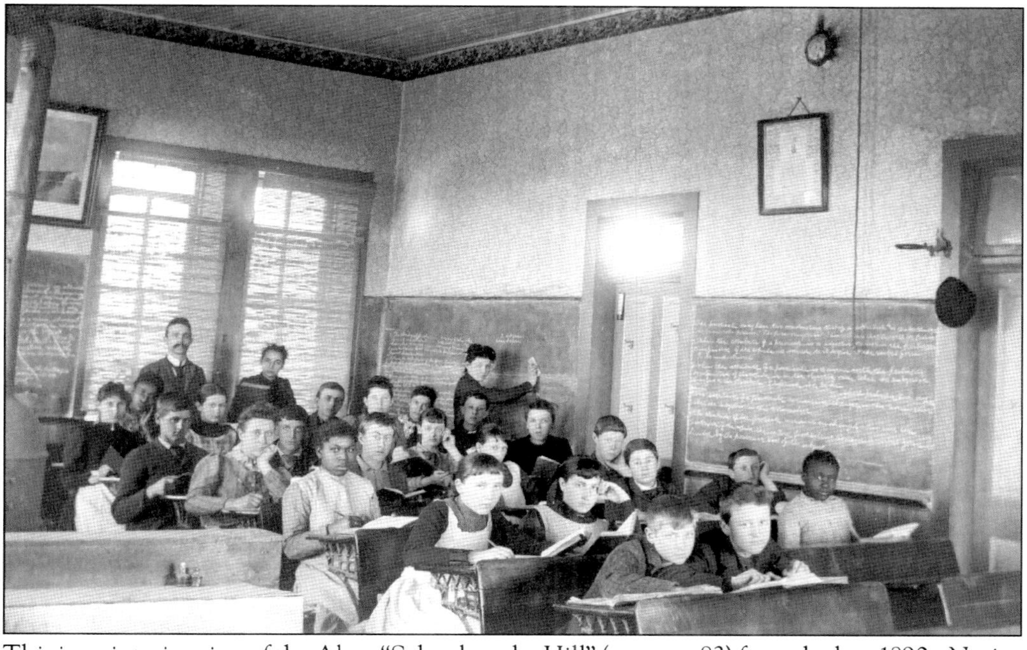

This is an interior view of the Alma "School on the Hill" (see page 83) from the late 1890s. Notice the Matt Thomson schoolhouse etching hanging on the wall over the blackboard. Thomson, a newspaperman and writer, was also superintendent of schools and placed one of his etchings in every school in the county (see page 84). (Courtesy of Wabaunsee County Historical Society.)

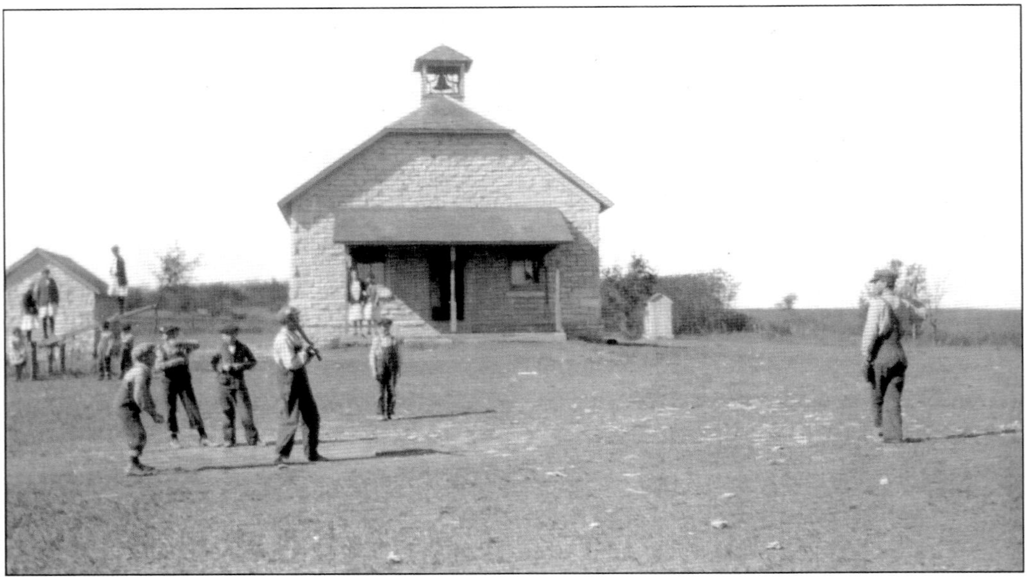

Students were enjoying time in the playground in this 1916 view of the District 3 school, located at 31514 Wabaunsee Road in Alma. Constructed in 1875, the building was used for township meetings after the school closed, until it burned in 2005. (Courtesy of Wabaunsee County Historical Society.)

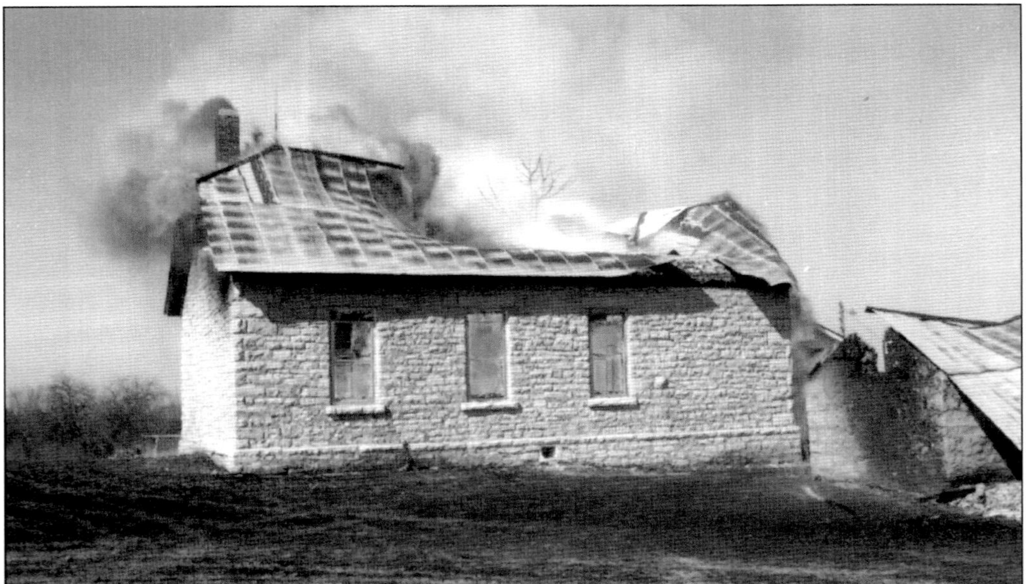

A raging pasture fire, fed by strong winds, destroyed the District 3 building on April 3, 2005. *Wabaunsee County Signal-Enterprise* owner Ervan Stuewe captured this photograph after going to the scene where firefighters were battling the blaze a half mile to the east, when the flames spread to the school grounds, engulfing the structure in minutes. (Courtesy of Wabaunsee County Historical Society.)

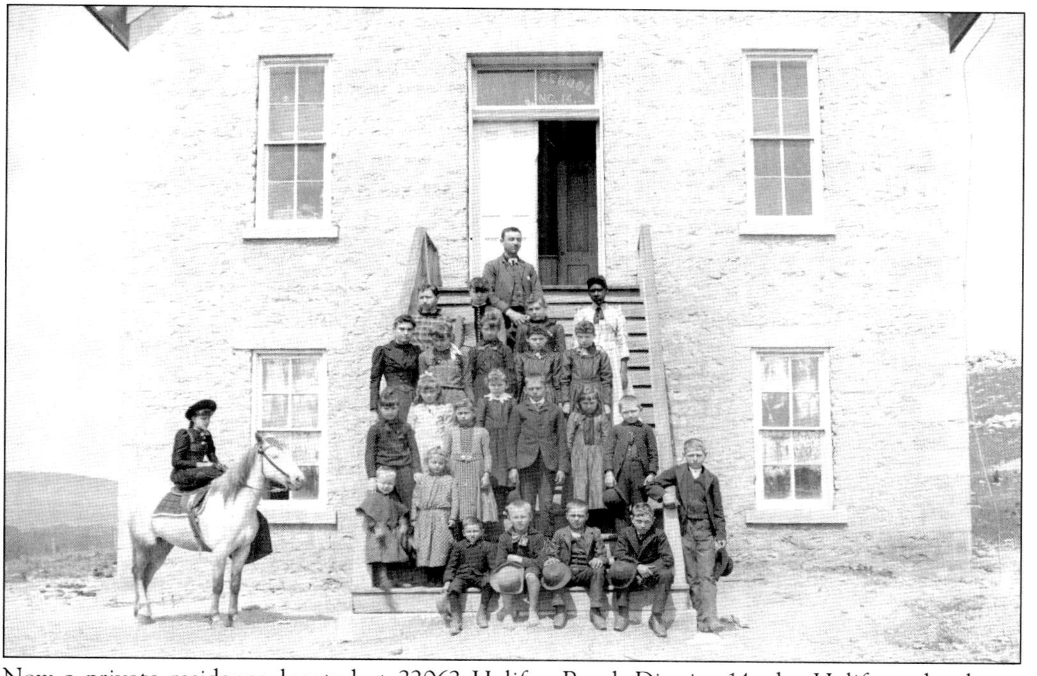

Now a private residence located at 22062 Halifax Road, District 14, the Halifax school was organized in 1862. The first school was a log structure before this building was constructed in 1881. (Courtesy of Wabaunsee County Historical Society.)

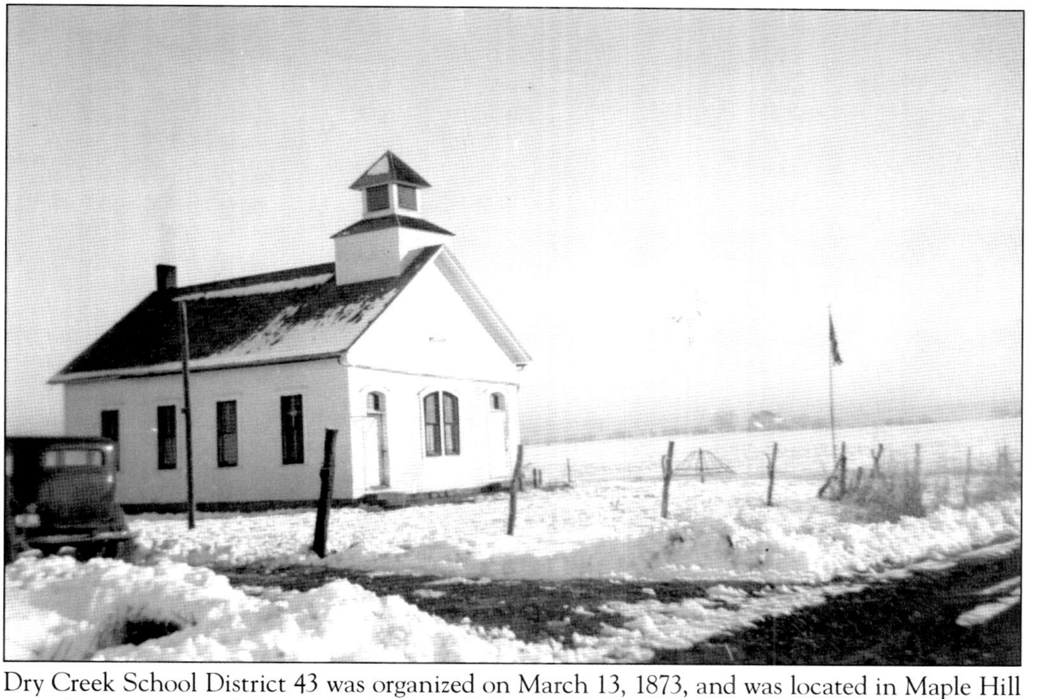

Dry Creek School District 43 was organized on March 13, 1873, and was located in Maple Hill township just west of Keene Road, one mile south of Interstate 70. (Courtesy of Wabaunsee County Historical Society.)

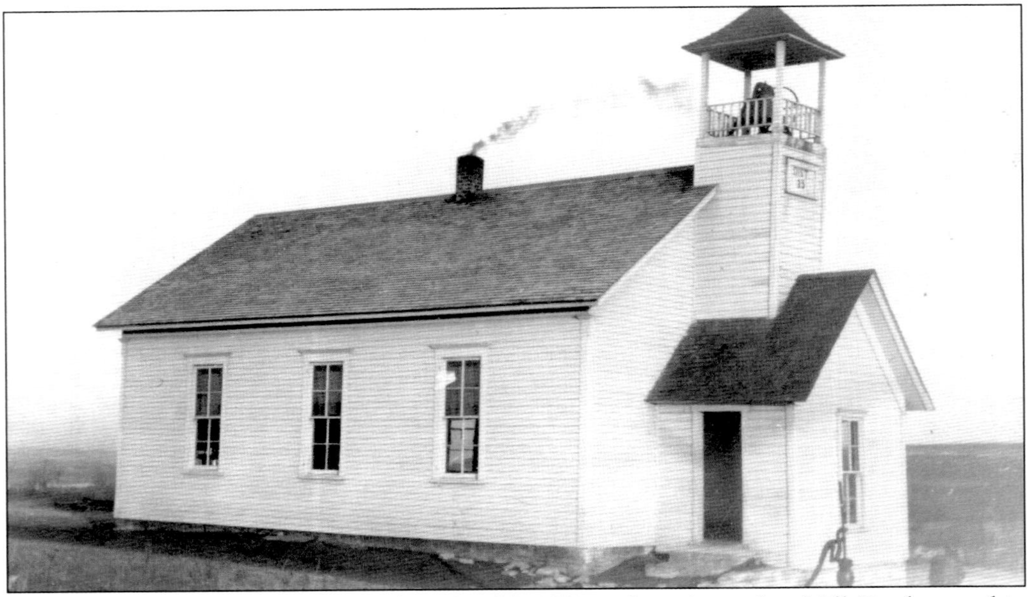

The District 35 school was organized on April 7, 1871, and was located in Mill Creek township on Skyline Road. The school burned in 1990. Notice the coal smoke coming from the chimney. Virtually all the 80 or so rural schools were heated with wood or coal stoves. Keeping the fires going was the job of the teacher, sometimes with the help of older students. (Courtesy of Wabaunsee County Historical Society.)

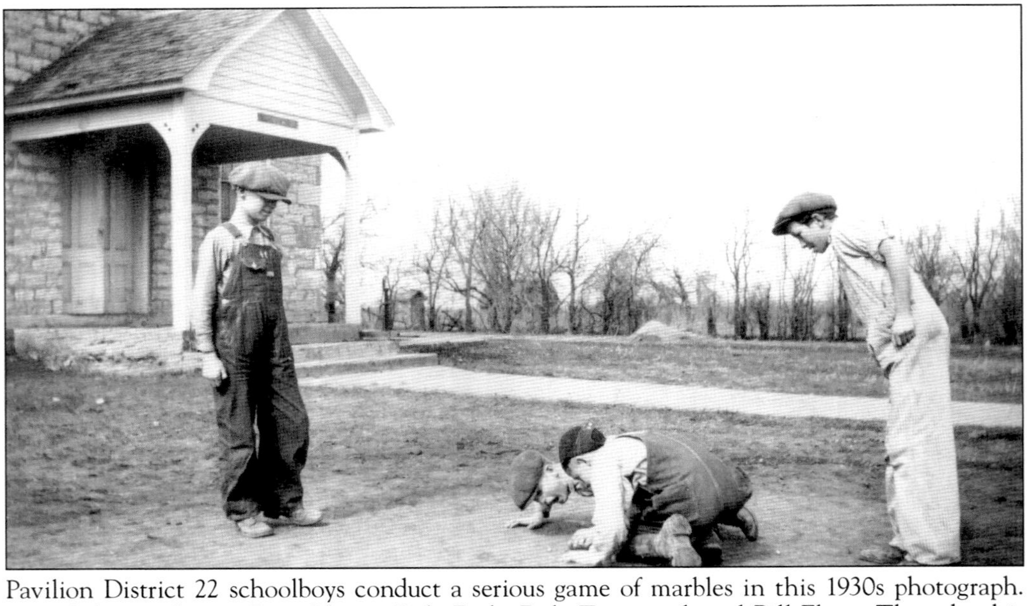

Pavilion District 22 schoolboys conduct a serious game of marbles in this 1930s photograph. From left to right are Don Glover, Dale Feyh, Dale Townsend, and Bill Ekart. The school is located at 35382 Antelope Creek Road. (Courtesy of Wabaunsee County Historical Society.)

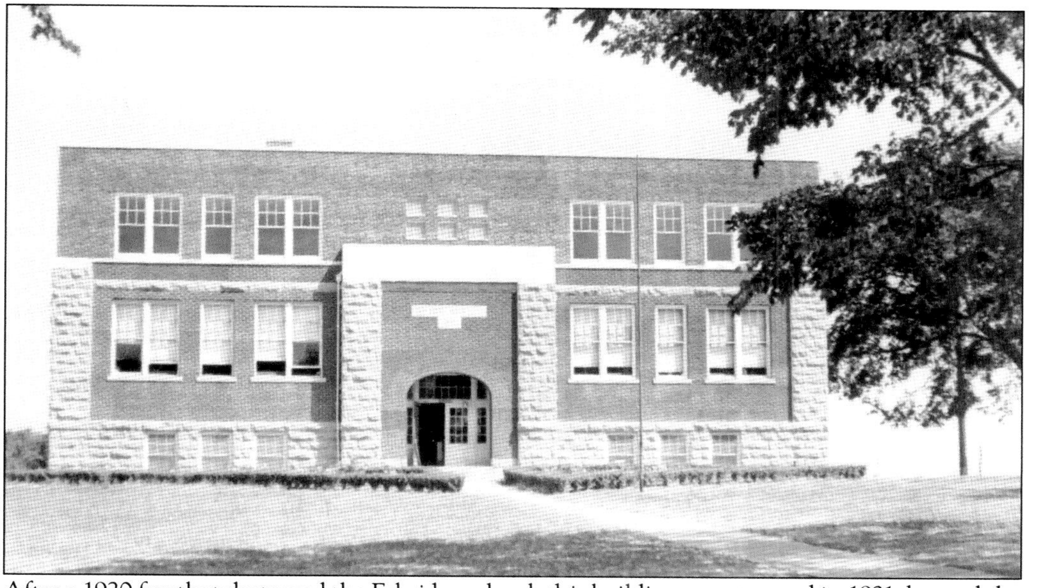

After a 1920 fire that destroyed the Eskridge school, this building, constructed in 1921, housed the Eskridge Grade School until 2004. Mission Valley School District USD 330 offered the building for sale by bids after its closing, and it is now in private ownership. (Courtesy of Inez Dunn.)

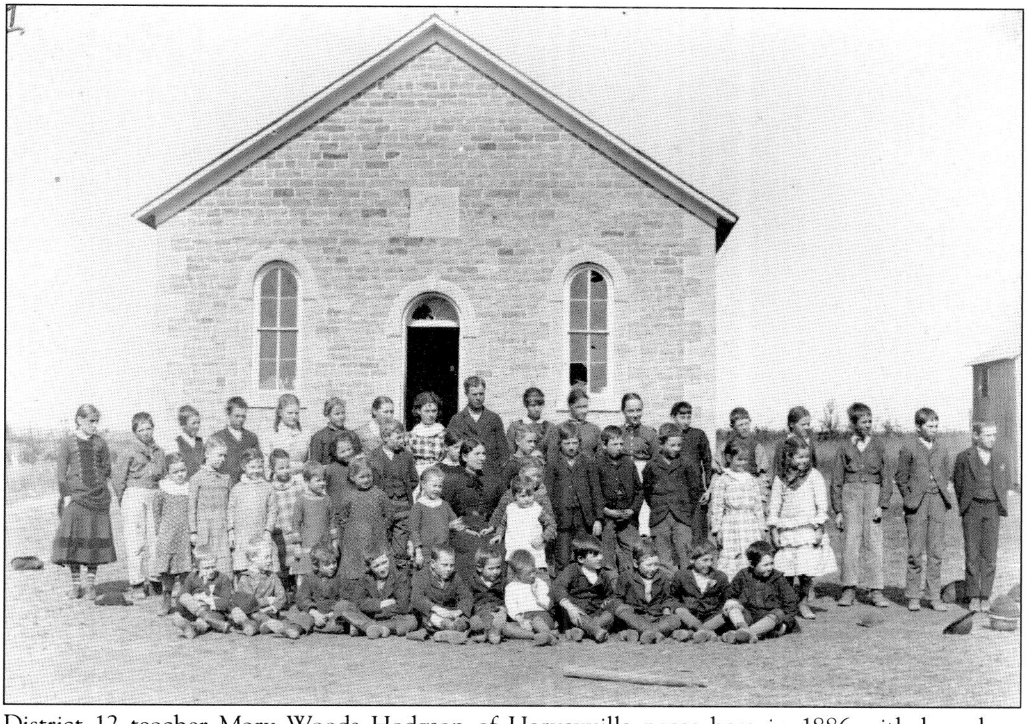

District 12 teacher Mary Woods Hodgson of Harveyville poses here in 1886 with her class. Amazingly, she seems to have 47 students. (Courtesy of Wabaunsee County Historical Society.)

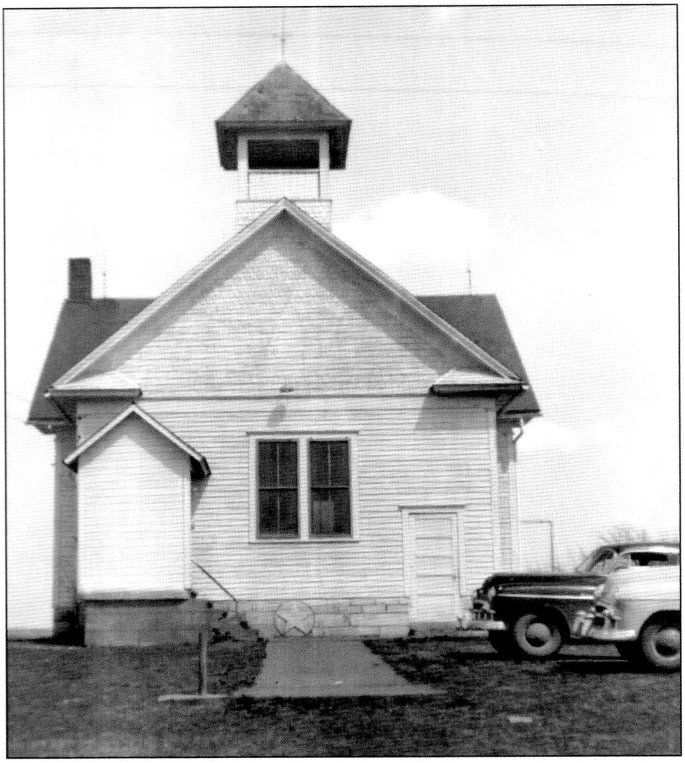

At left, the Star School District 40 building is seen here in the mid-1950s. Although in disrepair, the school still stands today and is located at 14469 Allen Road. Below, students pose for their photograph inside the Star school. From left to right, Sheila Jo Belt Nelson, Alice Romig Parsons, and Eugene Stephenson stand in front of the blackboard. Notice that a piano provides for music instruction, and the shelf of books behind the teacher's desk is the library. (Courtesy of Wabaunsee County Historical Society.)

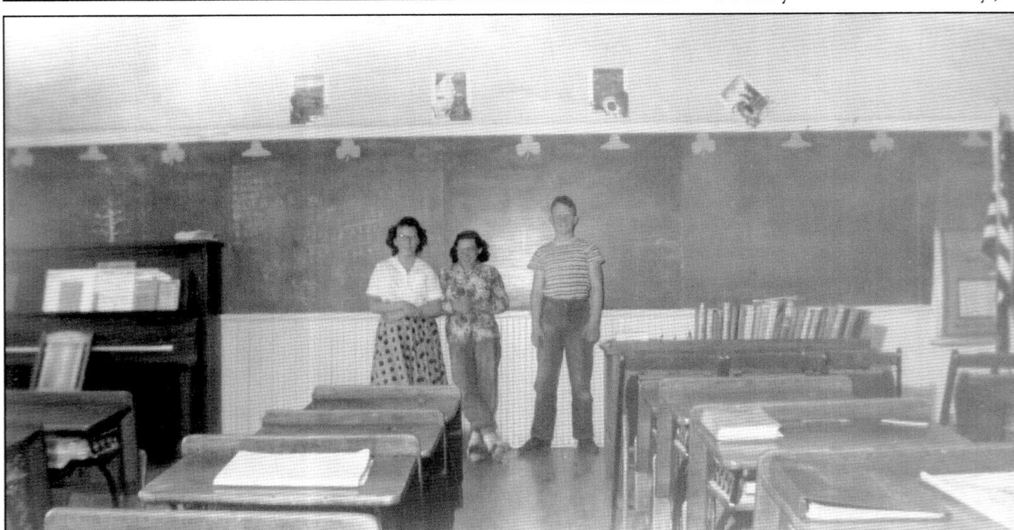

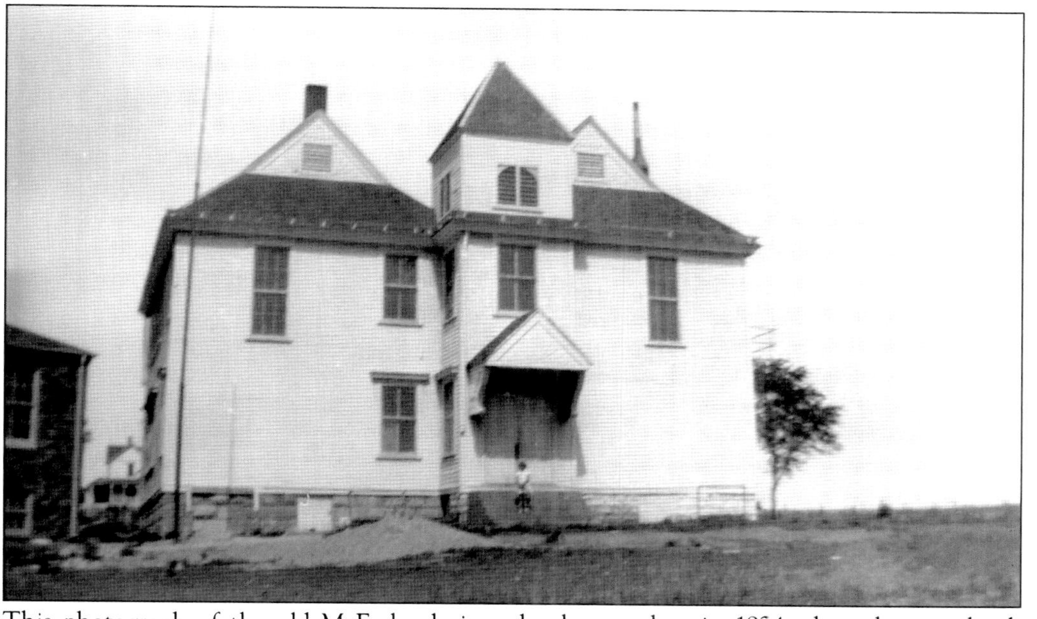

This photograph of the old McFarland city school was taken in 1934 when the new brick school had just been completed next door. The wooden school was located at 633 Main Street. (Courtesy of McFarland Heritage Center.)

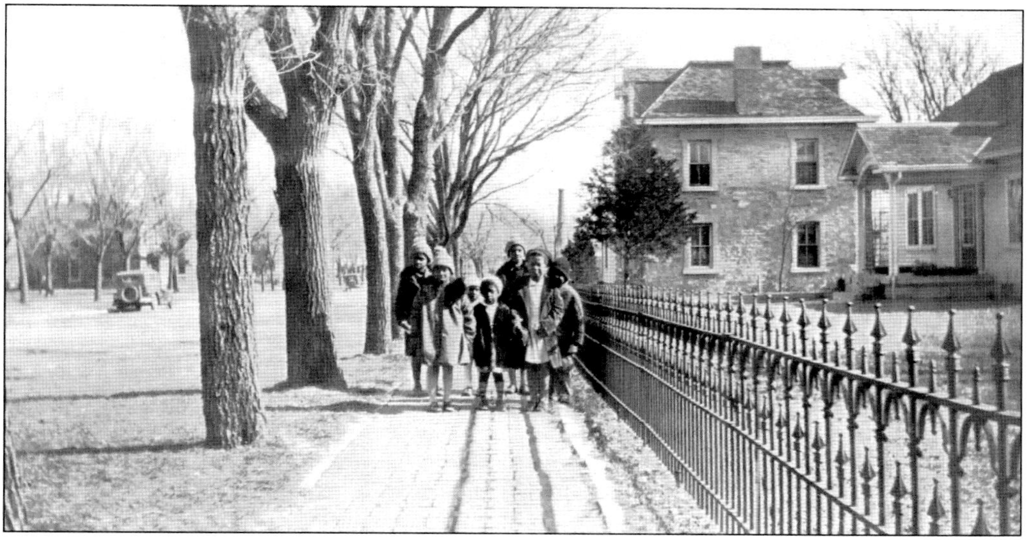

The Gardenhire kids are seen here walking to school down East Fourth Street in Alma in this 1930s view. Despite the fact that the nation's battle over segregation was waged just 35 miles away in Topeka in the landmark case *Brown v. Board of Education of Topeka*, segregation was never practiced in Wabaunsee County. Kids of all races attended the same schools, used the same restrooms (sometimes outhouses), and received the same instruction. (Courtesy of Wabaunsee County Historical Society.)

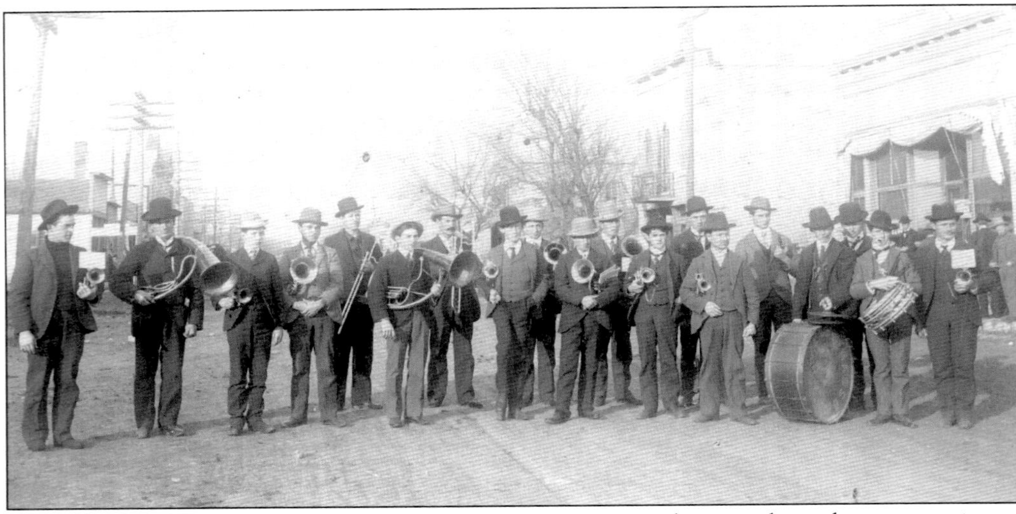

The Alma Volunteer Band is seen in this 1901 Gus Meier photograph at the intersection of Main (Third) and Missouri Streets, looking north. From left to right are Charlie Palenske, Theo Geisler, Charlie Thomson, John Degenhardt, Sam Mongerson, James Thomson, Dick Thoes, Ralph Sage, August Bandel, George Linss, William Speer, Louis Burt, Hugo Brandt, Charlie Dilley, Dick Hull, John Senge, Paul Geisler, Clarence Eck, and Guy Cleaveland. (Courtesy of Wabaunsee County Historical Society.)

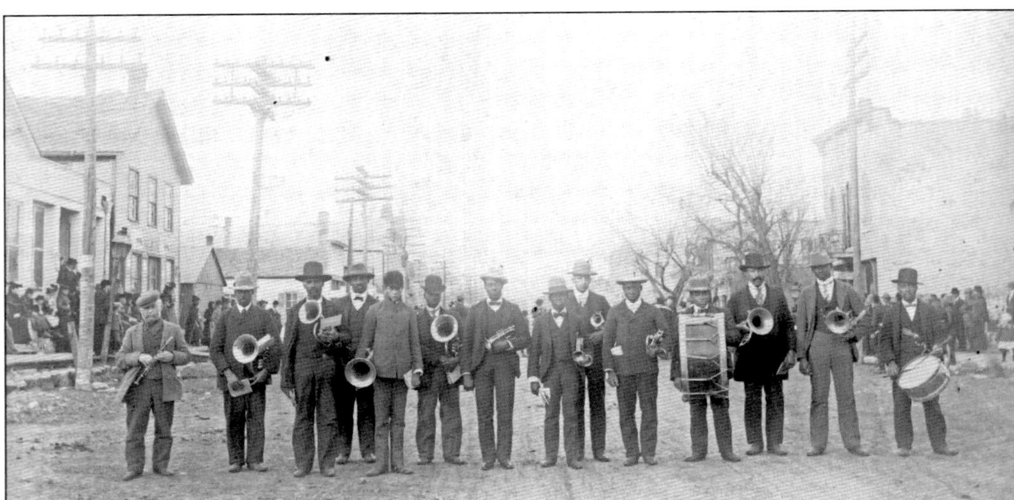

In a curious 1901 Meier photograph, taken at the same intersection as the photograph above, an all-black brass band performs at an Alma parade. Ferd Herrmann, a white Alma shoemaker, has joined this Alma troupe. One can see the Schmitz and Meyer store and the Kaufman building to the left. From left to right are Herrmann, Sully Wallace, John Goodpasture, Bill Goodpasture, Freddie Owens, Tom Wallace, Pickwith McDonald, Sam Bennett, Jim Cruters, Roy Wallace, Jessie Davis, Bill Cruters, John Holford, and Buddy Gardenhire. (Courtesy of Wabaunsee County Historical Society.)

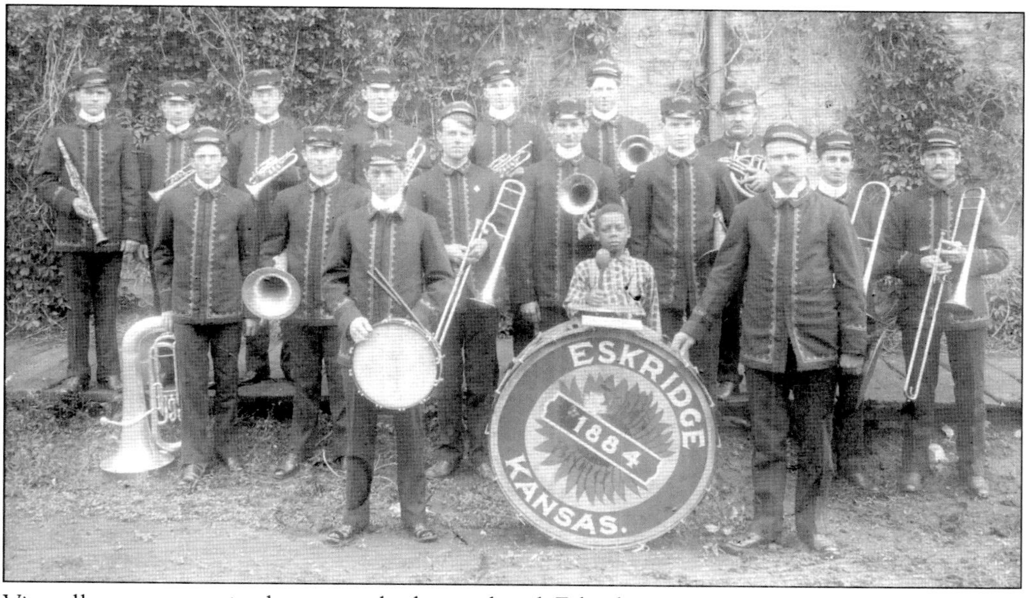

Virtually every town in the county had a city band. Eskridge was no exception. This view of the Eskridge city band is dated 1884, just four years after the town was platted and settled. (Courtesy of Inez Dunn.)

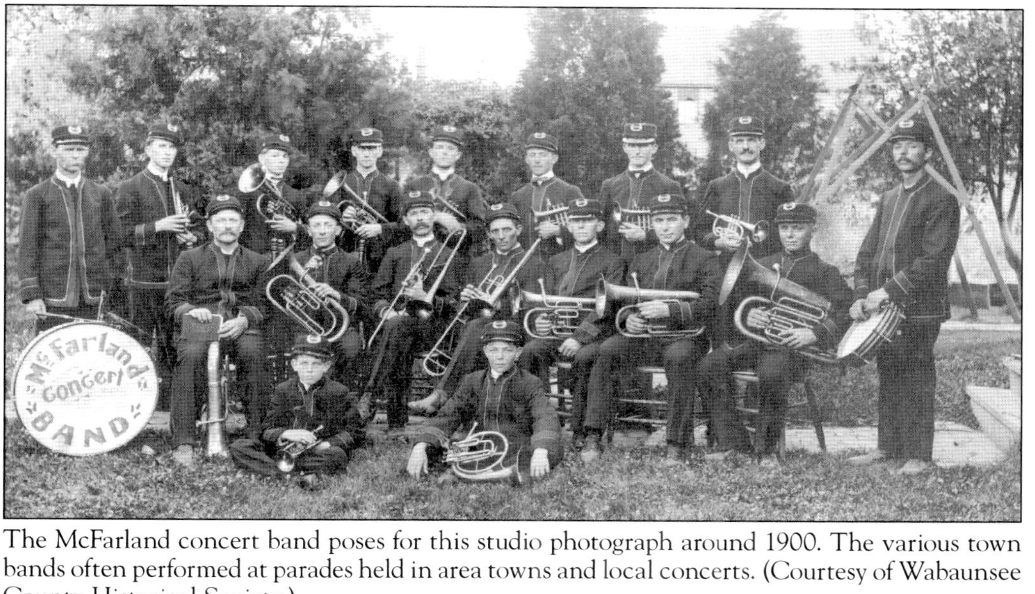

The McFarland concert band poses for this studio photograph around 1900. The various town bands often performed at parades held in area towns and local concerts. (Courtesy of Wabaunsee County Historical Society.)

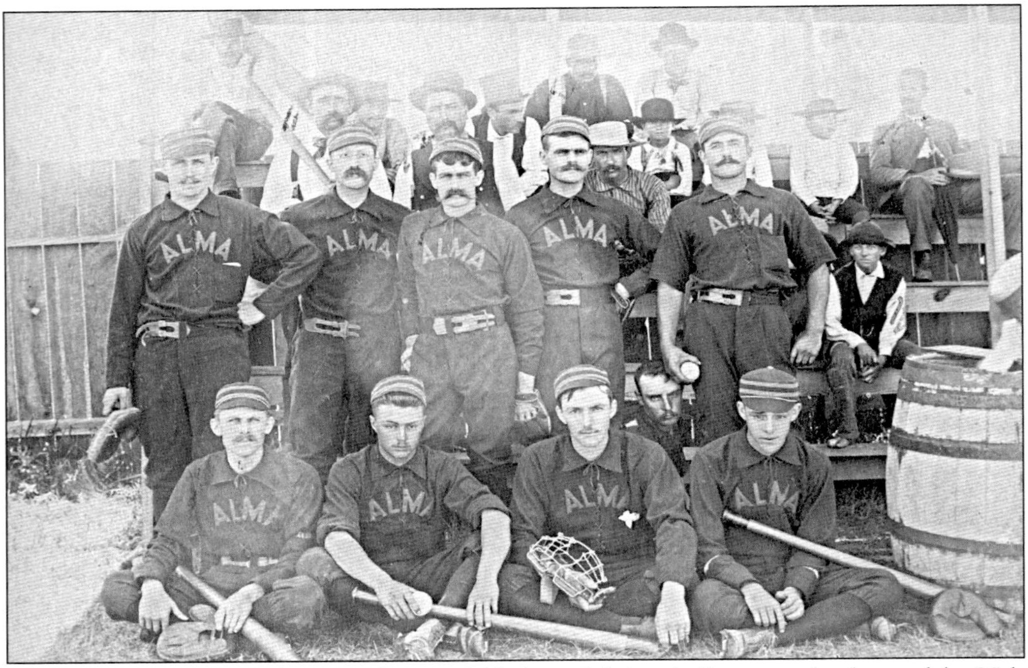

Almost every town in Wabaunsee County fielded an adult baseball team at the dawn of the 20th century. The Alma team is seen in this 1894 photograph. Team members identified are Carey Carroll, Bill Hughes, T. Gregory, Hugo Brandt, John Crafts, F. I. Sage, Charlie Henderson, Jim Henderson, Frank Mossman, Bill Horne, J. Fields, John Auer, S. Fields, John Horne, and C. O. Kinnie. (Courtesy of Wabaunsee County Historical Society.)

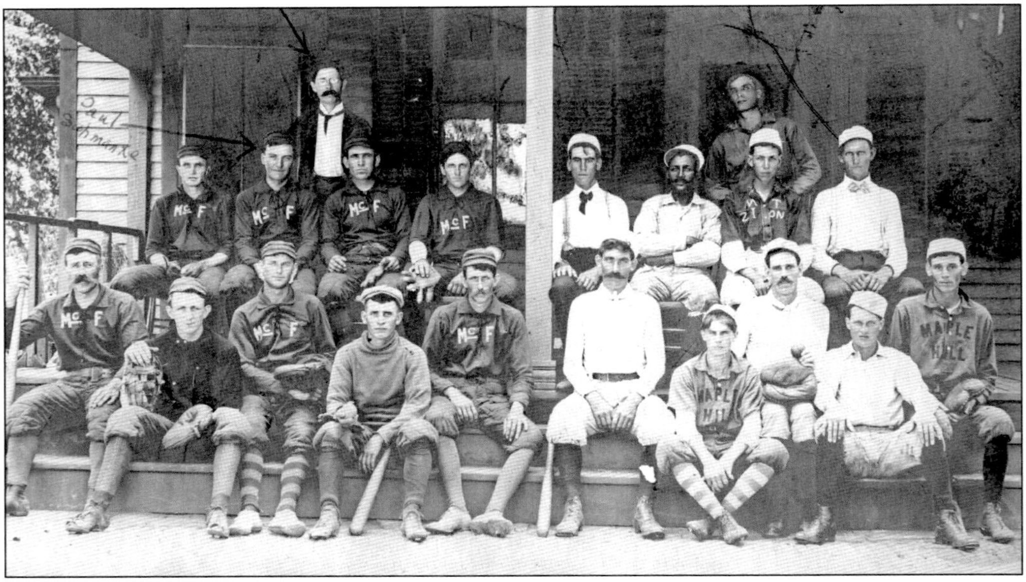

This photograph from the dawn of the 20th century shows both the McFarland and Maple Hill baseball teams. The only people identified are McFarland mayor Dr. Silverthorne, standing behind the McFarland team, and Paul Schmanke, second from the left in the second row of the McFarland team. (Courtesy of Wabaunsee County Historical Society.)

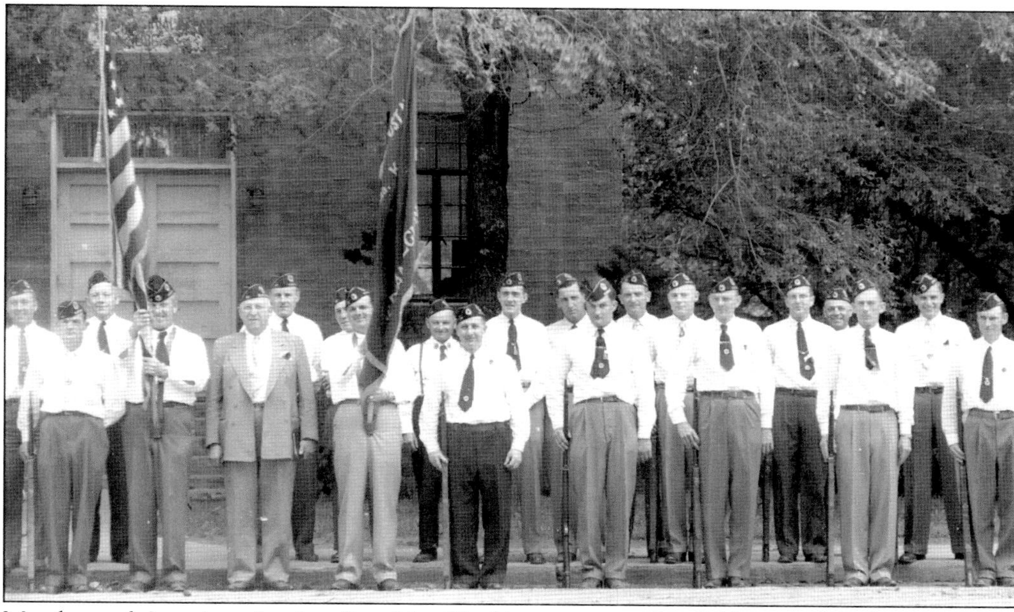

Members of American Legion Post No. 32, Alma, pose at the Soldiers and Sailors Memorial building, located at 504 Missouri Street. Pictured from left to right (first row) unidentified, Wally Gronquist, unidentified, Lawrence Richmond, Clarence Havenstein, John Haller, Arnold Bandel, Arnold Schmitz, and Oliver Diehl; (second row) Arnold Havenstein, Bob Grunewald, J. C. Edwards, Herb Mueller, Albert TenEyck, Harold Iott, Clarence Frank, Victor Zeckser, Mel Herren, Carl Diepenbrock, and Keen Umbehr. (Courtesy of Wabaunsee County Historical Society.)

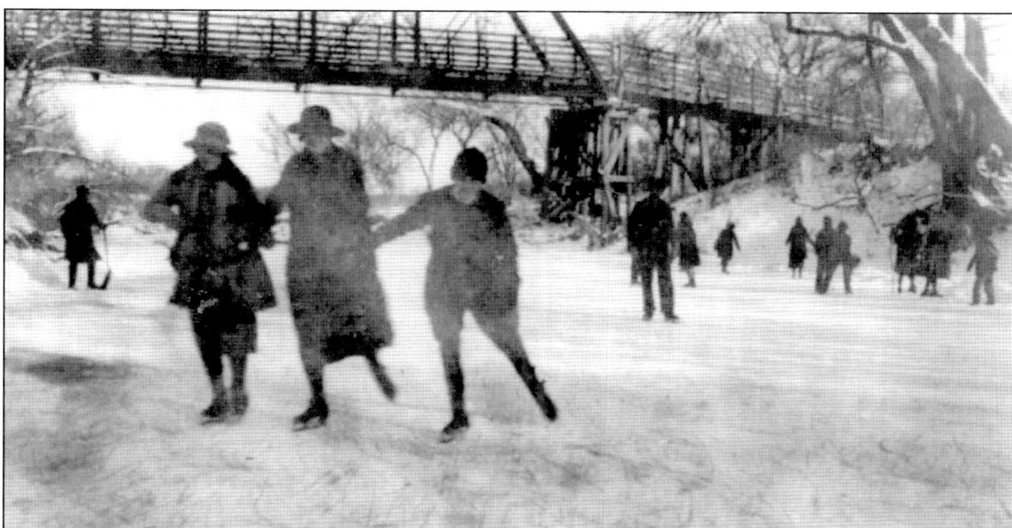

Ice-skating parties were popular on Mill Creek in the winter months. This group of skaters gathers at McFarland in this 1918 photograph. Notice in the background the Rock Island bridge, which was located behind the McFarland Stockyards. (Courtesy of McFarland Heritage Center.)

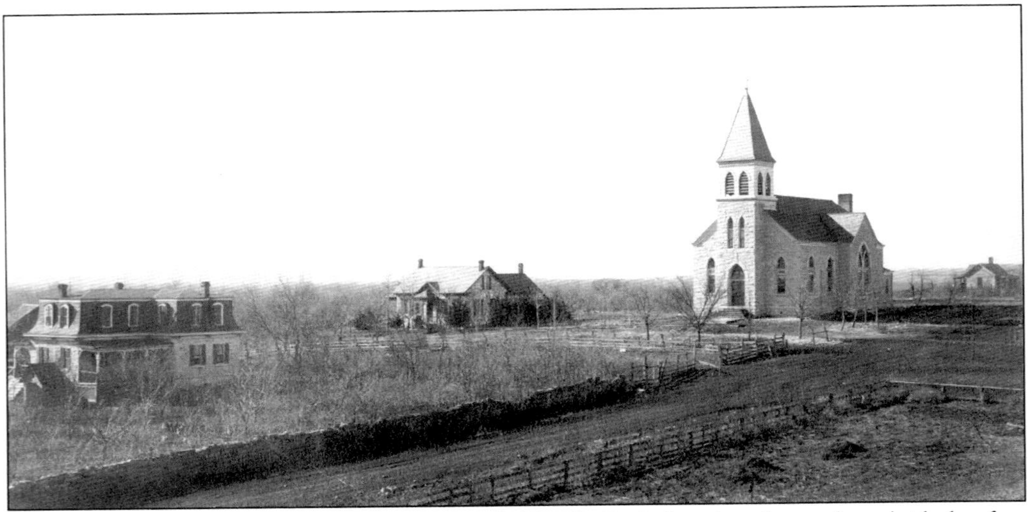

After a February 6, 1899, fire that destroyed Alma's Catholic church, workers laid the first cornerstone on August 27, 1899, for a new building and dedicated the new church on December 19, 1899. (Courtesy of Wabaunsee County Historical Society.)

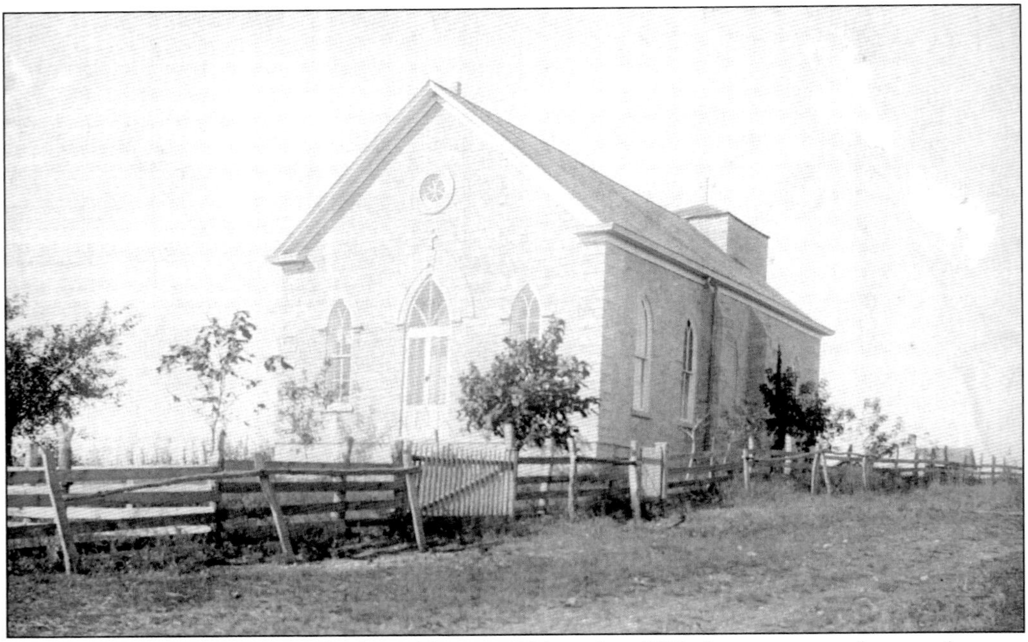

The first Catholic church was built in Alma in 1874, and in 1877, the tower, seen here at the rear, was erected. The first permanent priest arrived in 1880. The church was completely destroyed by fire on February 6, 1899. (Courtesy of Wabaunsee County Historical Society.)

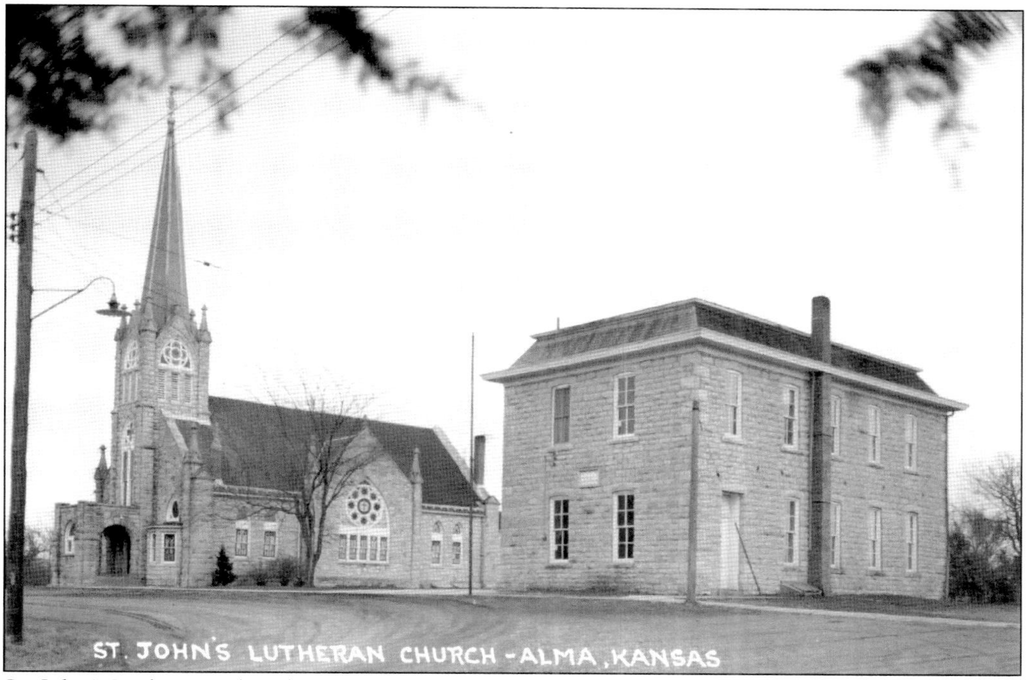

St. John's Lutheran Church and School are seen in this photograph postcard. The church was erected in 1908, during a boom in construction in Alma. (Courtesy of Wabaunsee County Historical Society.)

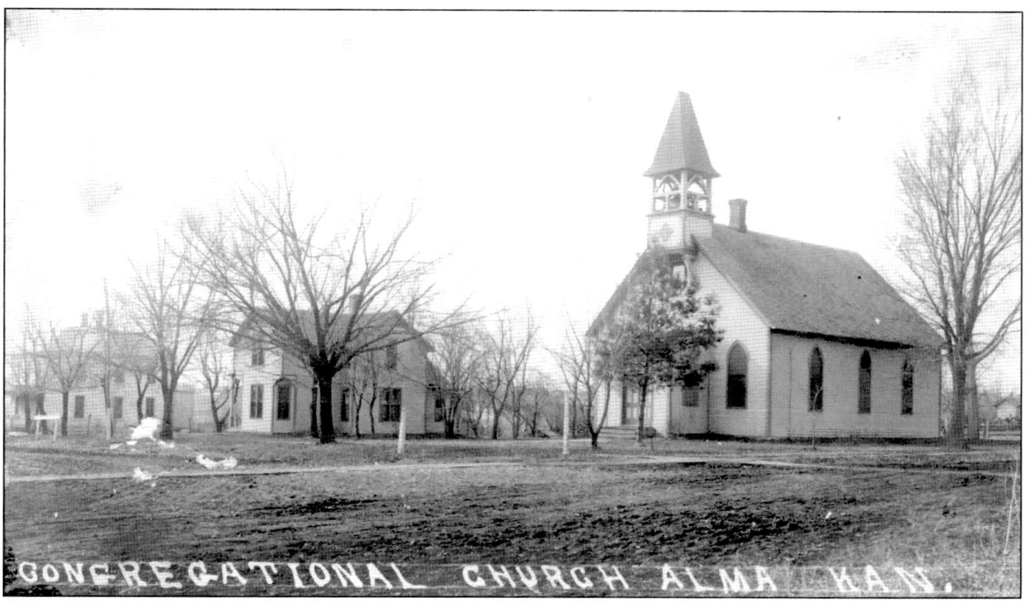

Alma's Congregational church was constructed in 1881 and is seen in this Gus Meier photograph postcard from about 1910. The church was razed, and a private residence was built on the site at 625 Ohio Street. (Courtesy of Wabaunsee County Historical Society.)

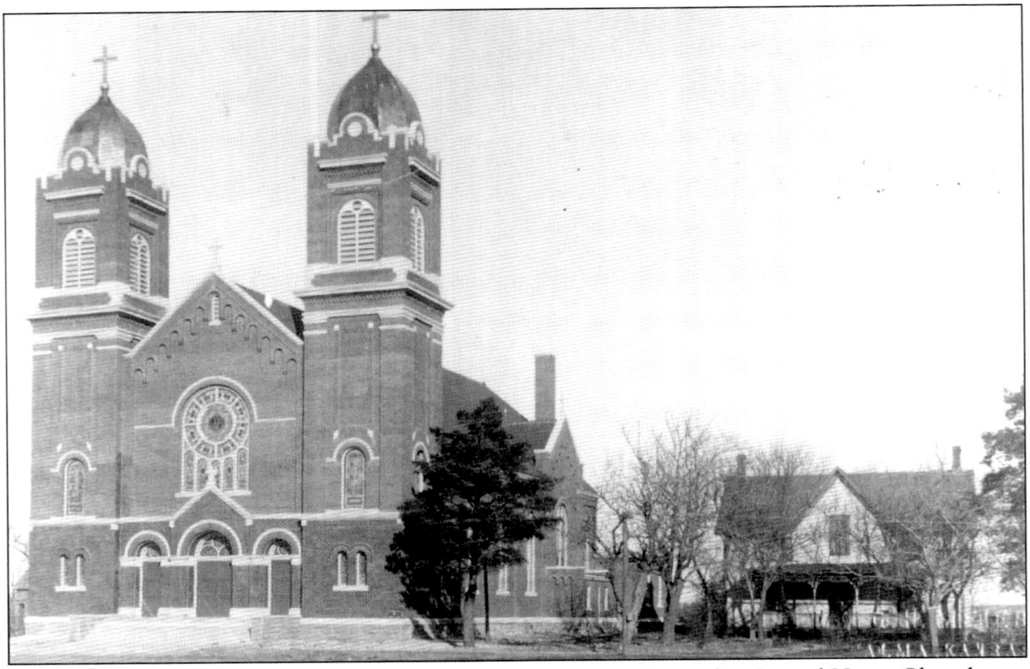

After a 1921 fire that destroyed the Catholic church at Newbury, this Sacred Heart Church was constructed next to the parsonage in 1922. This is a Gus Meier photograph postcard. (Courtesy of Wabaunsee County Historical Society.)

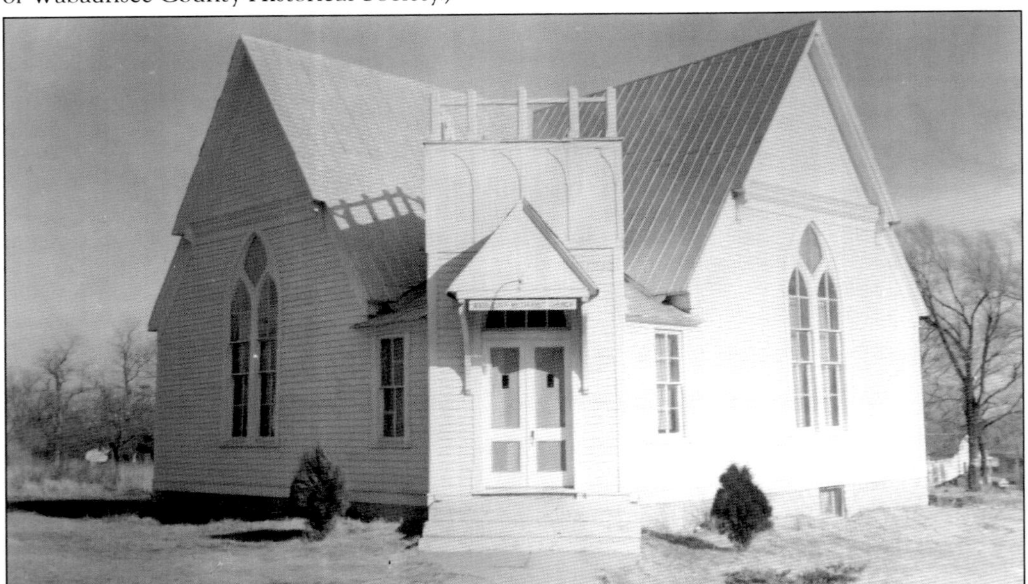

The Eskridge Wesleyan Church was constructed in the early 1880s during the boom growth period that the town experienced after the railroad came to town. The building is a private residence today, located at the northeast corner of West Third Avenue and Locust Street. The roof of this church can be seen in the early view of Eskridge on page 17. (Courtesy of Wabaunsee County Historical Society.)

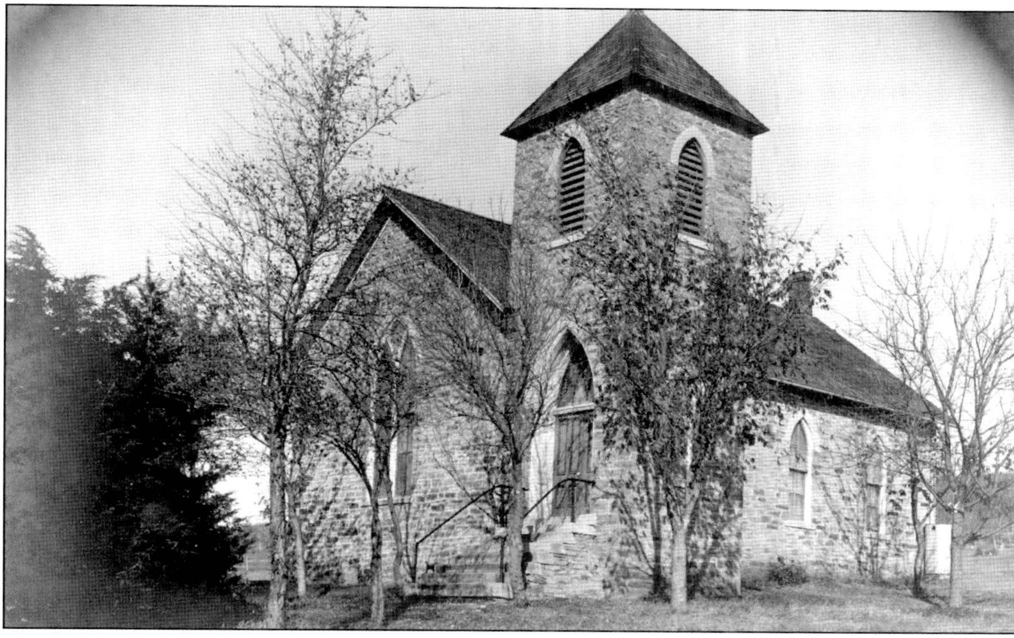

Construction of the Eliot Church, or the "Stone Church" as it is commonly known, was completed in August 1882. Although the building has no electricity, it is used even today for weddings and other special gatherings. The church is located at 15189 Old Stone Church Road in Maple Hill. (Courtesy of Wabaunsee County Historical Society.)

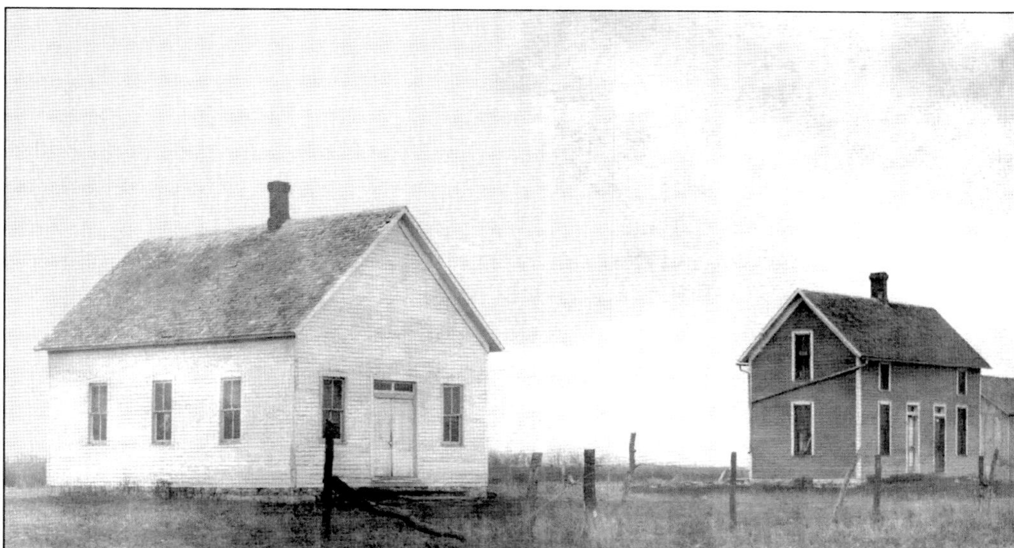

In May 1854, George Harvey took a claim on Dragoon Creek, becoming the first to file a claim in the county and the first Quaker to settle in the territory. More family members followed, and the area became known as the Harvey settlement. In 1874, the Dragoon Monthly Meeting was established and this meetinghouse was built at what is now 15991 Quaker Road. The meeting was disbanded in 1916. (Courtesy of Michael Stubbs.)

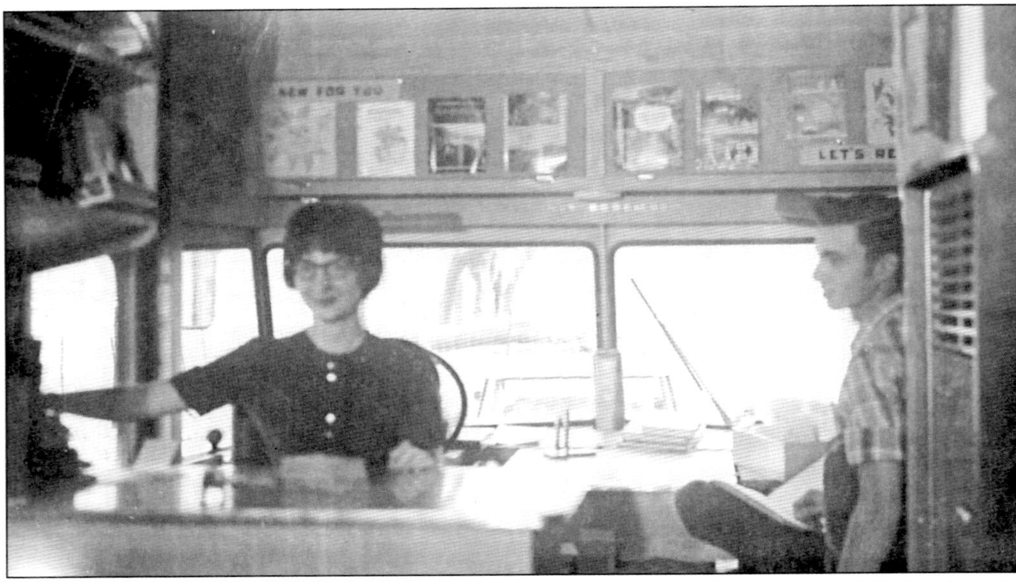

Otto Kratzer took this photograph of the interior of the bookmobile as it visited Volland in the early 1960s. From 1963 until 1995, the Pottawatomie Wabaunsee Regional Library operated a bookmobile to provide service to remote areas of the county. Created in 1962, it is the only two-county public library in Kansas. The headquarters was established in St. Marys in 1962. In 1963, the Alma branch opened, and in 1967, a branch opened in Eskridge. Mini libraries are located in Harveyville and Alta Vista. (Courtesy of Wabaunsee County Historical Society.)

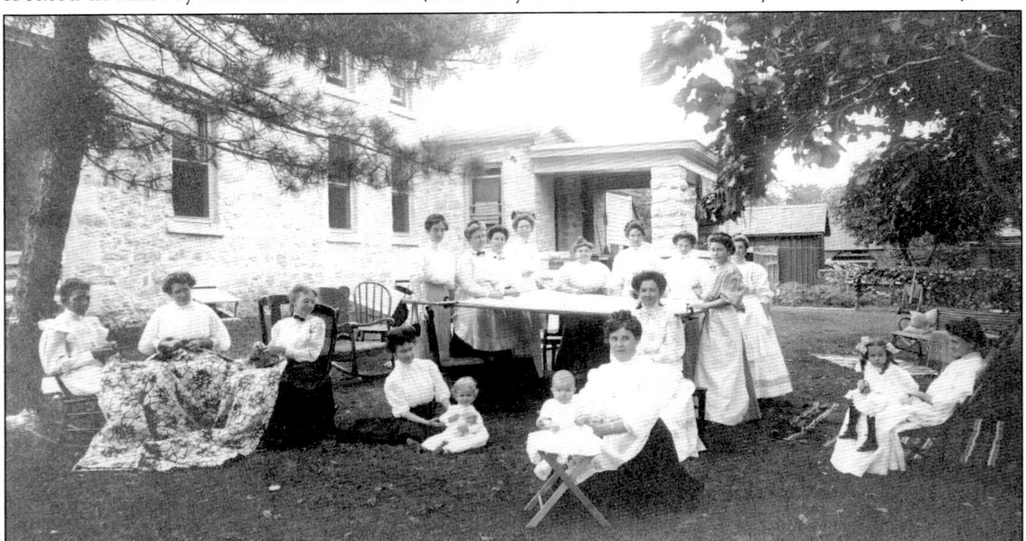

A group of women gather for a summer quilting bee in the yard at the Arthur S. Allendorph residence located at 205 West Seventh Street in Alma. Allendorph came to Wabaunsee County in 1888, entering into the cattle business. He leased thousands of acres of Flint Hills land and operated a large ranch about five miles northwest of Alma. He had extensive ranch holdings south of Alma near Halifax, and the Atchison, Topeka and Santa Fe Railway had cattle loading pens at Allendorph, about two miles southeast of Alma. (Courtesy of Wabaunsee County Historical Society.)

Five

Ghost Towns of Wabaunsee County

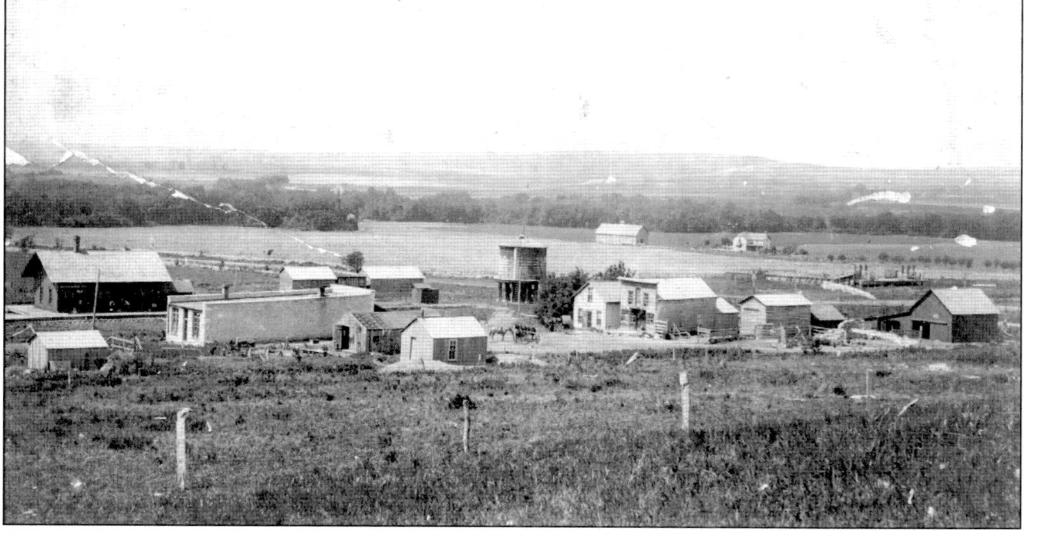

Among the county's ghost towns, Halifax is seen here around 1895. At the far left is the original depot that burned. To the right is Erickson's Blacksmith Shop and a store. In the background is Otto John Hess's home. One can also see the stockyards, where the second depot was later constructed. The post office changed the name of the town from Bismarck to Halifax in 1885, and after the post office closed, the Atchison, Topeka and Santa Fe Railway renamed the town Hessdale. (Courtesy of Wabaunsee County Historical Society.)

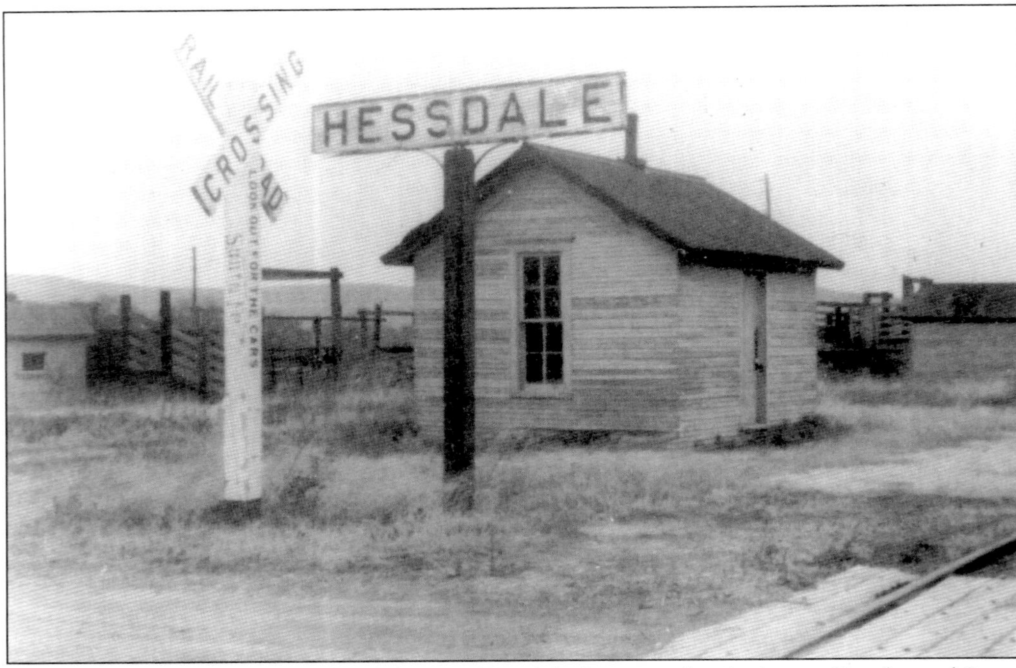

The stockyards can be seen behind the new Hessdale depot on the Atchison, Topeka and Santa Fe Railway. A historic marker stands today about where this depot was located. This depot was located at 22000 Hessdale Road. (Courtesy of Wabaunsee County Historical Society.)

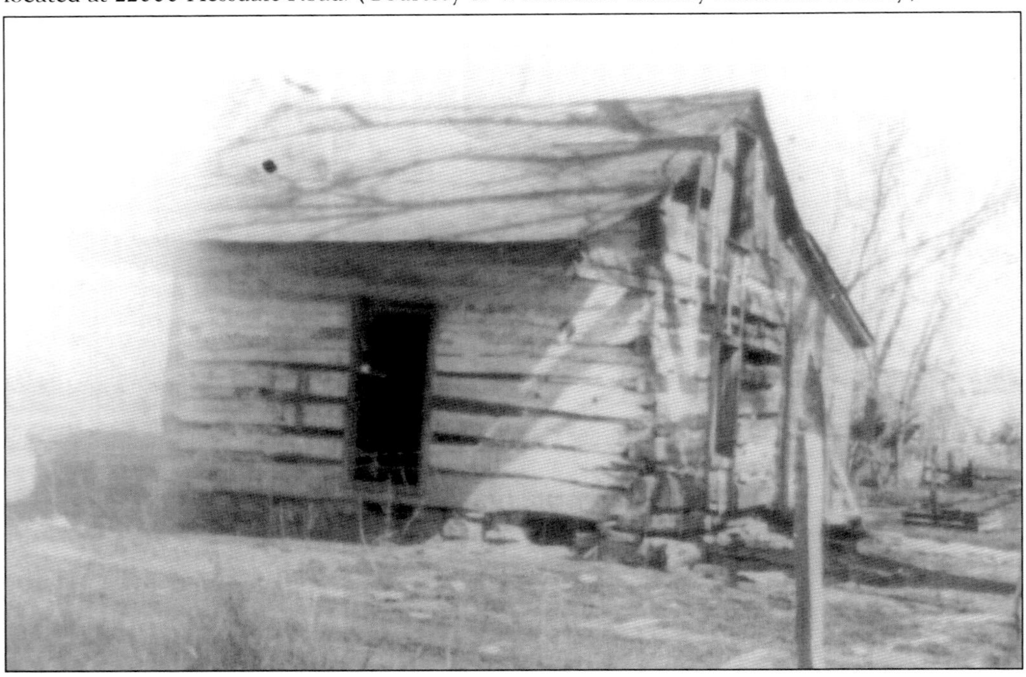

Above, the first Chalk store operated out of this log cabin. Like many of the ghost towns in Wabaunsee County, there is little left today that marks the town's existence, except photographs. (Courtesy of Wabaunsee County Historical Society.)

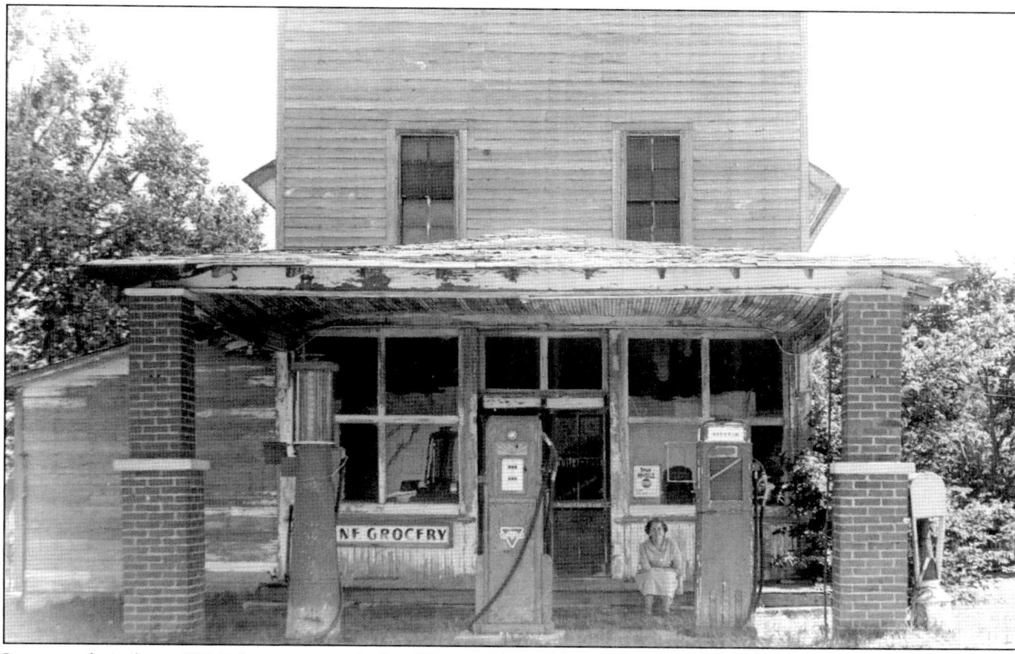

Lon and Arlene Wright operated the Keene Store for many years at 15026 K-4 Highway. The first Indian Agency store opened in 1858 just south of where this general store was constructed in 1874. The store burned in May 1996 after it was vacant. This photograph was taken by Bill Weidner in the late 1960s. (Courtesy of Rodney Allen.)

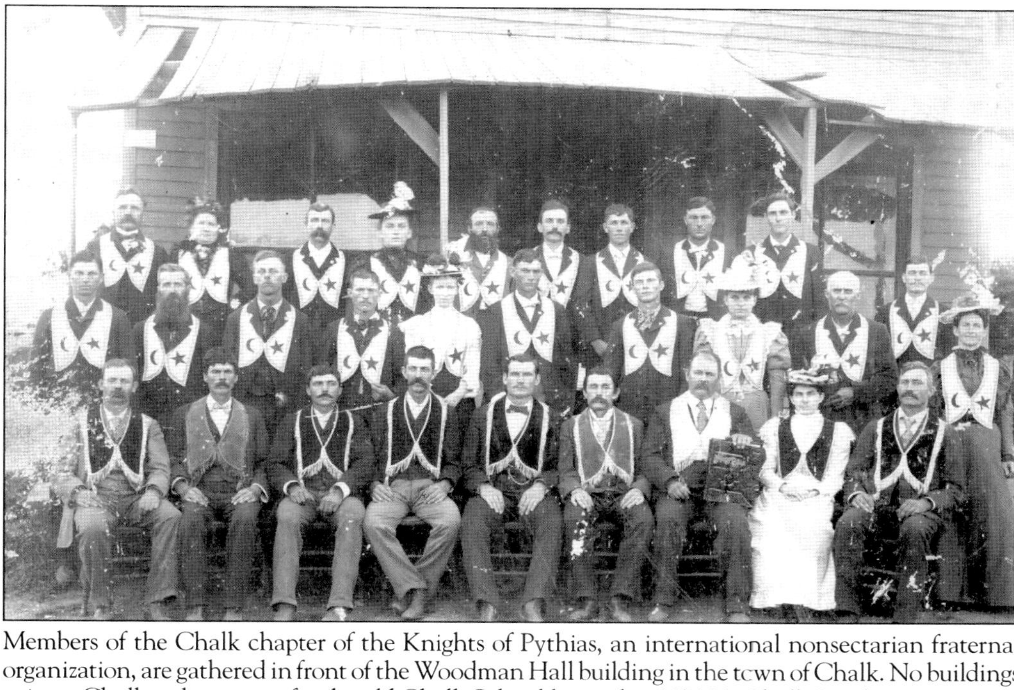

Members of the Chalk chapter of the Knights of Pythias, an international nonsectarian fraternal organization, are gathered in front of the Woodman Hall building in the town of Chalk. No buildings exist at Chalk today except for the old Chalk School located at 28720A Chalk Road approximately one mile east of the old town site. (Courtesy of Wabaunsee County Historical Society.)

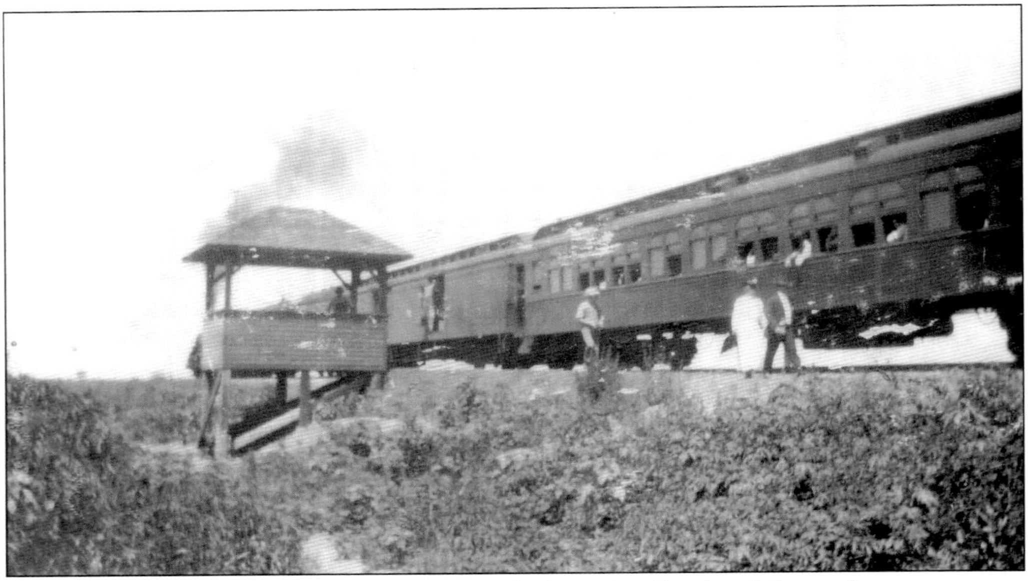

This view of the Vera depot, which was located where Vera Road and the tracks intersect, was taken in 1916. The facility offered only the barest of protection from the weather. (Courtesy of Wabaunsee County Historical Society.)

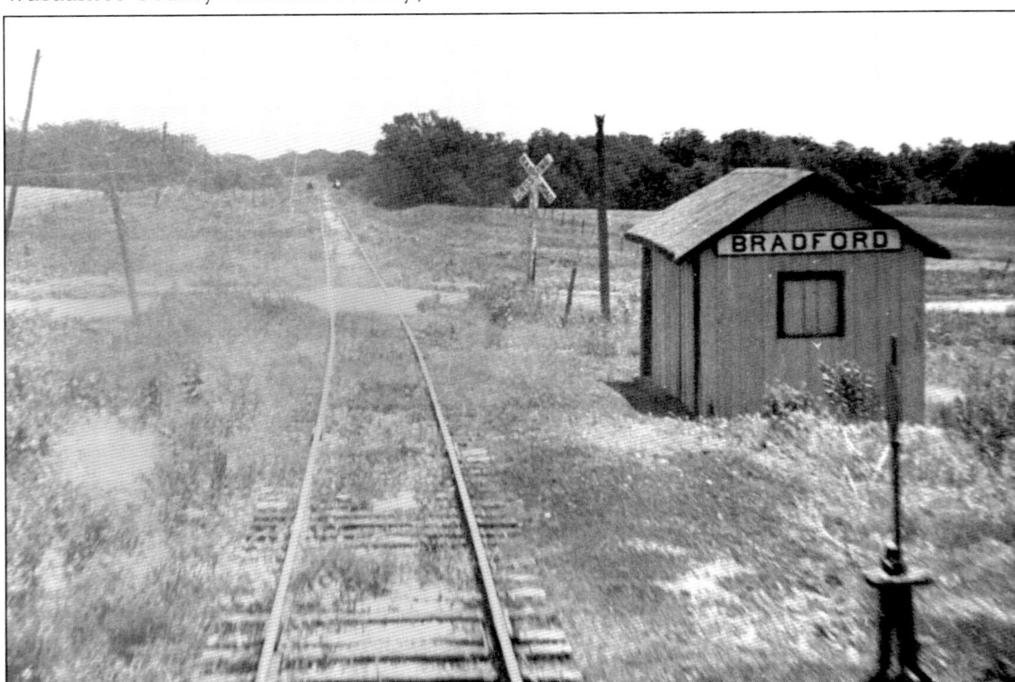

Above, the Bradford depot on the Atchison, Topeka and Santa Fe Railway line can be seen in this photograph. Bradford was once a growing settlement with hopes of becoming one of Wabaunsee County's towns. As things turned out, it became a ghost town, and today, with the railroad bed completely gone, it is even difficult to find a sign of Bradford. (Courtesy of Kansas State Historical Society.)

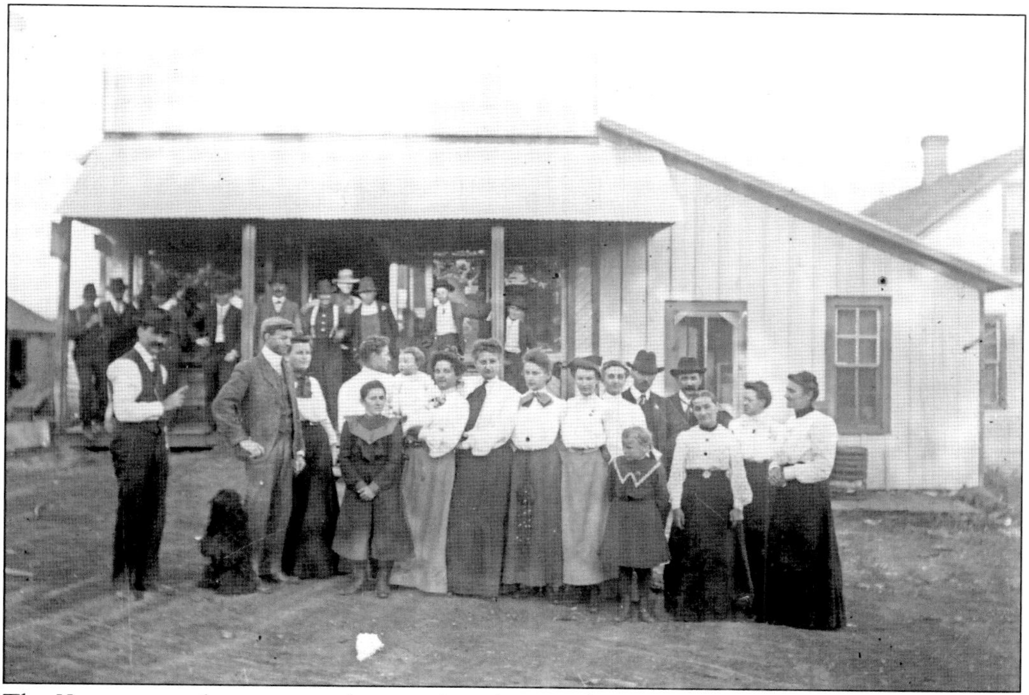

The Kratzer store became a gathering place for area farmers and ranchers and their families. This photograph, taken about 1910 in front of the old store, is illustrative of Otto Kratzer's love for photography and friends. He chronicled life in Volland for over 50 years on film. (Courtesy of Wabaunsee County Historical Society.)

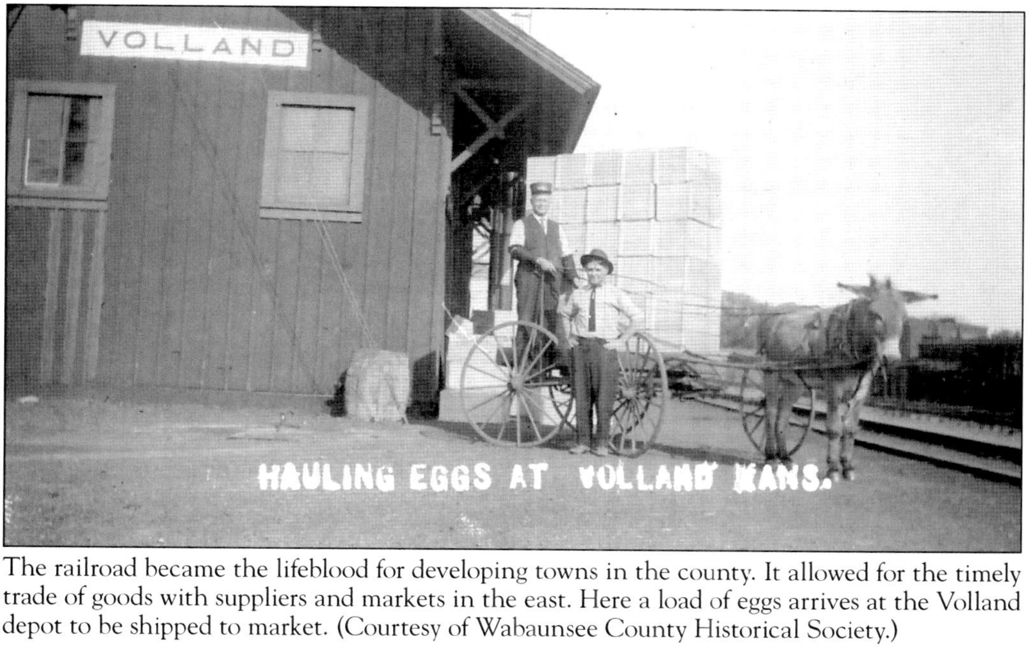

The railroad became the lifeblood for developing towns in the county. It allowed for the timely trade of goods with suppliers and markets in the east. Here a load of eggs arrives at the Volland depot to be shipped to market. (Courtesy of Wabaunsee County Historical Society.)

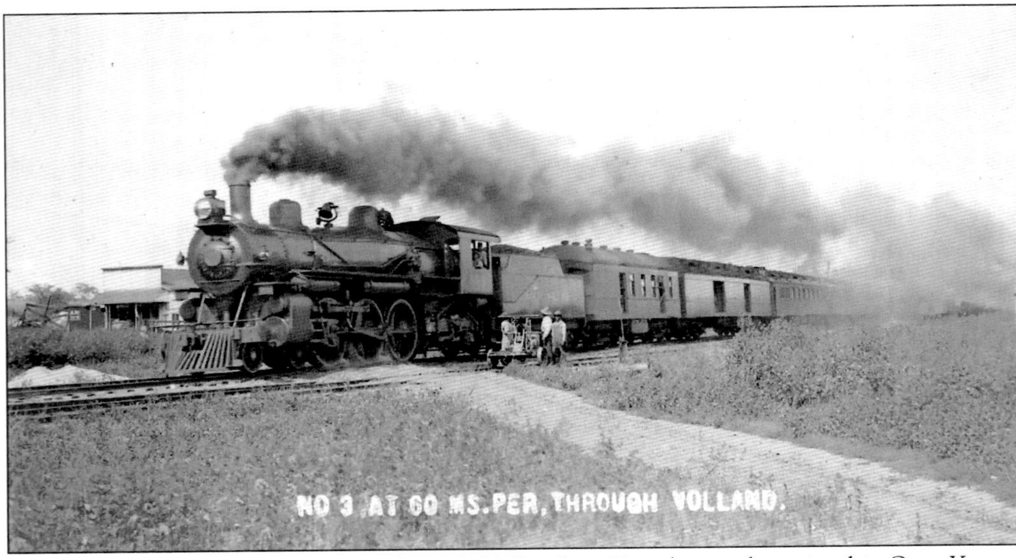

The Golden State Limited steams through Volland at 60 miles per hour in this Otto Kratzer photograph from about 1910. The No. 3 was an express train that ran westbound on the Chicago, Rock Island and Pacific Railroad line, seen here passing the old Kratzer store in the background. (Courtesy of Wabaunsee County Historical Society.)

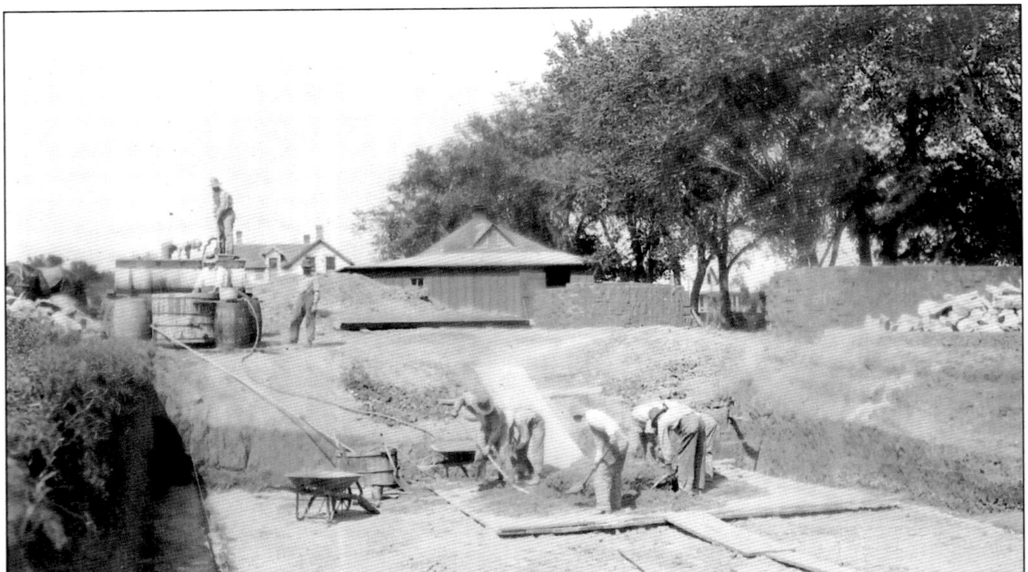

With the basement dug, workers mix mortar and prepare to lay the rock foundation for the new store. Notice the stacks of brick, pile of rock, and water barrels. (Courtesy of Wabaunsee County Historical Society.)

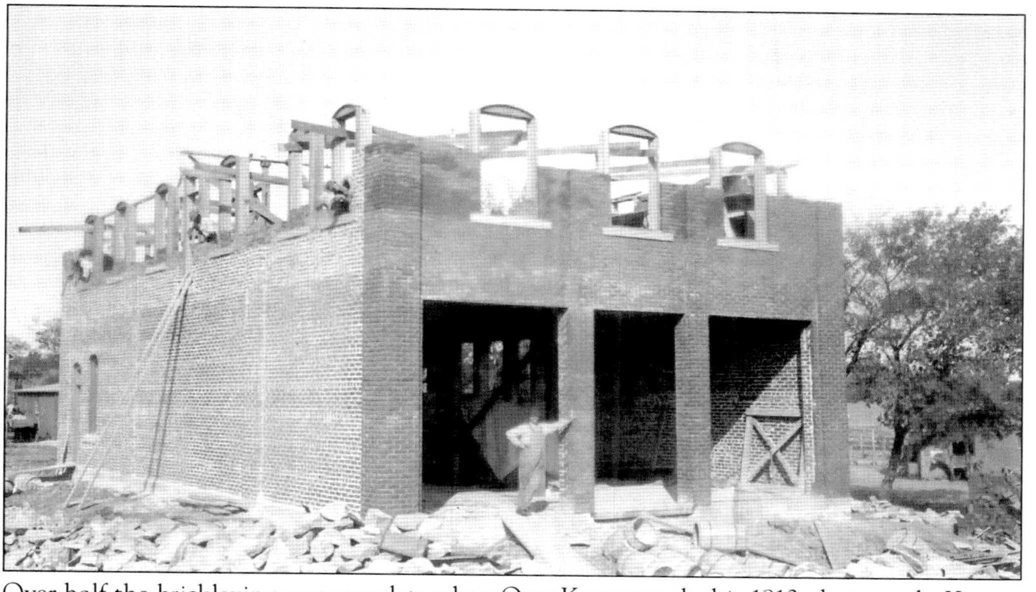

Over half the bricklaying was complete when Otto Kratzer took this 1913 photograph. Kratzer carefully recorded every step of the construction of this building. (Courtesy of Wabaunsee County Historical Society.)

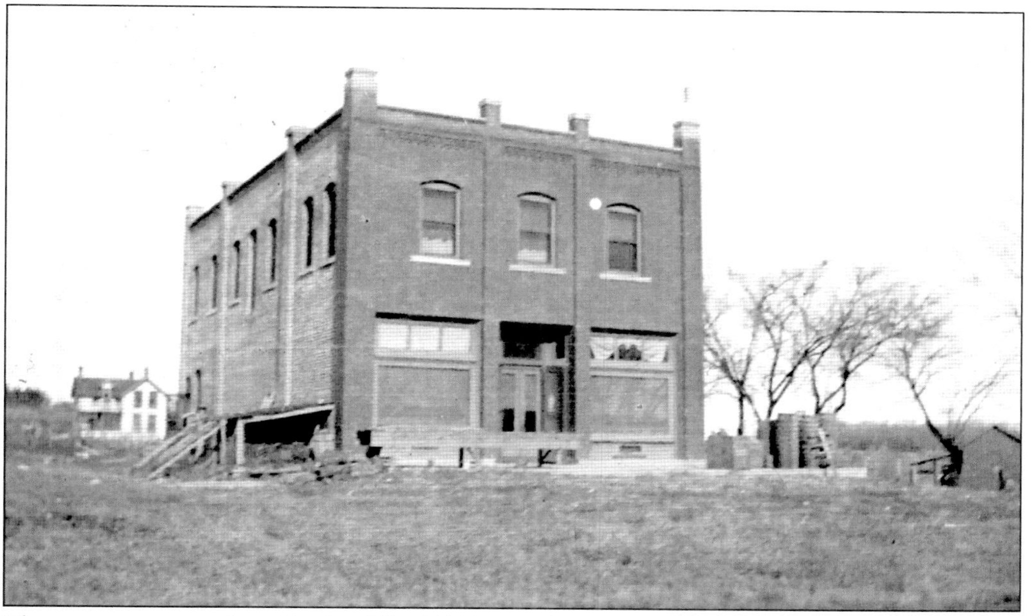

The new store, completed in the fall of 1913, was the center of commerce and the social scene in Volland. The store had telephones on both walls, one for the Alta Vista exchange and the other for the Alma exchange. The store was also the location of the Volland Post Office. After the coming of the diesel locomotive, trains no longer stopped at Volland, and then the passing train threw the mailbag on the ground and snatched the outbound mail from a pole. (Courtesy of Wabaunsee County Historical Society.)

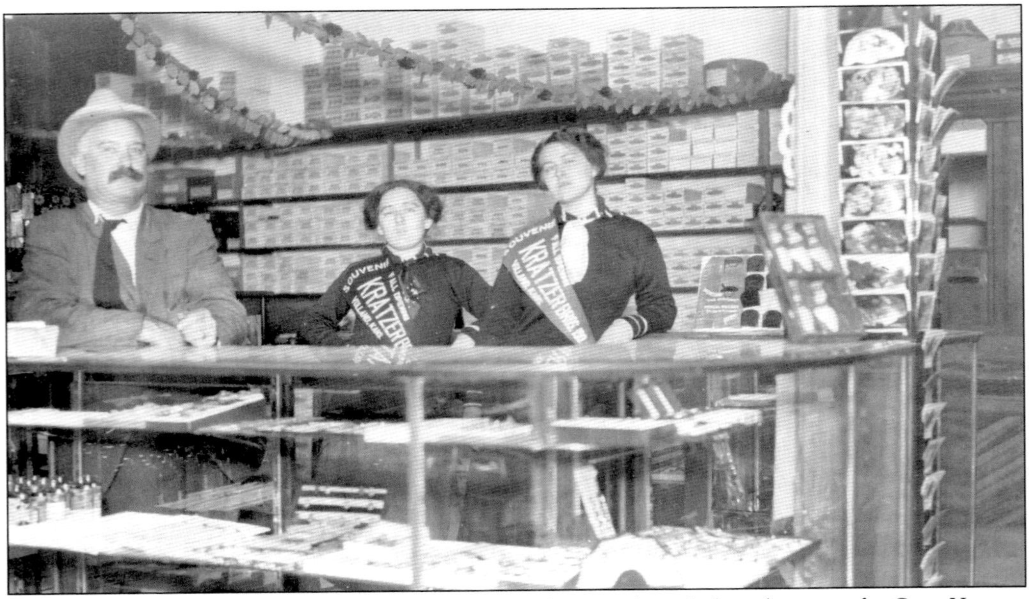

From left to right, Bill Kratzer, Louise Dittman, and an unidentified worker pose for Otto Kratzer on the opening day inside the new store at Volland in the fall of 1913. The store was the center of commerce and community for the residents of Washington Township for over a half century. (Courtesy of Wabaunsee County Historical Society.)

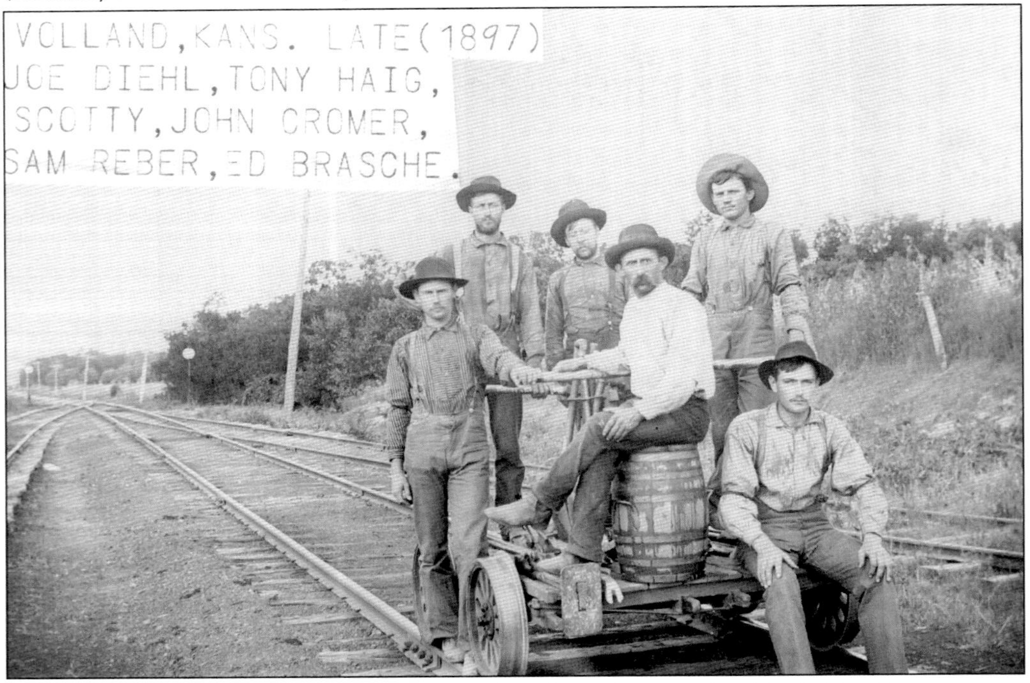

The Volland Rock Island section crew poses for Alma photographer Gus Meier. Section crews maintained and repaired the railroad tracks. The Volland section crew can be seen on a sidetrack as the Golden State passes through the Main Street crossing in the photograph on page 108. (Courtesy of Wabaunsee County Historical Society.)

Six

Disaster Strikes Wabaunsee County

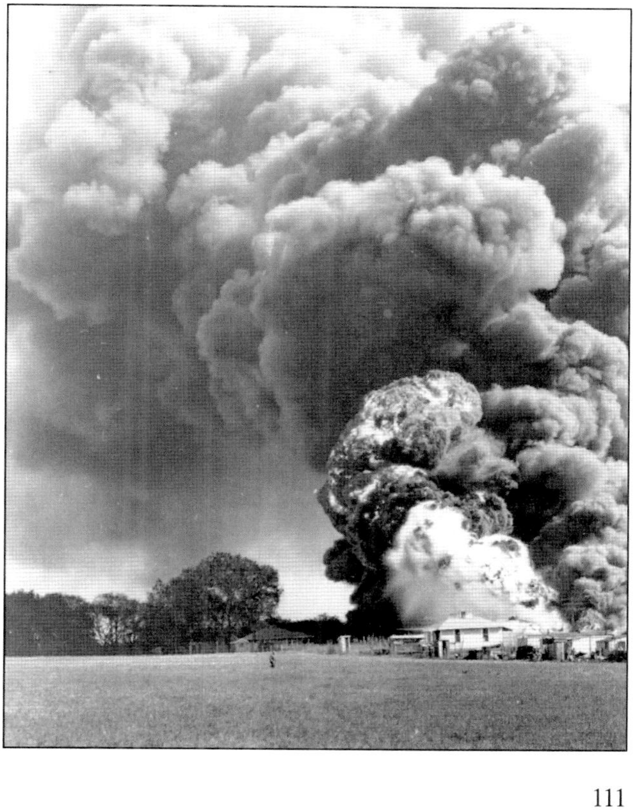

Throughout the county's history, its residents have faced disasters of many kinds, including fires, floods, tornadoes, and train wrecks. Despite the difficulties, citizens have always rebuilt and moved ahead. In this Otto Kratzer photograph, a train wreck at Volland in 1920 erupts in flames as oil tanker cars ignite. (Courtesy of Wabaunsee County Historical Society.)

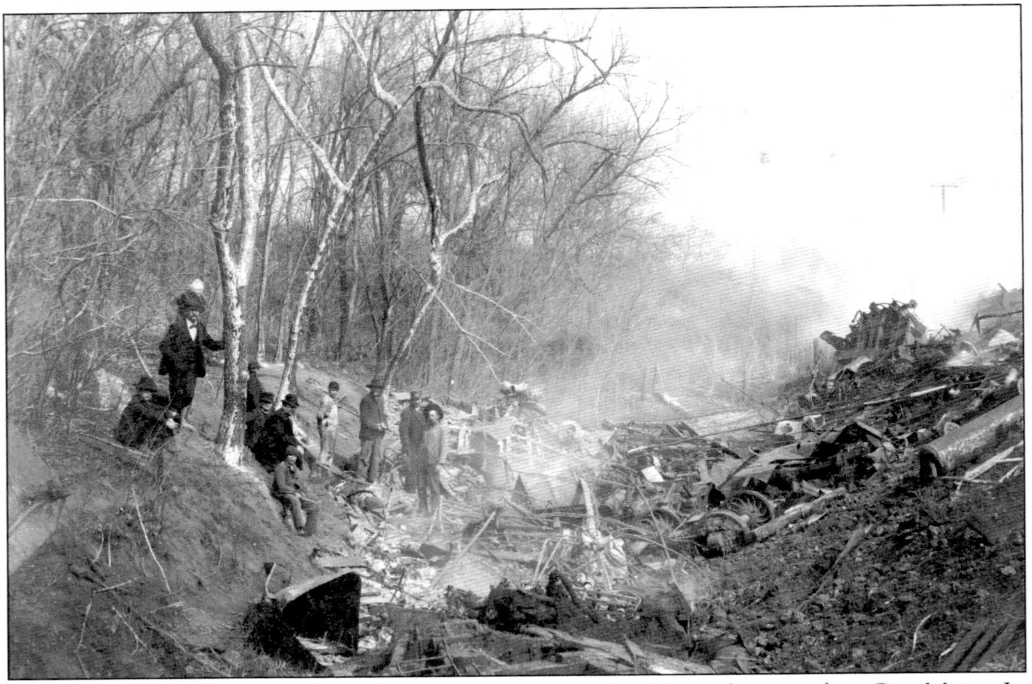

This 1899 train wreck at Volland was photographed by Alma photographer Gus Meier. In many cases, the greatest danger in a train derailment was the risk of fire. In this wreck, all that was not wrecked burned. The cause was washed-out tracks. (Courtesy of Wabaunsee County Historical Society.)

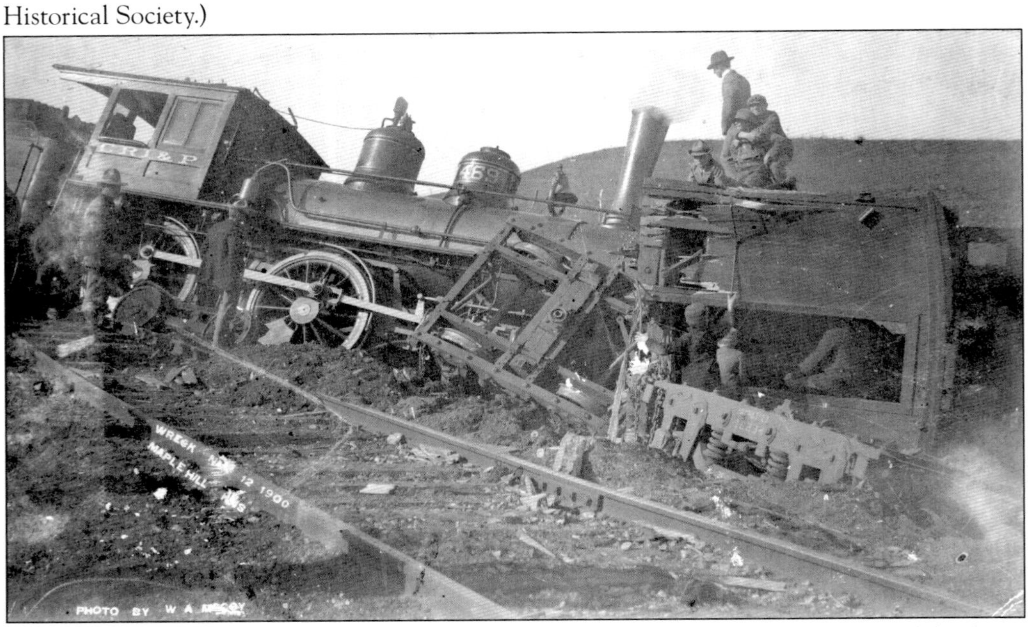

This 1905 derailment of a Chicago, Rock Island and Pacific Railroad train just west of the depot in Maple Hill provided a photo opportunity for Alta Vista photographer W. A. McCoy. Despite the frequency of wrecks, trains were the mainstay of transportation for the county for about 75 years. (Courtesy of Wabaunsee County Historical Society.)

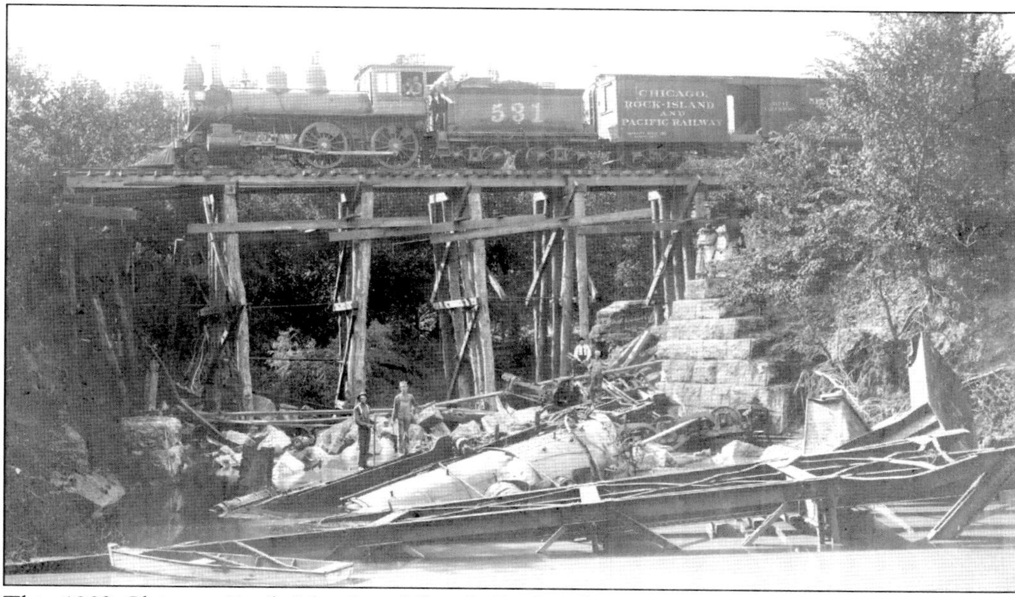

This 1903 Chicago, Rock Island and Pacific Railroad train wreck occurred where Hendricks Creek dumps into Mill Creek northeast of Alma. One of the two bridges over the creek had completely collapsed from floodwater, unbeknownst to the train crew. Crew members can be seen standing on the engine that plunged into Mill Creek. Wreckage from this locomotive still rests on the gravel bar where the accident occurred. (Courtesy of Wabaunsee County Historical Society.)

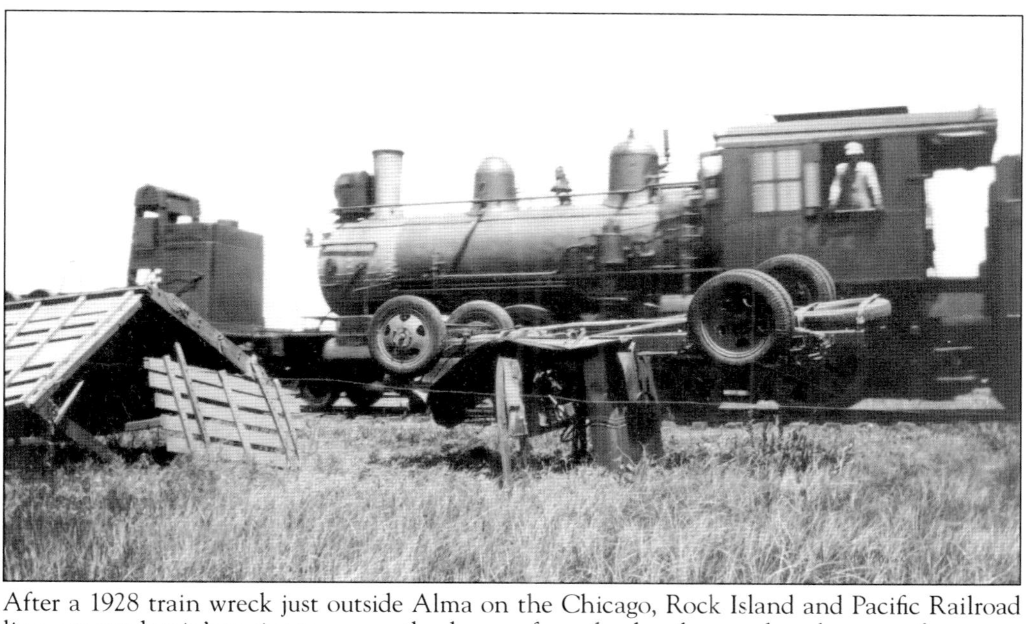

After a 1928 train wreck just outside Alma on the Chicago, Rock Island and Pacific Railroad line, a second train's engineer surveys the damage from the derailment where boxcars of new cars and trucks overturned, spilling new vehicles along the siding. (Courtesy of Jay Dee Miller.)

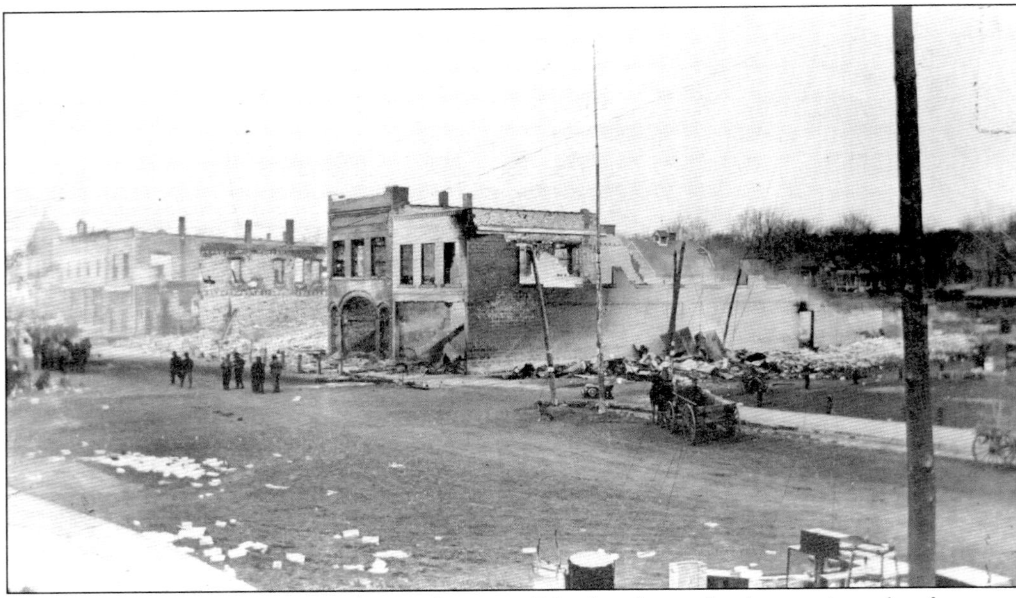

This 1913 Easter Studio image of Main Street in Eskridge shows the devastation after fire swept down the block, destroying 9 of the 12 buildings on the west side of the block. A March 12,1890, fire swept down the same side of the street. Both fires were contained at the Trusler building. (Courtesy of Inez Dunn.)

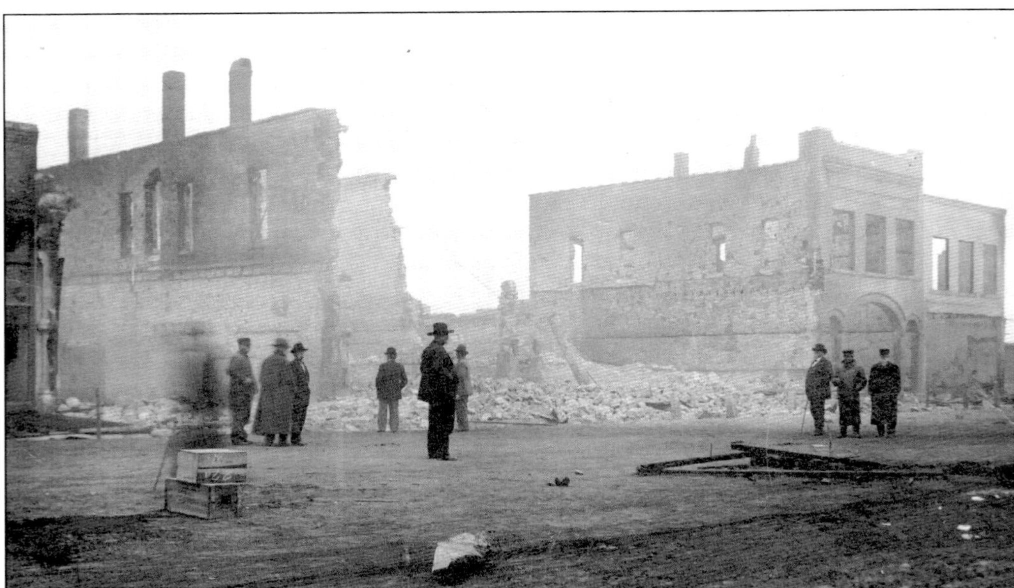

The morning after the devastating 1913 fire in Eskridge showed the business district in ruins. Compare this view with the pre-fire view on page 44. (Courtesy of Wabaunsee County Historical Society.)

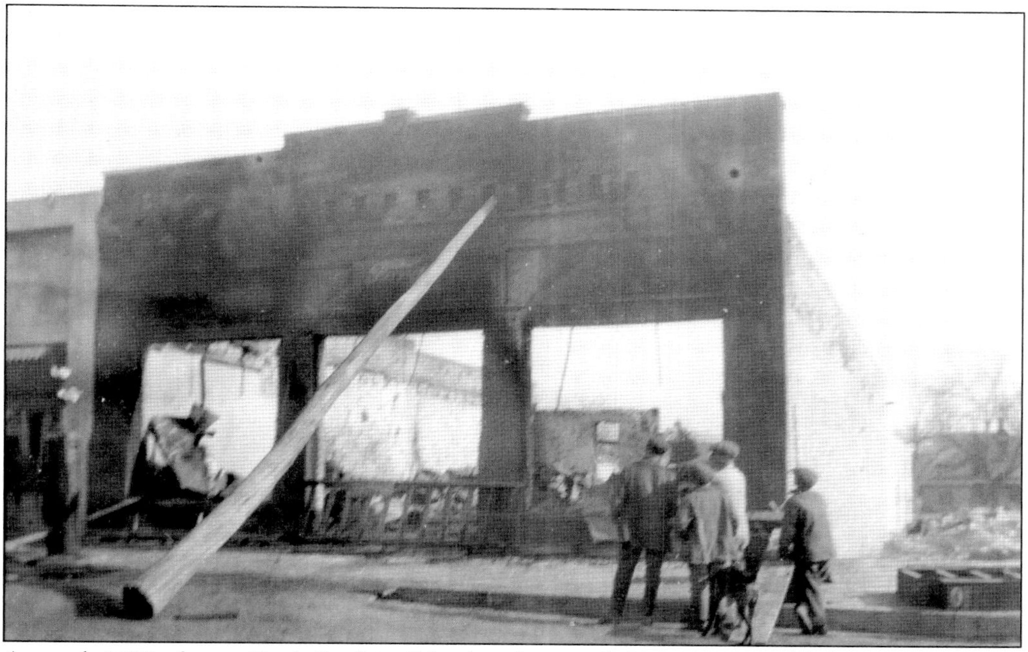

An early-1920s fire at Day's Ford in Eskridge destroyed the interior and left the face of this building in danger of collapsing. Amazingly, the building was rebuilt, the brick face was saved, and it stands today at 212 Main Street. (Courtesy of Inez Dunn.)

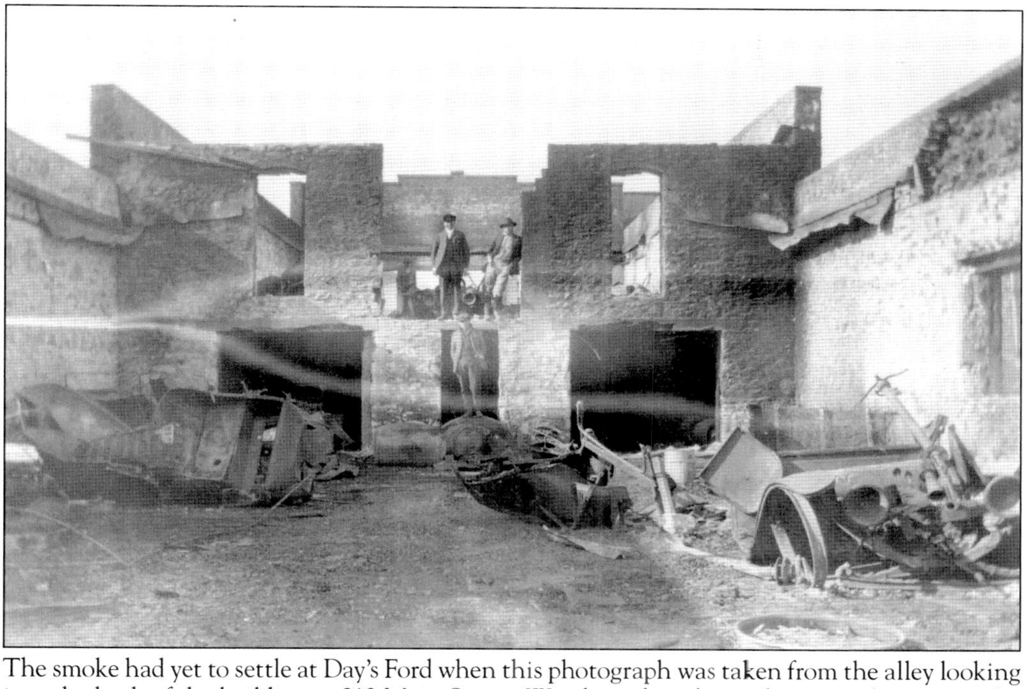

The smoke had yet to settle at Day's Ford when this photograph was taken from the alley looking into the back of the building at 212 Main Street. Wreckage from burned cars can be seen in the foreground. (Courtesy of Inez Dunn.)

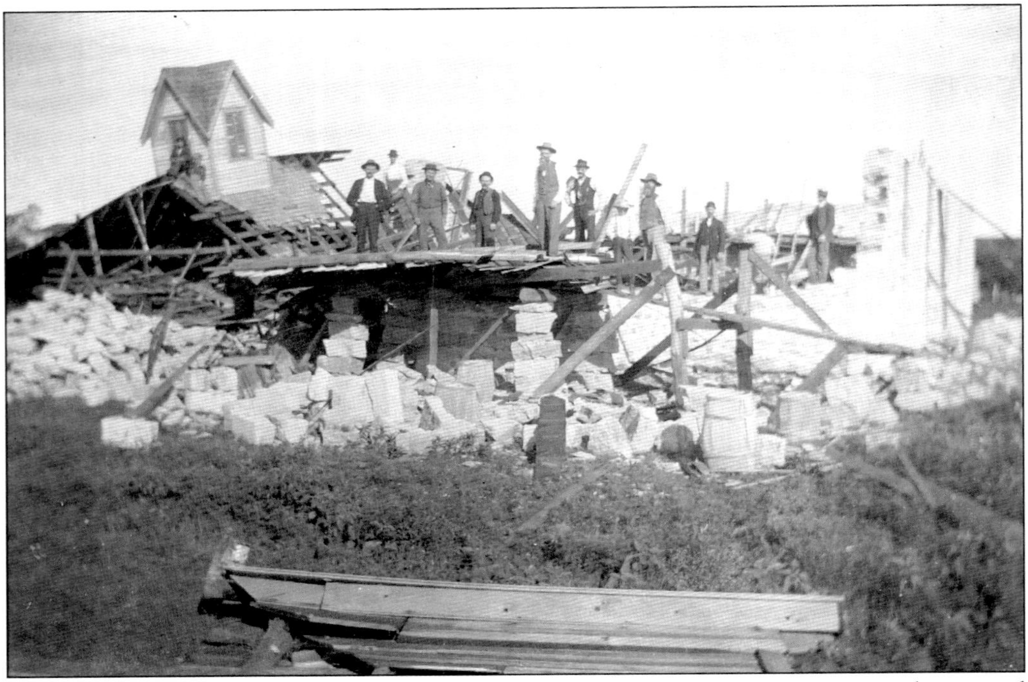

A powerful tornado struck Eskridge in 1911, destroying many structures. Easter Studio created a series of real-photo postcards of the damage, and this view shows the Baptist church destroyed by the violent storm. (Courtesy of Wabaunsee County Historical Society.)

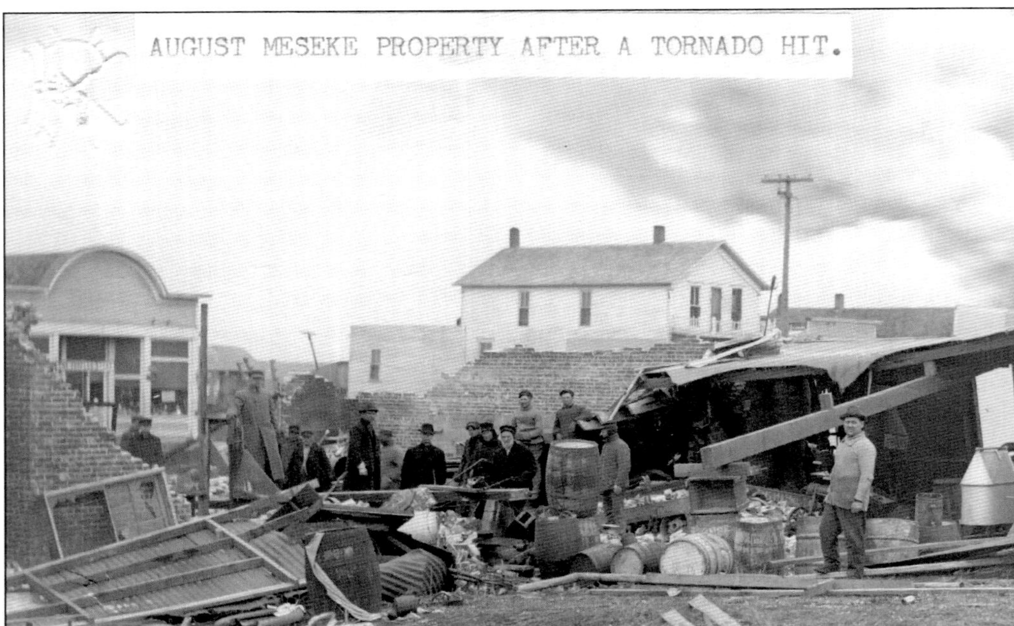

The sky still looks ominous as August Meseke (far right), a noted businessman in Alta Vista, and others examine the damage from the 1912 tornado. The business district in Alta Vista sustained considerable damage. (Courtesy of Wabaunsee County Historical Society.)

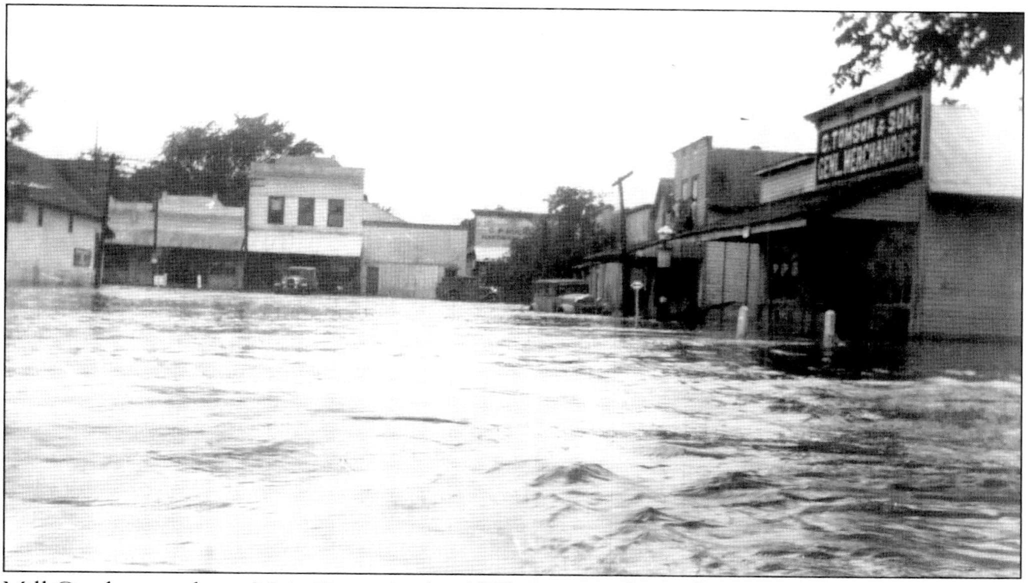

Mill Creek rages down Main Street in this 1935 photograph, as the stream overflowed its banks and swelled through Paxico. This view looks west down Main Street to Newbury Street in the center of the business district. Even today, residents of Paxico often face flooding conditions when torrential rains raise the tributaries to Mill Creek. (Courtesy of Wabaunsee County Historical Society.)

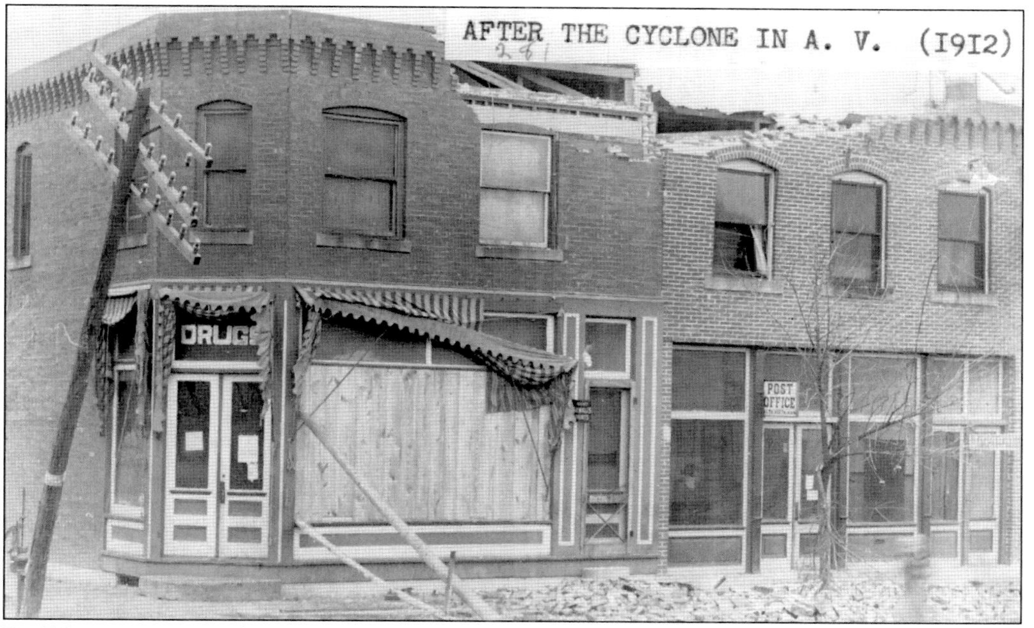

Dr. Edgerton's corner drugstore and the post office suffered severe damage from the 1912 tornado in Alta Vista. These buildings were new just a year earlier (see page 41). Notice the pile of bricks on the sidewalk in front of the building. This was just one of many structures badly damaged in the storm. (Courtesy of Wabaunsee County Historical Society.)

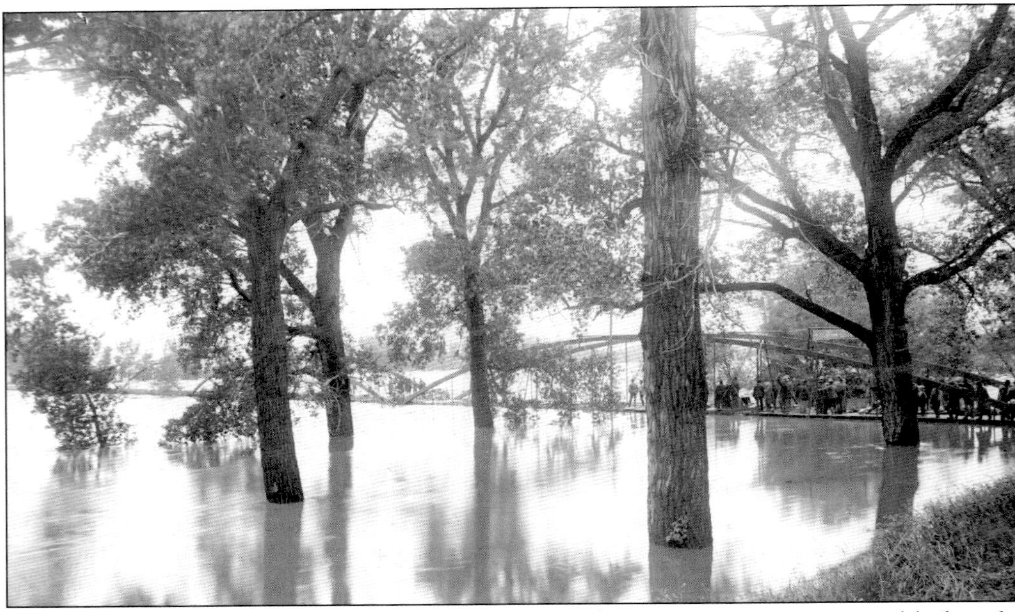

Prior to 1926, not a single lake existed in Kansas, and no major reservoirs existed before the flood of 1951. Likewise, very few ponds existed. For that reason, flooding along the Kansas River occurred several times a year. Some floods were severe, causing large property losses. In this 1903 view from the Wamego end of the Kansas River bridge, looking east, a number of people venture onto the flooded bridge. (Courtesy of Wabaunsee County Historical Society.)

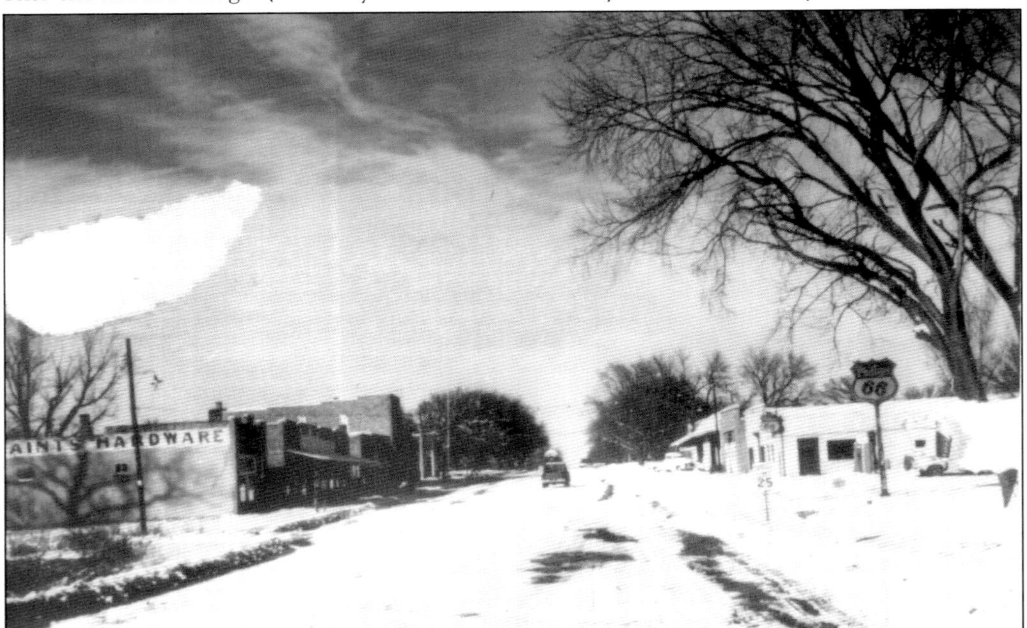

Weather has often brought disaster to Wabaunsee County by way of tornados and floods. However, a late freeze can be disastrous to farmers and ranchers. This unbelievable snow scene on Main Street in Maple Hill was taken on May 20, 1950. (Courtesy of Wabaunsee County Historical Society.)

Seven

Wabaunsee County Farm and Ranch Tour

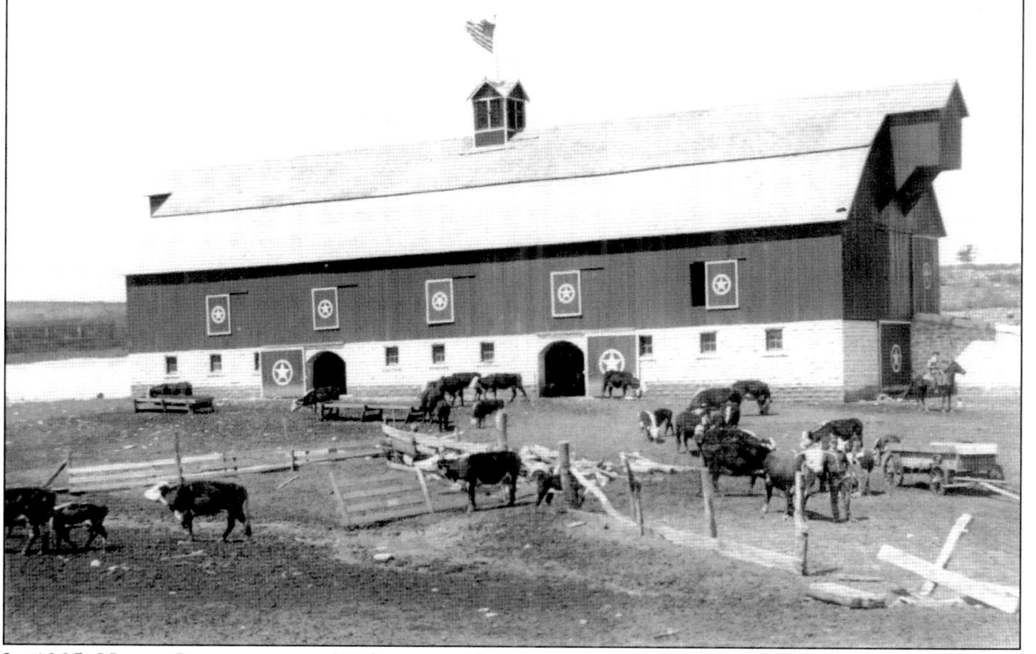

In 1905, Henry Sump came to Wabaunsee County and purchased Gus Droege's farm two miles south of Alma. He built this massive barn of native walnut, which became the center of his cattle-ranching operation. In 1920, Sump died on the farm after being struck by lightning. Sump's brother-in-law J. F. Terrass is seen at the barn in this 1920s photograph. The barn stands today on Highway 99 and is owned by Jimmie and Wendy Page. (Courtesy of Kansas State Historical Society.)

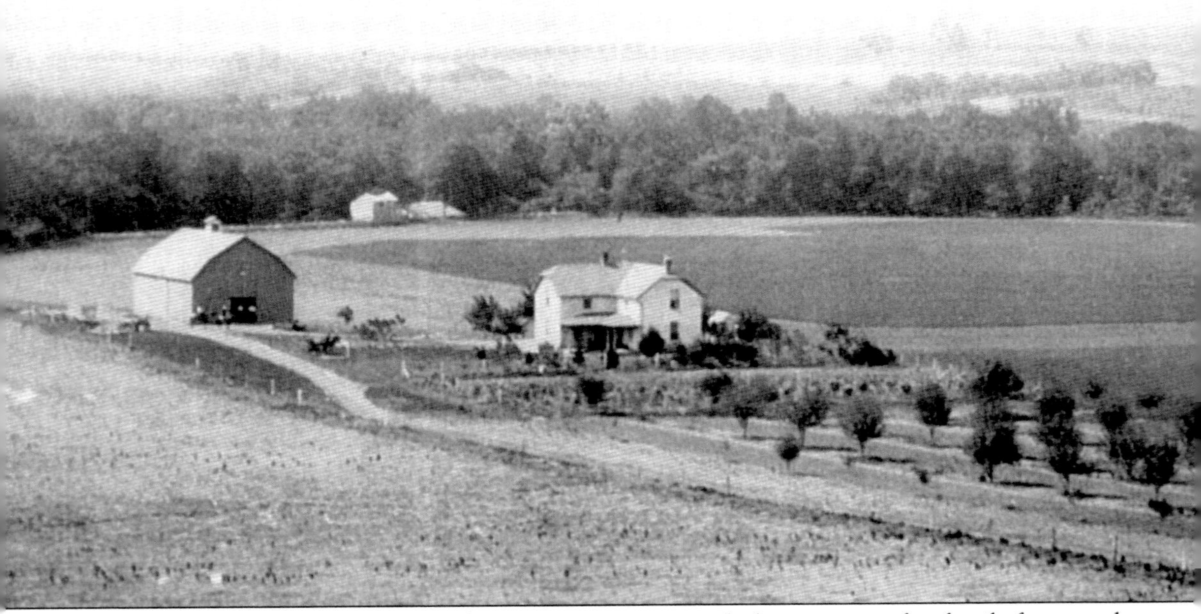

As Wabaunsee County is just reaching its sesquicentennial, there are very few family farms and ranches that have reached that same milestone. Among the grandest of all ranches currently in Wabaunsee County is one that began over 150 years ago. John Hess emigrated from Prussia in 1853 and married Gertrude Schmitz before settling in Wabaunsee County at Bismarck in April 1854. He was the first postmaster of Bismarck and was on the first school board for District 14, also known as the Halifax school (see page 89). The second youngest of their four children, Otto John, homesteaded on adjacent property to his father's and built the stone house seen in this photograph. Otto John's son Oliver Wendell Hess continued the ranching operation, becoming a prominent cattleman. Oliver Wendell's son Oliver Junior Hess and his wife, Virginia, continued the family ranching operation after their marriage in 1942. They live in the stone house seen above today. Their sons Jim and Alan Hess live next door and manage the 20,000-acre ranch today. (Courtesy of Jim Hess.)

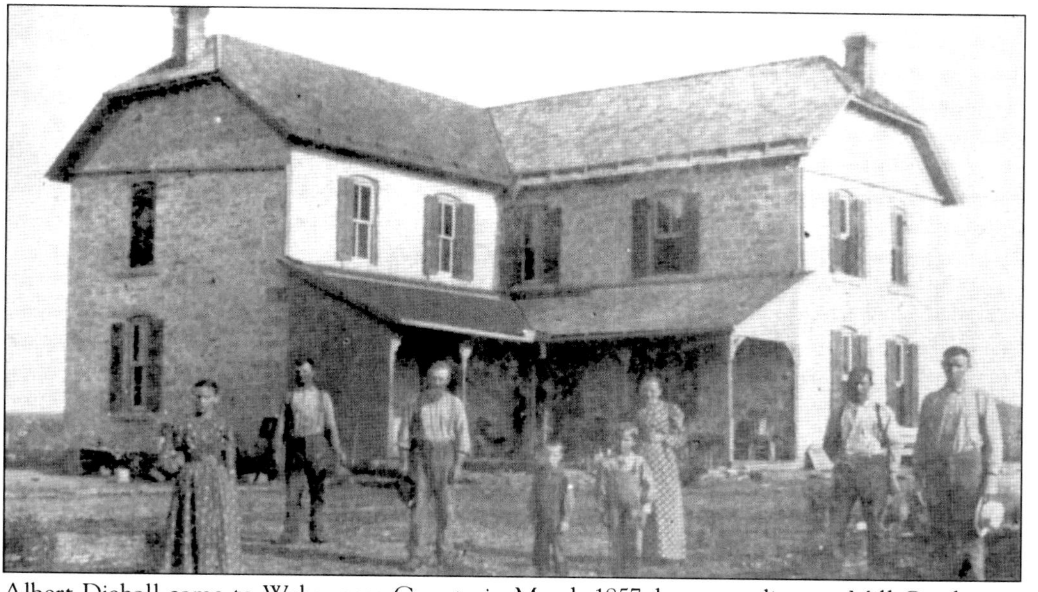

Albert Dieball came to Wabaunsee County in March 1857, homesteading on Mill Creek west of Alma. He built a stone house, above, on the homestead, where he settled. His son Albert Herman Dieball continued to farm and ranch the family homestead, and Albert Herman's son Don continues that ranching operation today, making this one of the longest-held family farms in the county. This house is located on Old K-10 Road. (Courtesy of Wabaunsee County Historical Society.)

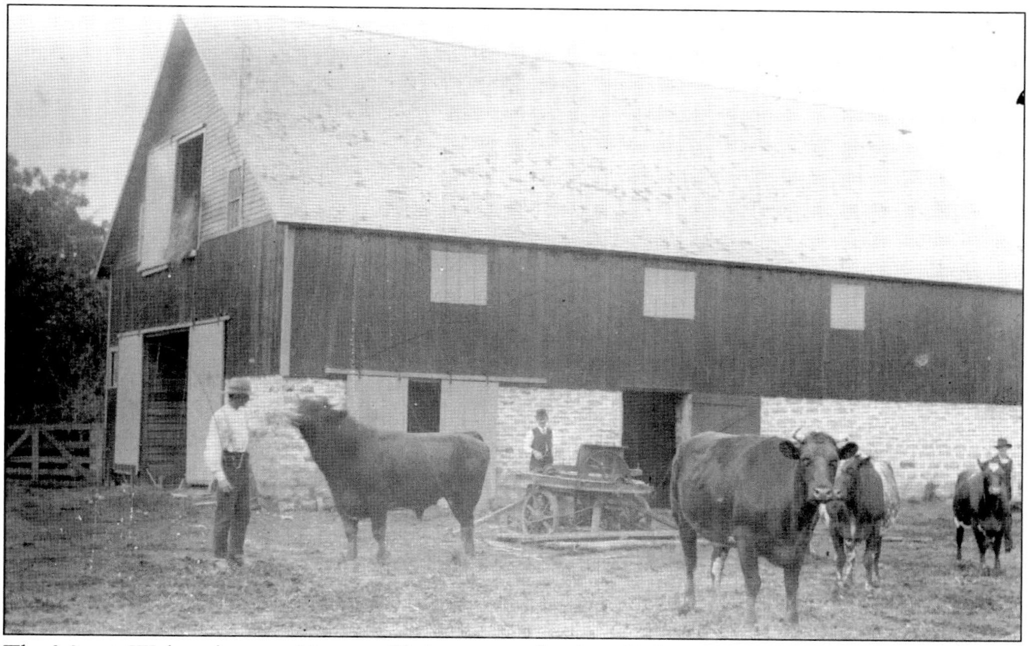

The Morris Walton barn at Harveyville is seen in this late-19th-century photograph. Walton was an active member of the Underground Railroad as well as being one of the earliest settlers in the Harveyville area. His name appears on county jury lists as early as 1864, and he played a role in local Republican Party politics until his death. (Courtesy of Wabaunsee County Historical Society.)

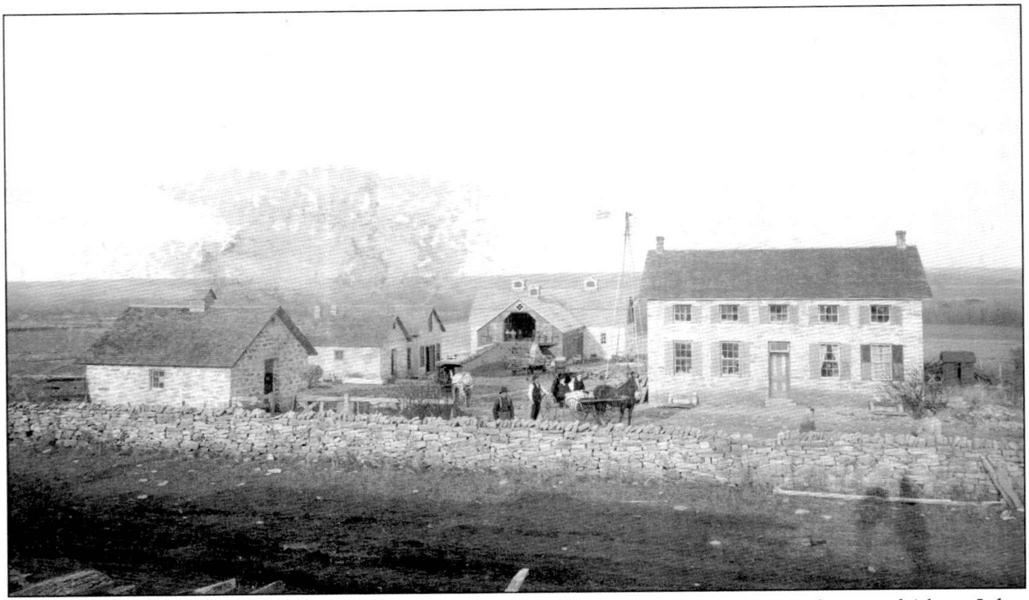

These are two views of the Schepp Ranch on Illinois Creek Road, six miles southwest of Alma. John Ludwig "Louis" Schepp lived on the ranch in the large stone house with his mother, Margaritha Muehlenbacher Schepp. His three uncles lived there as well, and when Louis was just a young boy, murdering thieves shot and killed his uncle Peter Muehlenbacher at the ranch. In later life, Louis became one of the wealthiest men in Wabaunsee County and had a massive barn constructed on his ranch. The barn still stands today along with several other barns and outbuildings. The house is gone. The ranch is now known as the Illinois Creek Ranch, owned by Ron and Kelly Lockton of the Kansas City area. (Courtesy Wabaunsee County Historical Society.)

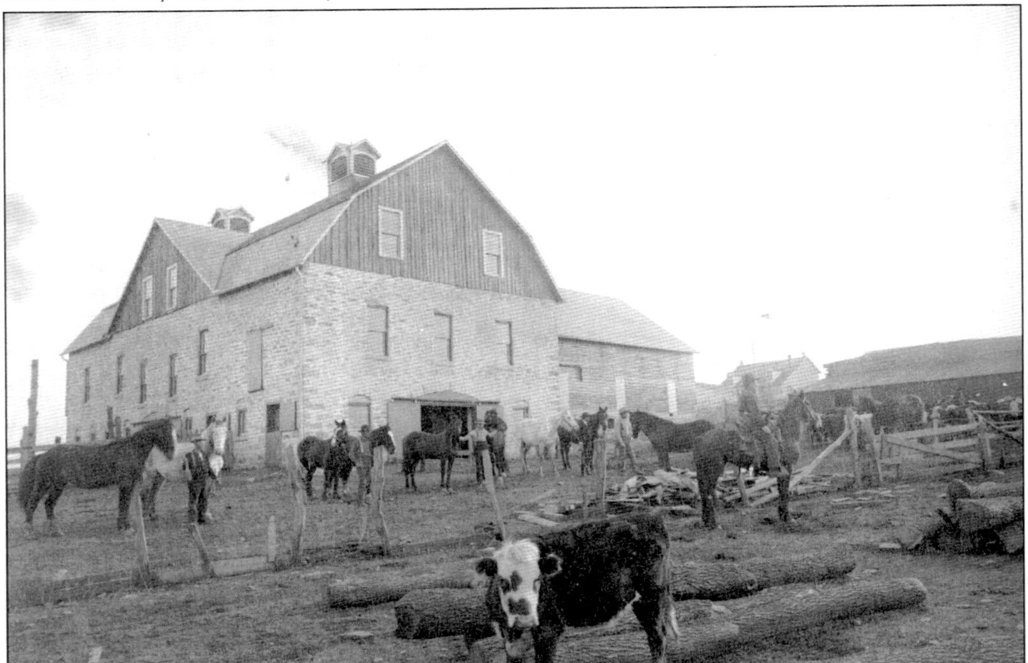

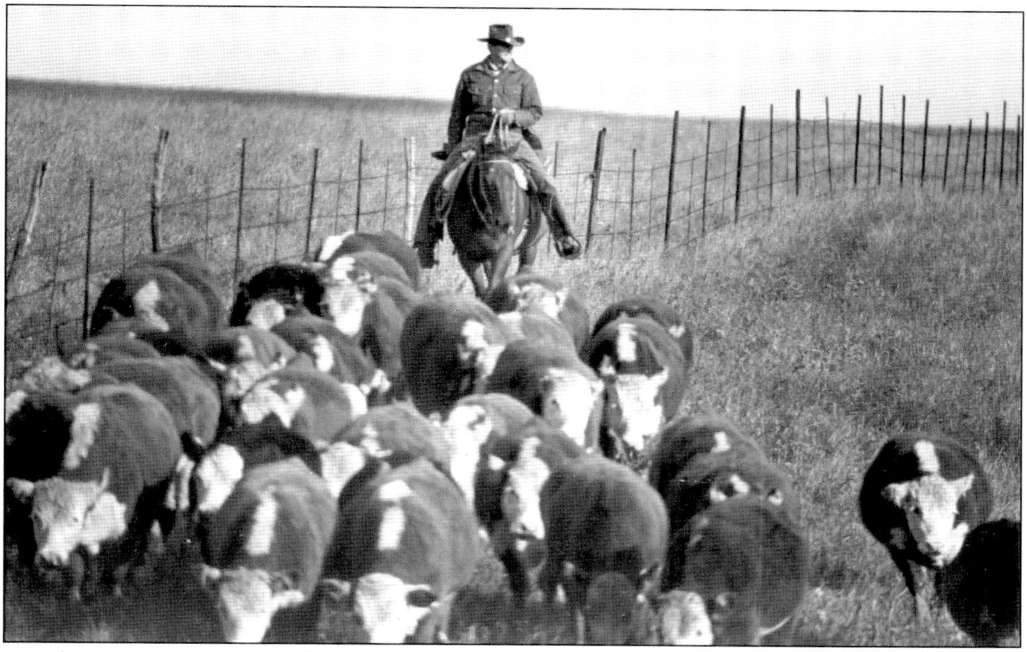

Ranching is timeless. The Flint Hills rancher today performs many of the same jobs and faces many of the same challenges that his father and grandfather faced, working the same ground. This 1985 photograph captures Jim Hess moving cattle at the Allendorph pens 12 miles northwest of Alma. (Courtesy of Jim Hess.)

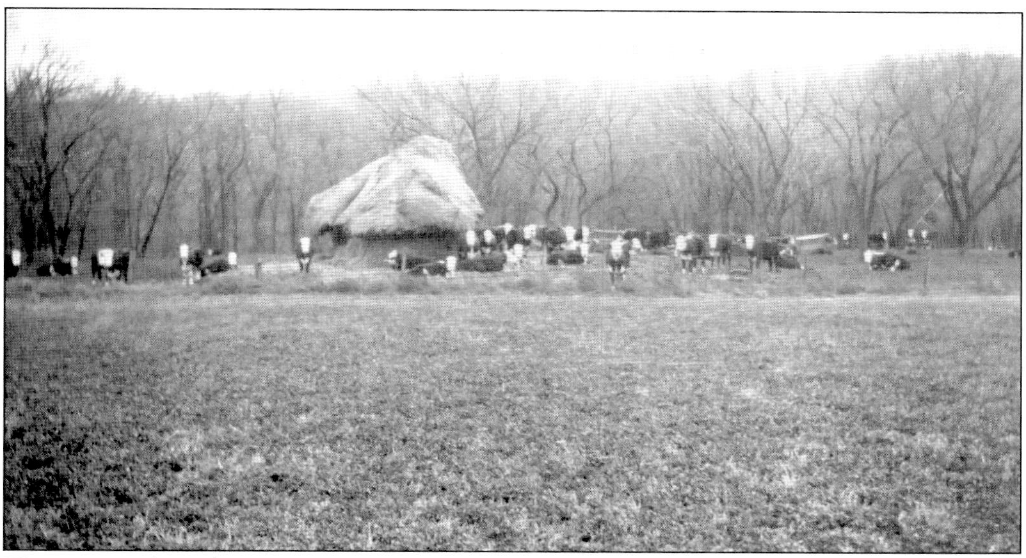

This is an early-20th-century view of cattle at the A. S. Allendorph ranch northwest of Alma. Allendorph came to Alma in 1888 and began acquiring land by purchase and lease and began dealing in cattle and pasture. His ranch consisted of over 5,000 acres, and he owned a fine home in Alma. The Atchison, Topeka and Santa Fe Railway had a cattle-loading stop just south of Alma at Allendorph because of the volume of cattle that was being shipped from that ranch. (Courtesy of Wabaunsee County Historical Society.)

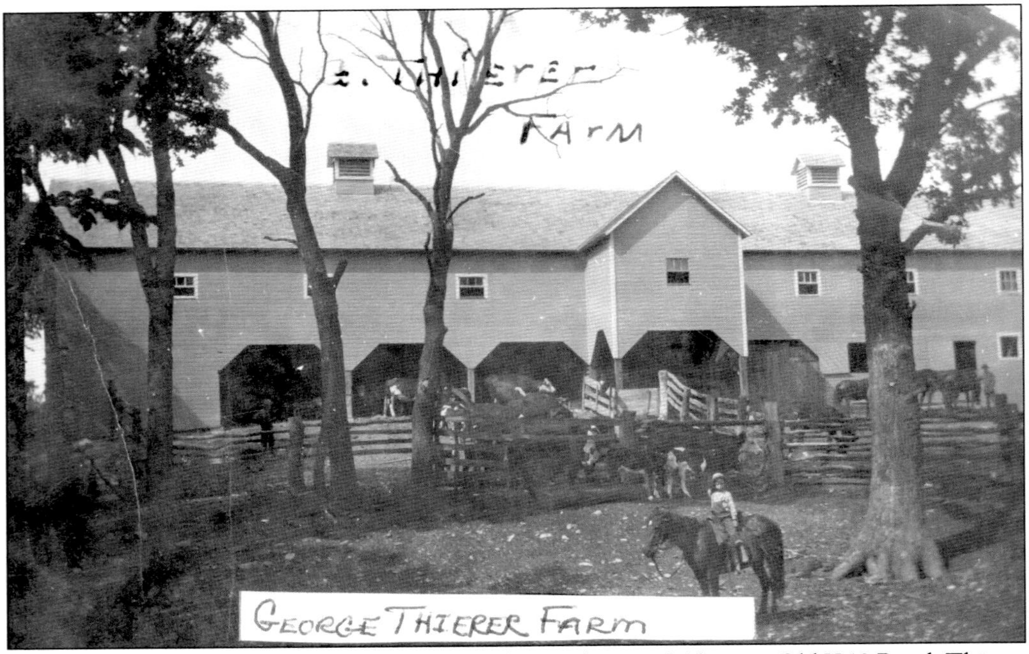

This is the Gus Thierer barn, located seven miles southwest of Alma on Old K-10 Road. Thierer came to Alma in 1869 and settled near Volland. In 1874, he married Rosa Fix of Volland, and the couple had five children. This massive barn was the site of many barn dances. The barn still stands, and the farm is still owned by the Thierer family. Thierer's great-grandson Larry and his family live on the farm. (Courtesy of Wabaunsee County Historical Society.)

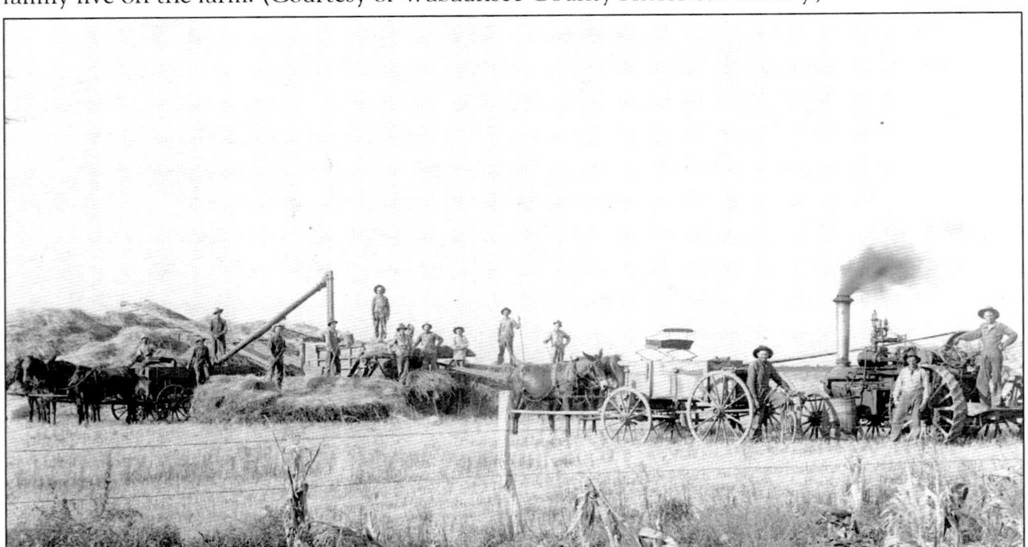

Written on the back of this photograph is, "Threshing at the Joe Sowers place at Wilmington, 1914." Wilmington was a very early settlement in Wabaunsee County; however, when the Manhattan, Alma and Burlingame Railroad chose to pass well north of Wilmington, the town of Harveyville was established on the rail line and most of the merchants at Wilmington moved to the new town. (Courtesy of Wabaunsee County Historical Society.)

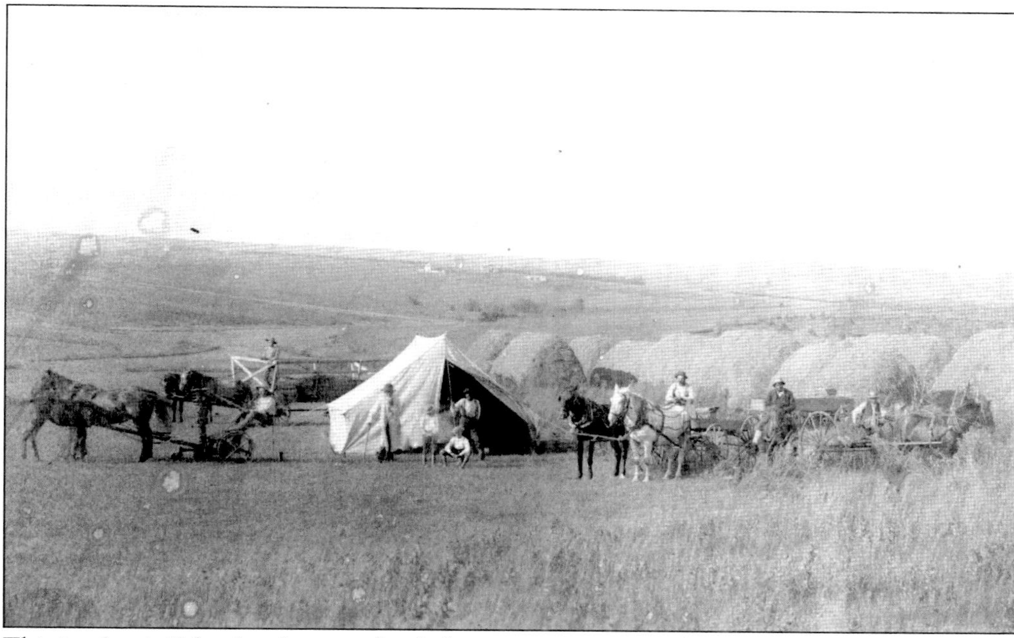

This is a Louis Palenske photograph of a haying operation on the H. J Palenske farm one mile south of Alma. This farm was the site of the early Pauly Mill at Alma, the first mill built on Mill Creek. Lorenzo Pauly bought the mill from Goettlieb Zwanziger, who first platted Alma. This photograph is from the late 1870s. (Courtesy of Wabaunsee County Historical Society.)

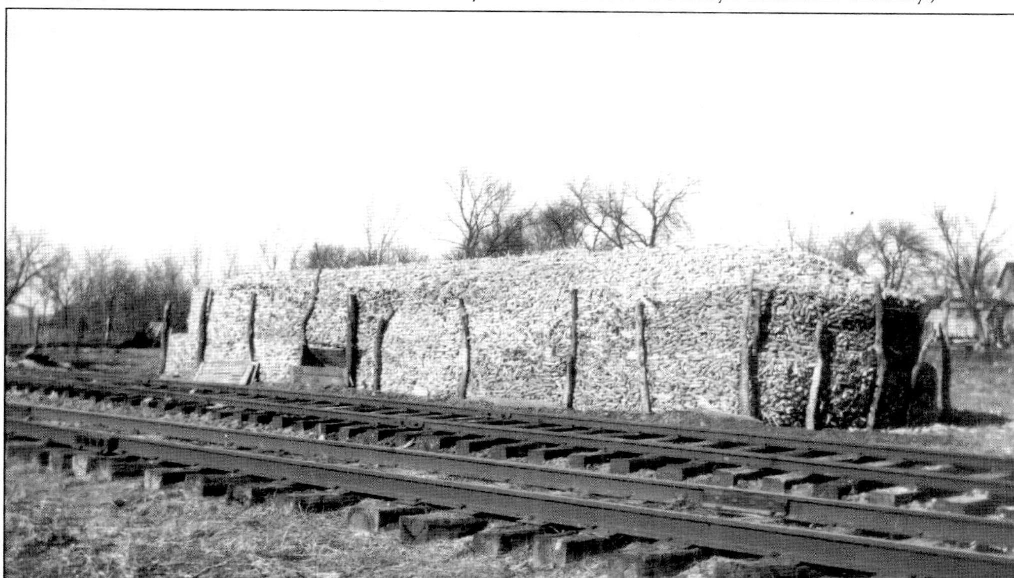

A corncrib stands next to the Atchison, Topeka and Santa Fe Railway tracks at Bradford, another ghost town in Wabaunsee County. Unlike some ghost towns, Bradford was on the rail line, but the town never experienced the boom that Eskridge and Harveyville experienced after 1880. Written on the back of the photograph is, "4,000 bushels of corn at Bradford." (Courtesy of Inez Dunn.)

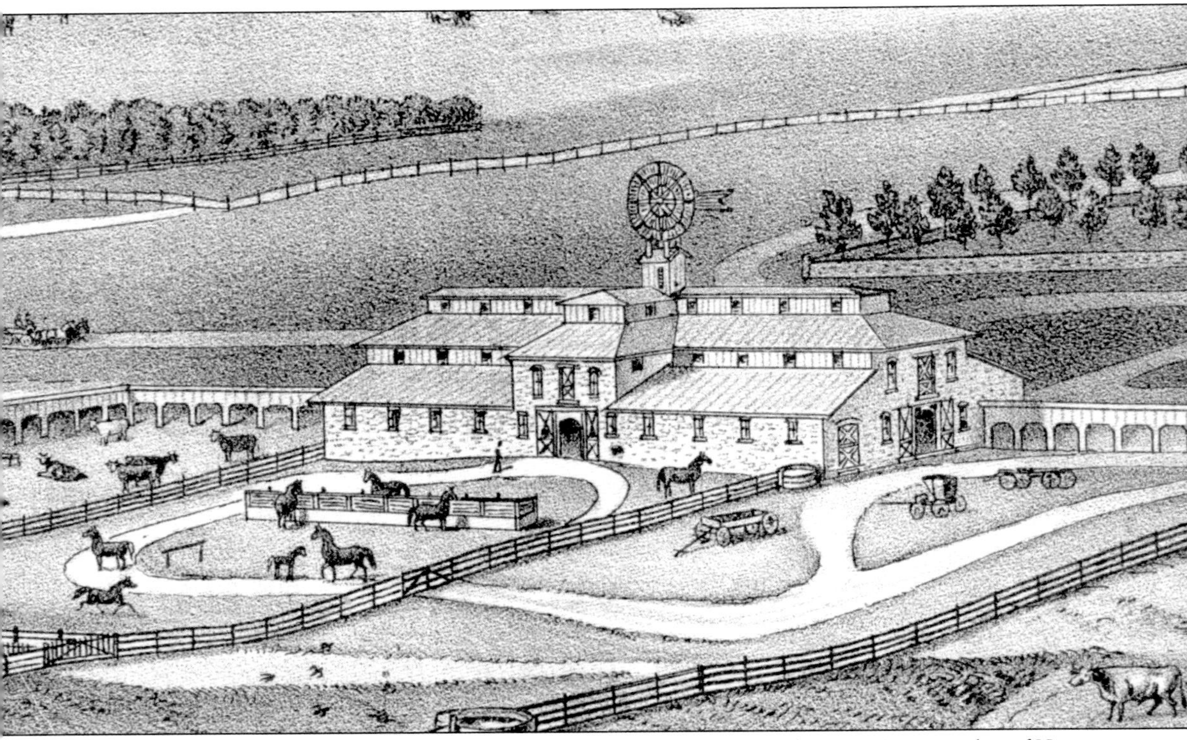

This etching of the J. P. Wiser barn and stock ranch appeared in the 1887 Everts atlas of Kansas. Wiser, of Prescott, Ontario, was known as the father of Canadian whiskey and was one of the largest distillers in that country. In his later years, his real interest was cattle ranching and horse ranching. He purchased a large ranch on the Wabaunsee-Lyon County line for that very purpose. The barn that he constructed is without a peer. Constructed of cut limestone, when the barn was completed, Wiser sent out engraved invitations to its opening, celebrated with a dance. Often, an erroneous story says that the barn was built to be a distillery; however, its design is specific for stock raising, Wiser's passion. Notice the windmill protruding from the roof. It powered wheels used to grind feed as well as pump water. After Wiser's death in 1911, his empire declined, and his ranch was sold to a group associated with the Swift meat company. The barn still stands today in virtual ruin in the 10,000 block of Allen Road. (Courtesy of Wabaunsee County Historical Society.)

BIBLIOGRAPHY

Baughman, Robert W. *Kansas Post Offices, May 29, 1828, to August 3, 1961.* Topeka, Kansas: Kansas Postal History Society, 1961.

Bisbey, J. M., et al. *Pioneering in Wabaunsee County.* Vol. 11. Kansas State Historical Society, 1910.

Business Directory and History of Wabaunsee County. Topeka: Kansas Directory Company, 1907.

Connelley, William. *A Standard History of Kansas and Kansans.* Chicago: Lewis Publishing Company, 1918.

Cutler, William G. *The History of the State of Kansas.* Chicago: A. T. Andreas, 1883.

Hoots, Greg A., *The Complete History of Lake Wabaunsee,* Alma, KS: Flint Hills Publishing, 2008.

Hoots, Greg A., ed. *Flint Hills Special.* Alma, Kansas: Wendy Page, 1998.

Magee, R. Sorren. *Magee's History and Directory of Wabaunsee County, Kansas.* Winchester, KS: Argus Job Printing Office, 1885.

Pantle, Alberta, ed. "The Connecticut Kansas Colony: Letters of Charles B. Lines to the New Haven (Conn.) Daily Palladium." *Kansas Historical Quarterly* 22, Spring 1956 and Summer 1956.

Spear, Stephen Jackson. *Reminiscences of the Early Settlement of Dragoon Creek, Wabaunsee County.* Vol. 13. Kansas State Historical Society, 1914.

Thomson, Matt. *Early History of Wabaunsee County, Kansas, with Stories of Pioneer Days and Glimpses of Our Western Border.* Alma, KS: self-published, 1901.

Turnbull, Roderick. *Maple Hill Stories.* Kansas City, MO: Lowell Press, 1961.

———. *More Maple Hill Stories.* Kansas City, MO: Lowell Press, 1974.

Wabaunsee County Historical Society. *New Branches from Old Trees: A New History of Wabaunsee County.* Alma, KS: Wabaunsee County Historical Society, 1976.

———. *Stories of the Past: the Third Edition of Wabaunsee County History.* Alma, KS: Wabaunsee County Historical Society 2000.

Discover Thousands of Local History Books Featuring Millions of Vintage Images

Arcadia Publishing, the leading local history publisher in the United States, is committed to making history accessible and meaningful through publishing books that celebrate and preserve the heritage of America's people and places.

Find more books like this at
www.arcadiapublishing.com

Search for your hometown history, your old stomping grounds, and even your favorite sports team.

Consistent with our mission to preserve history on a local level, this book was printed in South Carolina on American-made paper and manufactured entirely in the United States. Products carrying the accredited Forest Stewardship Council (FSC) label are printed on 100 percent FSC-certified paper.

MADE IN THE USA